MURD

Criminal Conduct
in
Old Alexandria, Virginia, 1749-1900

By T. Michael Miller

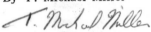

HERITAGE BOOKS, INC.

Published 1988 By

HERITAGE BOOKS, INC.
1540E Pointer Ridge Place, Bowie, Maryland 20716
(301)-390-7709

ISBN 1-55613-115-1

A Complete Catalog Listing Hundreds Of Titles On
History, Americana, And Genealogy
Available Free Upon Request

TABLE OF CONTENTS

INTRODUCTION

Historical studies involving Alexandria have traditionally focused on socio-economic and political questions. In addition antiquarians and students have penned numerous monographs on architecture, archaeology and local house histories. Yet, no one has previously investigated the impact of crime and deviant behavior on Alexandria society. How did this Virginia town curb its criminal element and what types of punishment were meted out to guilty offenders?

Eighteenth and nineteenth century Alexandria entailed more than birthnight balls, barbecues, horse races and elegant receptions. Beneath this chimerical cloud there also lurked segments of society who engaged in robbery, arson and even murder to advance their malevolent schemes. As a seaport community, Alexandria was populated by a diverse mixture of sailors from foreign ports. Different dialects could be heard as Spanish, French and Portugese sailors plied the town's cobblestoned streets and alleys in search of good rum, women and amusements. Many frequented taverns and ordinaries which dotted almost every corner of the community. After a few drams of rum, the inebriated clientele became raucous and rowdy, engaging in fisticuffs, brawls and knifings. For entertainment of the more sensual variety these motley characters flocked to back alleys and seedy houses of ill repute. Especially during the Civil War when Alexandria was thronged with thousands of Union soldiers, there were more than forty of these dens of inquity which catered to the whims of many a lonely soldier. In the 1880's and 90's the 300 block of North Lee street was known as Alexandria's red light district. The neighborhood brothels were finally closed in 1916.

The majority of crimes committed in nineteenth century Alexandria involved minor offenses for petty larceny, public drunkenness and assault and battery. These acts were so recurrent that the author chose not to chronicle them. Instead the inquiry focuses on the major felony categories of murder, rape, infanticide, seduction, bigamy, etc. The study does not proport to be scientifice or all inclusive. Most of the vignettes have been extrapolated from the *Alexandria Gazette* newspaper. Also a search of grand jury proceedings from 1800 to 1900 were instrumental in verifying the verdict of juries and the form and penalities imposed.

The administration of justice in colonial Alexandria was primarily the responsibility of the local sheriff. Appointed by the Fairfax County Court after 1752, he was charged with keeping the peace, maintaining the jail and trying local law breakers. To assist him with his workload a number of constables policed various geographic regions of the county and Alexandria. Apparently the incidence of serious crime in early Alexandria was nil. Most offences were of a less serious nature such as gaming, swearing profanely, drunkenness or selling liquor without a license. Donald Sweig, writing in *Fairfax County, Virginia - A History*, has compiled a listing of crimes from several court order books. He notes, for instance, that in 1749 there were five cases of assault and battery; five women charged with having bastard children of whom Rebeckah Davis was sentenced to fifty lashes and Margaret Webster to twenty-five. In the 1750's there were one hundred eighty-eight cases of assault & battery; one hundred instances of women having bastard children and five of fornification: Thomas Lewis with Eliz. Harris, Col. John Colville with Mary Cary, Wiatt William with Isabelle Sankstone, Michael Melton with Martha Evans, Simon Pearson; three cases of adultery, John McDaniel & Margaret Gooding, William May with his housekeeper and Joseph Cash with Josephene Hith. Of a more serious nature, Daniel Foot was charged with assaulting and ravishing Ann Sheel. Also, the *Virginia Gazette* of April 10, 1769, reported that the body of a white man was found floating in the river just off Alexandria. The first verifiable murder transpired in June 1752 when Thomas Kelley confessed in Fairfax County Court to killing one Thomas Davis. (*Fairfax County Court Order Book*, 1749, p. 207) The 1760s were punctuated by forty-six cases of assault & battery; one of fornification involving Simon Pearson and Pelitah Grafford; three cases of adultery including Joseph Watson, Cecilia Trig & Simon Pearson and finally thirty-two cases of bastardy. (Donald Sweig, *Fairfax County, Virginia - A History*. (Fairfax, Virginia: Fairfax County Board of Supervisors, 1978), p. 51, 60, 74.)

Criminals were generally fined or required to post bonds. But on other occasions local justice could be more severe. When Wm. Edges, a convict servant owned by merchants Jno. Carlyle and John Dalton, received a stolen sheep from a slave he was sentenced to thirty-nine lashes on his bare back at the public whipping post. (Thomas Preisser, *18th Century Alexandria, Virginia, 1749-1776*. Ph.D. diss., Wm. & Mary College, 1977, pp. 226-234.)

The criminal justice system and prison facilities were removed from Springfield near current Tysons Corners to Alexandria in 1753. The jail was physically situated near the courthouse on market square along with stocks and a pillory. The security at the prison left much to be desired and the local sheriff frequently complained about the jail's derelict condition which resulted in numerous escapes.

When Alexandria was incorporated in 1779, the city police department fell under the jurisdiction of an elected City Council. In 1780 there was one day policeman and two night watchmen who received a salary of $150 per annum. As the town became increasingly urbanized, there was a need for better police protection. At a lecture given by the Society for the Promotion of Useful Knowledge in 1790 the subject of inquiry was "What improvements were necessary to be made to the police of Alexandria" (*Alexandria Gazette*. 10/14/1790, p.2.)

By December 1796, City Council passed an act which raised revenue to support a night watch. It stated:

WHEREAS it is necessary for the preservation of property in the town of Alexandria, and for the good order and government of the said town, that a regular Watch should be established therein, Be it enacted by the Mayor and Commonalty of the..Town of Alex. andria. That four watchmen shall be annually appointed in such manner as the Council shall direct; one of whom shall patrol each ward every hour, between the hours of 10 o'clock at night and day-break, throughout the year; and that each watchman shall receive, as a compensation for his services, a sum not exceeding one hundred and fifty dollars per annum, to be paid quarterly.

An be it further enacted, that a Superintendent of the watch shall be annually appointed by the Common Council in such manner as they shall direct; whose duty it shall be to oversee the watchmen, that they perform their duty faithfully and attentively - to assign to them the wards they are respectively to patrol - and to receive and take charge of such disorderly and suspicious persons as may be apprehended by the watchmen. And the said Superintendent shall receive, as a compensation for his services, a sum not exceeding two hundred and fifty dollars per annum, to be paid quarterly.

And be it enacted, That it shall be the duty of the several watchmen...to suppress all disorderly meetings and to take him or her, or them so found on their patrol or in disorderly houses, to the superintendent who shall confine such person or persons in the watch house, or goal, until the morning; and then take him or them, before some magistrate of the town to be examined.

And, for defraying the Expence of the said Watch, Be it enacted, That there shall be paid annually - By every Wholesale Merchant in the Dry Good, Grocers, or Produce line in the Town of Alexandria, a tax of ten dollars - By every Retail Storekeeper, Druggist or Apothecary, five dollars - By every Shopkeeper or Huckster, two dollars and fifty cents - By every occupier of a dwelling house, storehouse, or warehouse, for each store of said house, one dollar. By every occupier of a brew house, distillery or biscuit bakehouse, five dollars.

And be it enacted, That if any person shall keep a wholesale store and also a retail store, in separate houses, he shall pay the tax imposed on a Wholesale Merchant and Retail Store-keeper. And if any person shall keep more stores or shops than one in the town, he shall be liable to a tax for each store or shop... ("An Act - For establishing a Watch in the Town of Alexandria, and raising revenue for the Support thereof." *The Columbian Mirror and Alexandria Gazette*, 12/27/1796, p.2.)

In 1805, Alexandria boasted a superintendent of police, 6 watchmen and 1 officer which cost the city $1,650.00 per annum. (*Alexandria Gazette*, 8/19/1876, p.2.) By January of the same year another ordinance was passed which allowed the Mayor to appoint additional constables at his own discretion. (*Alexandria Gazette*, 1/26/1805, p.3.) Each constable was required to post a bond of $300 for the faithful performance of his office. (*Alexandria Gazette*, 6/18/1805.)

Legislation was passed by the Common Council in 1810 which specified that 4 constables would be appointed annually every April. They were charged with: (1) preventing noisy or riotous conduct in the street; (2) attending market every morning during the busy hours to keep order and prevent the tumult and robbery of idle boys and negroes; (3) attending Sunday market and dispensing the crowd by 9:00 a.m.; (4) preventing the assemblages & riotous play of boys of every description; (5) going through their wards and making note of persons and orphan children who by law ought to be sent to the poorhouse; (6) attending the fish market from sunrise in the morning until 10 o'clock at night; (7) suppressing all species of gambling. (*Alexandria Gazette*, 4/16/1810, p.3.)

Alexandria was an occupied city during the tumultuous Civil War. For four long years the citizenry suffered under the yoke of Northern oppression. Indeed, Alexandria endured the longest military occupation of any town during this conflict. With the influx of so many soldiers there was great excitement and pandemonium.

General Slough, the Military Governor, wrote in 1862: "...there as there had been for days previous, a reign of terror in Alexandria. The streets were crowded with intoxicated soldiery; murder was of almost hourly occurrence, and disturbances, robbery and riot were constant. The sidewalks and docks were covered with drunken men, women and children, and quiet citizens were afraid to venture into the streets and life and property were at the mercy of the maddened throng - a condition of things perhaps never in the history of this country to be found in any other city." (Wm. Hurd, *Alexandria, Virginia 1861-1865* [Alexandria Virginia:City of Alexandria, 1970] p. 26.) After order was restored Alexandrians literally walked their streets as strangers. They were not permitted to go out at night, their mail was intercepted and passes were required to travel to Washington and outlying environs. Those who failed to swear obedience to the U. S. Government were suspected of treason and arrested on the slightest pretext. In addition, violators of the occupation ordinances were hauled before a military provost marshal. Some were fined, orders sent to the slave pen jail at 1315 Duke Street or to the Old Capitol Prison which occupied the site of the current U. S. Supreme Court building.

After the conflict, the civil police department was re-organized in April 1865. A bill was passed by Council which called for 8 police, "4 to go on duty at 1 o'clock p.m. and to serve till 1 a.m., the other 4 to go at 1 a.m. and to remain until 1 p.m. Other provisions provided for the appointment of a Chief of Police and officers' salaries were raised from $300 to $600 per annum. To avoid conflict of interest, personnel were strictly forbidden from engaging in any other business activities. (*Alexandria Gazette*, 4/29/1865, p.3.)

The contemporary police department had its origins in an 1870 reorganization act. That year City Council established a police board consisting of two individuals from the Board of Aldermen and two from the Common Council. The board was mandated to hear all complaints against the police and to suspend any officer for misconduct. By the terms of the new law the force was expanded to 21 members at an annual salary of $500; 1 captain of police, at a salary of $600; 1 lieutenant of police at a salary of $500. In addition the police force was uniformed at their own expense and each "officer ordered to wear a badge in the form of a star, made of blank tin and numbered in the center." (*Alexandria Gazette*, 7/15/1870, p.3.)

Before the first 21 officers were sworn in, a jurisdictional dispute erupted between the Mayor and the new police board over whether officers should be bonded. (*Alexandria Gazette*, 7/19/1870). An additional conflict arose when both the Mayor and Council claimed the right to elect officers. This resulted in a dual police force and James Webster having been elected captain and John L. Smith, lieutenant at a joint session of council, they both attempted to perform their duty and were sent to jail by the Mayor. Smith and Webster remained there but a few hours and were later released by the issuance of a writ of habeaus corpus.

The Embroglio made its way into the courts with the result that it splintered the local democratic party machine. Some citizens sided with the Mayor while others favored the City Council. Thereby, Wm. N. Berkley, a moderate Republican, was elected in the 1872 Mayoral election. (*Alexandria Gazette*, 7/23/1918.)

Expenditures to finance the police department from 1805 to 1876 included the following sums:

```
1805 ------------------$1,650.00
1852 ------------------ 2,488.00
1855 ------------------ 3,758.08
1859 ------------------ 6,042.14
1860 ------------------ 6,117.84
1869 ------------------ 8,945.10
```

NEW POLICE

```
1871 --------------- $12,903.92
1872 --------------- 12,613.97
1873 --------------- 11,551.90
1874 --------------- 13,359.08
1875 --------------- 11,123,63
1876 --------------- 10,184.96
1877 --------------- 9,500.00
```

Source: *Alexandria Gazette*, 8/19/1876, p.2.

Unfortunately very few police department records are extant prior to 1870. However, a log of the arrest records can be gleaned from the *Alexandria Gazette* as early as 1861. Listed under happenings of the Police or Mayor's Court, they detail who was arrested, what charge was lodged against the individual and what penalities or fines were imposed.

An inspection of grand jury and arrest records also reveal that there was a higher incidence of all categories of crime after the Civil War. The destruction of the old antebellum "ancien regime" and its replacement with a new social order no doubt was a contributory factor to the increased crime rate. Another variable was the effect the Emancipation Proclamation had on the negro population in Virginia. A large influx of non-native blacks known as contraband settled in and around Alexandria after the war. They were generally less restrained in their behaviour, having recently won their freedom.

The aggregate figures for male (M) and female (F) Negroes (N) and whites (W) arrested and sent to jail exist for the period 1886 to 1900. These figures indicate the number of persons arrested and sent to jail, by race, and are as follows:

1886
1,269 arrested
181 sent to jail
61 subject to the chain gang

1887
1,302 arrested
233 sent to jail
117 subject to the chain gang

1888
? arrested
302 sent to jail
148 felonies, 154 misdemeanors,
17 insane.

1889
? arrested
? (W) - ? (N) sent to jail

1890
1,562 arrested
119 (WM), 4 (WF) sent to jail
168 (NM), 17 (NF) sent to jail

1891
1,672 arrested
121 (WM), 2 (WF) sent to jail
212 (NM), 17 (NF) sent to jail

1892
1,743 arrested
83 (WM), 1 (WF) sent to jail
244 (NM), 9 (NF) sent to jail

1893
2,043 arrested
105 (WM), 2 (WF) sent to jail
271 (NM), 7 (NF) sent to jail

1894
1,960 arrested
136 (WM), 2 (WF) sent to jail
315 (NM), 10 (NF) sent to jail

1895
1,912 arrested
117 (WM) - 316 (NM) sent to jail

1896	2,201 arrested
	244 (WM), 5 (WF) sent to jail
	349 (NM), 13 (NF) sent to jail
1897	1,791 arrested
	179 (WM), 10 (WF) sent to jail
	330 (NM), 36 (NF) sent to jail
1898	? arrested
	99 (WM), 2 (WF) sent to jail
	235 (NM), 3 (NF) sent to jail
1899	957 arrested
	56 (WM) sent to jail
	257 (NM), 3 (NF) sent to jail
1900	1,124 arrested
	34 (WM), 3 (WF) sent to jail
	150 (NM), 3 (NF) sent to jail

(Of the 190 persons sent to jail, twelve were adjudged insane.)

TOTALS: Arrested – 19,536
Whites sent to jail – 1,394 males and 31 females.
Negroes sent to jail – 2,847 males and 117 females.

Sources: *Alexandria Gazette*, 12/31/1886, 1887, 1888, 1890, 1891, 1892 1893, 1894, 1895, 1896, 1897, 1898, 1899, 1900.

An analysis of the data clearly reveals that twice the number of negro males (2,847) and three times the number of negro females (117) were sent to jail as compared to white inmates (1,394 males) (31 females). Overall, minus missing data, there were 19,536 arrests from 1886 to 1900. Whether the figures reflect that more crime was committed by blacks is debatable and is beyond the scope of this inquiry. No doubt there was a backlash after the Civil War as white Southerners regained political control of Alexandria. Also, tensions between the races were heightened with the passage of Jim Crow laws in the late 1890s. With the exception of the Christmas riot of December 1865, race relations were at their nadir from 1897 to 1900 when two negroes were lynched in Alexandria without having been given the benefit of a fair trial.

Listed in the appendix is a compilation of constables and police personnel who served in Alexandria and Fairfax County from 1749 to 1904. In addition, there is a descriptive sketch and short history of the Alexandria jail.

Having concluded these remarks, the author invites the reader to explore the wide diversity of crimes which were perpetrated in Alexandria from 1749 to 1900. The large majority of Alexandrians, both black and white, were law abiding citizens and these vignettes in no way besmirch their many and notable accomplishments.

CHAPTER ONE

Abortions & Infanticide

INQUEST - An inquest was held by Coroner Neale, on Sunday afternoon, at the upper end of Duke street, on the body of an infant male child, (lately born) of Sarah Roles. The mother asserted that the child was born dead; but the usual tests applied by physicians, it was ascertained to have been born alive. The jury, therefore, returned a verdict that the child "came to its death from want of proper attention on the part of its mother." The examination was made by Drs. Brown and French. (*Alexandria Gazette*, April 14, 1857, p.3.)

^^*^*^*^*^*^*^*^*^*^*

CORPORATION COURT - When the *Gazette*'s report of yesterday's proceedings of the Corporation Court closed, a jury was being impaneled for a new trial of Newton Smith, colored, charged with the murder of an infant child, the progeny of himself and a white girl.

Martha Ferguson was examined and testified: The child was born Monday morning about 10 o'clock early in December 1870; on Tuesday or Wednesday following went to see Smith and he acknowledged the child to be his; promised to take it to his mother at Mt. Vernon and have it cared for; on same night he came to my house and went into the room where my daughter and child were; asked him if it was his child and he said yes; my daughter said he was the father of the child; the night following, at 9 o'clock, Smith came to my house to get the child, saying that he had obtained a place near Diagonal pump for the child to board till he could take it to his mother's near Mt. Vernon, to be raised and cared for; I said he had better leave it with me till he could take it directly to his mother; he said no, he would take it then and carry it to the place near the Diagonal pump; when I asked him who was the woman that was to take care of the child, he said he had forgotten her name; it was a girl child; was in a healthy condition when given by me to Smith; was clothed in a white flannel skirt, white cotten dress and white skirt; its waist was bandaged with a piece of white flannel, which was fastened with pins; the child was wrapped up in a shawl when I gave it to Smith; afterwards I identified this shawl at the Mayor's office; I offered to put more clothing around the child but Smith objected; said he had a cape on and would protect it with that; the child was very near white and not deformed; had a fine suit of long straight black hair; my daughter was a servant at Mansion House

1

and Smith who is a mulatto, lived there at same time; she had been there nearly a year. I fed the child on milk and water from its birth to the time Smith took it; before giving it to Smith I gave it some toddy; my daughter was 15 years of age at the time of the birth of the child.

Cross-examined: Never knew this thing was happening until the birth of the child; never saw child afterwards, nor any of the clothing except the shawl.

Hugh Latham was called and testified; I am Mayor of Alexandria city; have known Smith as a servant at Mansion House; I don't know Harriet Ferguson; I had a conversation with Smith at Mayor's office in December 1870; from information I had received, I sent for Smith to come to me; I asked what he did with the child he took from Mrs. Ferguson's; he said he had taken it to his mother's, near Mt. Vernon, and that he returned same night in time to perform his duties at the hotel; I told him that he must go after the child next day and return and produce the child to me; the afternoon following about five o'clock as I was going out of the outside door of my office on my way home, as I opened the door Smith was there and walked in; I invited him into my private office, and I said, Smith where is the child? why didn't you bring it? said he, Mr. Latham I couldn't; I have not been for it: I then said, Smith, I fear that the child found down on the commons is the child you took from Mrs. Ferguson's; what is the name of Heaven made you do so? His reply was Mr. Latham I don't know, I didn't know what I was doing; he was then committed for further examination, and subsequently Smith was examined by Justice May and committed for trial; I was present and asked Smith how he came to strip the child; he replied, Mr. Latham do you suppose I would strip the poor little thing; I asked him what he did with the shawl which was around the child when Mrs. Ferguson gave it to him; he said it was at the Mansion House and designated the room and locality in the room; he said the shawl was under a bed or mattress; the shawl was sent for and found and identified by Mrs. Ferguson.

The jury was then adjourned till today when the case was resumed.

Thomas Grove testified: never knew Smith till December 1870; about 11 o'clock a.m. I was walking along the river shore and found a child in a pond of water; it was a female child and it was lying on its face in the water; the water was at that time little over two feet deep; there was some trash from the tide lying by it; the child was resting on the bottom; the water was clear and I could see it easily; it had on one piece of clothing; it looked like a shirt; when I saw the child I went home and afterwards to the office of Mr. Beach, the Coroner and reported that I had found this dead child; I saw the child again at the inquest, after it was taken out of the water; I did not see who took the child from the water; it was taken from the pond on the hill to a place near Mr. Snowden's; the nearest house was a square off; the child was bright; I don't know whether it was a white or black man's child; the pond of water was right on the river shore; the water at high tide flowed into this pond; at low tide the water of the river would be some ten or fifteen yards off, but it would leave the pond full of water.

Samuel Beach, Coroner, testified: I was a Coroner in December, 1870; I held an inquest on December 16, 1870, upon the body of a female infant found dead near the ship yard; I had it removed from the pond to a place very near opposite Mr. Snowden's where I held the inquest; Dr. R. C. Powell attended the inquest; the child had on one garment when I removed it from the water; I do not remember whether the garment was cotton or woolen; ...the garment was not removed till the doctor arrived; the garment was not removed until the child had been taken into a house before the inquest was held; my impression is that the doctor used his knife to cut a band that was around the child; I do not recollect what was done with the clothing; I think the parties in whose house the inquest was held clothed the child for burial; I think the name was Davis; ... at the time of finding this child I knew nothing of Newton Smith having obtained the child from Mrs. Ferguson's; the hair of the child on which the inquest was held was black; have no recollection of the child being deformed; my opinion is that the child was well formed; I have no recollection of the child having any peculiar or birth marks; the child was buried by Mr. Wheatley.

Dr. D. M. French testified; I have been a practising physician for nearly 23 years; in December, 1870, I knew Mrs. Ferguson; she lived near the corner of Princess and Alfred streets; I was at the house at the confinement of Mrs. Ferguson's daughter in December, 1870; she gave birth to a female child alive; ... the mother of the child was white, and child had the appearance of a bright mulatto; first saw Newton Smith to know him when he came to my house with Mrs. Ferguson; at the time of the birth of an infant it is very red if the circulation through the lungs is free and healthy; I think that this was the case with this child; it cried lustily when born I remember; I don't think I saw the infant again after its birth; it had very dark and long hair; I was satisfied that the child had African blood in it; in a conversation with Mrs. Ferguson and Smith at my house Smith informed me that he was the father of the child Miss Ferguson gave birth to and that it was right and proper that he should take care of it; Smith also said he had or would make arrangements to have it sent to a house near the diagonal pump to be nursed till he could send it to his mother's near Mount Vernon; I told him that I had no objection provided the child was properly cared for; I was in Philadelphia when the inquest was held over the body of the child found near the ship yard and was gone about a week; I heard of the finding of a dead child from a police officer, and I then communicated to Mayor Latham what had occured at Mrs. Ferguson's house...

Dr. R. C. Powell testified: I have practised medicine constantly since 1862; was present at the inquest on the body of a female infant; ... I thought at first the child was white, but there was a peculiarity about the hair, which was curley; the peculiar appearance of the hair made me express the opinion that the child was the offspring of one white and one mulatto parent; from an examination I made I was satisfied that the child was born alive and drowned; I suppose from the appearance of the child that it was from one to six days old when drowned, and there were no signs of mortification; I can not tell with any certainty how long the child had been in the water; my opinion is that it had been there less than eighteen days; at that season of the year the body of an infant would not decay or show signs of mortification in eighteen days; I was fully satisfied from the signs exhibited in the examination of the body that the child came to its death by

3

drowning; ... infants ... if exposed on the ground where this child was found, in the month of December, if the thermometer was down to feezing point, could not live at the furthest, I think more than a few hours; ...

Geo. W. Jones testified: I am a member of the Alexandria police force, and was in December 1870; I know Newton Smith; took him from jail to the Mayor's office for trial on the way I broached the question to him about this child; he seemed much concerned about it; I asked what he carried the child down there for, when he said he was going to take it to his mother, and he said that he laid it down there thinking that some one would get it and take care of it; I asked him if the child was alive when he left it there; he said it was; I asked him if he did not think that the child would freeze before any one found it, it being cold weather; to this he made no answer; ...

Examination for defence – Maj. Hewey E. Alvord testified: I have known Smith for 10 years; his reputation was good as a boy and man; found his mother at Tappahannock and brought her to this city; she with her husband located somewhere near Mt. Vernon; she is now dead....

...the jury after having been instructed by the Court, were sent to their room to consult of their verdict at a quarter to eleven o'clock last night, and after being absent from the Court room for near an hour, returned into the Court with the following verdict: "We, the jury, find the prisoner guilty of murder in the second degree, and fix his term of imprisonment in the penitentiary to be ten years. The prisoner then moved for a new trial.... (*Alexandria Gazette*, April 10, 11, 1872, p.3.)

^^*^*^*^*^*^*^*^*^*^*^*^*^*

THE SENSATION produced yesterday when the news was noised around town that the mutilated remains of an innocent babe had been found in a cellar on lower Prince street brought to mind other instances of such discoveries which have from time to time been made. In the larger cities infanticide is so common that it has long since ceased to excite comment, the more appalling, or what is regarded as the more appalling crimes, throwing this species of inhumanity in the shade, though, after all, what crime is more heinous than that of taking the life of an innocent babe? About fifteen years ago a colored man barely escaped the gallows here for committing this brutal crime. It will be remembered that what was believed to be his offspring, or rather its lifeless body, was found in a pond of water near Battery Rodgers, and before and since that time numerous other cases have been brought to light, though it seemed impossible to bring the guilty to justice. About the most notable case, however, which has come under our observation happened twenty-five years ago – in the spring of 1861 and though wars and rumor of war had nearly stifled every other matter of interest, it produced some sensation. On the lower end of Wolfe street there stands an old brick house, two stories and a half high, with an extensive back building. It now belongs to the Virginia Iron and Shipbuilding Co. who have painted the front red and otherwise rejuvenated it. At the time referred to it was rather a dingy looking place, lathered over with yellow wash, and the abode of those who

4

doubtless could afford no better habitation. An old man named Taylor, a waterman, was one of the tenants, and a report was started, either by him or others who lived in the house, that the premises were haunted, it being asserted that supernatural noises occasionally emanted from certain rooms. One day Taylor pulled some of the loose wainscoting from the wall for the purpose of adjusting it more securely, and was startled and horrified to find the skeletons of several infants concealed behind the boards. The bodies had been packed in lime and encased in old trowsers legs, and the boards having been removed the lifeless forms had been stuck in between the wall and wainscoting. Who the unnatural parents were was never learned and the affair after having been duly discussed, ran its course as a nine days' wonder, and was soon forgotten. (*Alexandria Gazette* April 21, 1886, p.3.)

∧∧*∧*∧*∧*∧*∧*∧*∧*∧*∧*

THE NEW BORN negro baby found in the yard of the county court house early yesterday morning, and given in charge of a colored woman named Ann Triplett, by the police, died yesterday evening about five o'clock. After investigation by Capt. Webster, of the police force, it was ascertained that the mother of the child was a negro woman named Ella Thompson, alias Ella Day, who lives on Queen between Washington and Columbus streets, and who admitted, when questioned, that she had thrown the baby over the fence of the court house yard, shortly after it was born, without caring what became of it. A coroner's inquest was held upon the body this morning by Dr. R.C. Powell, and the jury rendered a verdict of death from criminal negligence. A warrant for the mother's arrest on a charge of murder had been issued, but in consequence of her condition she will not be taken into custody until her health permits, but is under police surveillance. She is only about nineteen years of age. (*Alexandria Gazette* June 10, 1886, p.3.)

July 13, 1886 - Ella Thompson who stands indicted for murder was led to the bar in custody of the jailor and being arraigned pleaded NOT GUILTY to the indictment; thereupon came a jury to wit...and having heard the evidence and arguments of counsel, retired to consult of their verdict and after a time returned into court with the following verdict to wit: "We the jury find the prisoner guilty of involuntary manslaughter and fix the penalty at 6 months confinement in the county jail and a fine of $5.00. Therefore it is considered by the Court that the said Ella Thompson do pay a fine of $5.00 together with the costs of the prosecution and be imprisoned in jail for the term of 6 months and the said Ella Thompson is remanded to jail. (*Alexandria Corporation Court Minute Book*, Vol. 7, July 13, 1886, p. 88, 89)

∧∧*∧*∧*∧*∧*∧*∧*∧*∧*∧*

CHARGED WITH INFANTICIDE - Lula Thomas, a colored girl between 18 and 20 years of age, living in the southwestern portion of the city, was arrested yesterday, charged with infanticide. It appears that the girl had been in the service of a family living on Lee street, near

5

Prince and on Tuesday last manifested signs of indisposition, subsequent to which she repaired to an outhouse. The lady of the house, seeing she was in no condition to fulfil her household duties, sent her home, and soon after was informed that the body of a newly born infant was in the sink of the outhouse. Suspecting the girl of having deposited her offspring in the sink, she sent for the suspected one's mother and acquainted her with the facts in the case, in the meantime ordering her to remove the body. The mother, Julia Thomas, complied and took the remains to her home, where she buried them. The police in the meantime were informed of the affair and proceeded to the residence of the suspected parties, but the mother denied the charge of infanticide brought against her daughter, and pretended that her trouble was but the result of a common contingency in approaching maternity. It was finally discovered that the body had been buried in the back yard, and the woman was arrested. This morning the Coroner, Dr. Purvis, held an examination at Mr. Demaine's undertaking establishment, where the body of the infant had been taken. A number of witnesses were examined, but a case of infanticide could not be proved, though the verdict of the jury and the opinion of Dr. Smith, was that the child's death was due to gross neglect on the part of its mother. Dr. Smith stated that the child had never breathed. A warrant for the arrest of the girl was issued and the case will be tried in the Mayor's office tomorrow. In the meantime Julia Thomas, the mother of the suspected girl is held at the station house with her nursing infant. (*Alexandria Gazette*, June 5, 1891, p.3.)

POLICE REPORT - The Mayor this morning disposed of the following cases: ... Julia Thomas, colored, for burying the dead infant of her daughter in her yard, was fined $5.00. (*Alexandria Gazette*, June 6, 1891, p.3.)

^^*^*^*^*^*^*^*^*^*^*^*

BODY FOUND - This morning while two boys - John Walsh and John Coleman - were wading in Hunting creek, between the bridge and the brick yard, they found the body of a white female child in a bag with a stone attached. They reported the matter to Constable Sipple, who had the body removed to Undertaker Demaine's establishment, and this evening Dr. Purvis, the Coroner, held an inquest. Nothing whatever could be learned concerning the body, and the jury - Messrs. James McCuen, French Smoot, J. W. Carr, Geo. Hinkin, C. T. Helmuth and R. S. Windsor - returned a verdict that the child had been killed with a blunt instrument, having been struck on the head and the skull fractured, and afterwards placed in the bag and weighted as found. (*Alexandria Gazette*, July 23, 1891, p.3)

^^*^*^*^*^*^*^*^*^*^*^*

While workmen were tearing down an old row of frame houses on Gibbon street, between Columbus and Alfred, a few days since they found a box in which were the remains of an infant which had evidently been there for a long time. The houses for a long time had been occupied by colored people. (*Alexandria Gazette*, October 13, 1892, p.3.)

^^*^*^*^*^*^*^*^*^*^*^*

A FOETUS FOUND - This morning while a little girl was passing down the west side of Royal street between Prince and Duke she saw a neat little box lodged between the palings of a fence and proceeded to examine it. Upon opening the box she was rather surprised to find concealed in it an embryonic specimen of the genus homo in the shape of a perfectly formed foetus about four inches long. She informed John Dogan, colored, who lives nearby, of her discovery, and later Mr. B. F. Turner, who happened to be in the neighborhood at the time, turned the defunct Lilliputian over to Dr. Purvis, the Coroner, who will investigate the matter. (*Alexandria Gazette*, November 4, 1892, p.3.)

^^*^*^*^*^*^*^*^*^*^*^*

THREATENED TO KILL THE CORONER - A young colored woman living on Wolfe street, between Patrick and Alfred, yesterday gave birth to an illegitimate child, and was attended by a colored midwife named Abbie Williams. The head of the child was not properly formed, and from this and other causes it was said it expired as soon as born. Dr. W. R. Purvis, the coroner, was notified, and in making an examination he discovered that the umbilical cord had been so arranged that in time it would have proved fatal to the child, while the operation had been properly enough performed to insure safety to the mother. The doctor having had his suspicions aroused on several other occasions by the apparent death of colored infants from neglect, concluded that this was a case which demanded investigation, and he interrogated the "granny" closely. The latter undoubtedly understood the modus operandi resorted to on such occasions, and being closely pressed by questions from the Coroner finally said she couldn't see very well and supposed she had performed her duty satisfactorily. The doctor finally had the woman arrested for criminal neglect. Later William Williams, son of the accused, learned of the interview between his mother and Dr. Purvis, and becoming exasperated said he would knock the Coroner in the head with a cobble stone on sight. Officer Howson later found the bellicose individual and carried him to the station house and locked him up. This morning Mayor Strauss held him in the sum of $100 to keep the peace for twelve months. There is every reason to believe that the crime with which the midwife in this case is charged is committed with impunity in this city, and that the infants whose worldly career is thus rendered ephemereal are buried at the city's cost, while their improvident and depraved parents prowl the city night and day leading lives of immorality, laziness and dishonesty. An inquest was held this morning over the remains of the infant referred to above. Dr. W.M. Smith made the autopsy. A verdict was rendered to the following effect: "The jury render a verdict that the child was born dead and that there was no foul play, except neglect on the part of the midwife, and recommend that all midwives be required to be registered at the auditor's office. (*Alexandria Gazette*, December 19, 1893, p.3)

^^*^*^*^*^*^*^*^*^*

ANOTHER CHARGE – Dr. Purvis, the Health Officer, today discovered evidence of criminal neglect on the part of another colored midwife who had officiated at a birth. The woman had paid no attention to the safety of the child, but had arranged everything conducive for the safety and comfort of the mother. (*Alexandria Gazette*, December 22, 1893, p. 3.)

^^*^*^*^*^*^*^*^*^*

DESTROYED HER CHILD – The mystery surrounding the finding of the body of a dead infant in the sewer on St. Asaph street, between Wilkes and Gibbon, has been explained by the arrest of a young colored woman named Ruth Carroll. Today information was obtained by Officer Beach sufficient to warrant a search for the woman, and she was found at her service place by that officer, who was soon afterward joined by Constable Webster and taken to the station house, where she made a full confession. She said she was 19 years old and that since last summer she has been leading a wayward life. While walking on St. Asaph street Wednesday night, and when near the man–hole of the sewer where the body was found it became evident to her that she would pass through a crisis before she could reach home. Not desiring that her mother should know anything about her condition, she attempted to perform her own obstetrics, and her ordeal being over she took the fruit of her waywardness to the man–hole and dropped it in. She undertook to qualify this statement afterward by saying the infant slipped out of her hand into the sewer. She at first pretended the child was born dead, but upon being closely questioned admitted it was alive and that she heard it cry. The woman was locked up and she will be sent on to court to answer the charge of murder. Ada Carroll, mother of the prisoner, was subsequently arrested. (*Alexandria Gazette*, April 6, 1896, p.3.)

Ruth Carroll, colored, charged with murdering her infant child, was sent on to the grand jury. Ada Carroll, colored, mother of the accused, suspected of being a party to the murder, was dismissed. (*Alexandria Gazette* April 7, 1896 p.3.)

VERDICT – Commonwealth vs. Ruth Carroll – ...The defendant was led to the bar and pleaded NOT GUILTY. And a Jury came to wit and having heard the evidence returned the following verdict: "We the jury find the prisoner guilty of voluntary manslaughter and fix her punishment at one year in the penitentiary." The court then sentenced her to one year in the penitentiary. (*Alexandria Corporation Minute Book* Vol. 12, January 29, 1897, p. 129).

^^*^*^*^*^*^*^*^*^*

SUSPECTED OF INFANTICIDE – Bettie King, a seventeen year old

8

colored girl, was arrested yesterday on suspicion of killing an infant child of which she is supposed to be the mother. On Saturday night the girl called on Dr. Purvis and requested him to visit her as she was indisposed. The doctor went to her house on Commerce street, where he found the dead body of an infant about two days old hidden in the corner under some rubbish. The girl was placed under arrest, but her condition rendered it necessary to place her at the Infirmary. The body of the infant was taken to Mr. Demaine's undertaking establishment, and an autopsy was held yesterday morning by Drs. Purvis and Jones. Evidences of violence were found, it being apparent that the child had been struck on the head and subsequently choked to death. The accused claims that the child was born dead, but the doctors say it lived several hours after its birth. Amy Clark, a colored woman, who was found in the house, was placed under arrest, it being believed that she is a party to the alleged crime. The case was called in the Police Court this morning, but it was continued. An inquest was held this morning with Mr. R. E. Knight as foreman. Several witnesses were examined. Dr. Jones, who made the examination, stated that the child's head and face were bruised and there were evidences of strangulation. He did not think, however, that its death was due to criminal intent, but to neglect. The jury returned a verdict that the child came to its death at the hands of its mother, Bessie King, through criminal neglect. The mother, who is still at the Infirmary, has been turned over to the city authorities. (*Alexandria Gazette*, December 13, 1897 p.3.)

^#^#^#^#^#^#^#^#^#^#^#^#^#

BODY FOUND - The dead body of a colored infant was found in an alley bounded by Duke, Wolfe, Columbus and Alfred streets early last night by Alice Munday, colored. The body was wrapped in paper and had been placed in an ash pile. The police investigated the matter and the child was carried to the undertaking establishment of Mr. William Demaine, where an examination was made this morning by Dr. Purvis, the coroner, who discovered that the child had been born dead and that no crime had been committed. The body was subsequently interred. (*Alexandria Gazette*, April 7, 1898, p3.)

CHAPTER TWO

Adultery & Bigamy

BIGAMY – A man named John Beach has been arrested in this place, charged with having married a woman in Montgomery County, Maryland, he at the same time having a wife and children here. He has been committed to jail, to await his examination before the County Court. (*Alexandria Gazette*, January 17, 1865, p.2.)

THE BIGAMY CASE – In the Corporation Court, Judge E.M. Lowe, today, the case of the Commonwealth vs. Thos. R. Bird, indicted for bigamy, was called and the trial proceeded with D.L. Smoot, Commonwealth's Attorney, appeared for the prosecution, and Messrs. Kilgour and Ball for the defence. The prisoner was led into Court and with the assent of the Commonwealth's Attorney, the accused was allowed to sit by his counsel. The indictment charging that on the 16th day of January, 1868, in the city of Washington, D.C. the said Bird did marry one Mary Broden, and take her as his wife, and that afterwards, to wit: on the 1st day of March 1871, in the city of Alexandria, Virginia, he did feloniously marry one Henrietta Godwin, the said Mary Broden being then alive and still the wife of the said Thos. R. Bird, was then read to the accused, to which he plead "not guilty."

...The Commonwealth's Attorney then stated the facts of the case substantially, as laid down in the indictment, and read the law of the State denouncing a punishment for the crime of bigamy, such punishment being imprisonment in the penitentiary for not less than 3 nor more than 8 years. The counsel for the defence having no statement to make at this time the witnesses both for the prosecution and defence were then called to the Book and sworn.

The first witness called for the prosecution was Father P. F. McCarthy, who testified that he lives in Washington; is pastor of the Church of the Immaculate Conception; has been for 5 years; knows both Thos. R. and Mary Bird; the latter's name was formerly Mary Broden; she is now T.R. Bird's wife; that he married them January 16th, 1868, at his (McCarthy's) residence in Washington city; they were married under authority of a license; Bird brought him the license; they were married according to the laws and customs of his church and of the District of Columbia; keeps a record of all marriage licenses among his church papers; (a copy of a license was then shown the witness) and he stated that it was similar to the one brought

11

him by Bird, and under authority of which he performed the ceremony making Bird and said Mary, man and wife; it is the kind of marriage license used in Washington.

Cross examined: First saw Mary Broden a few days before her marriage; had a conversation with her in regard to the coming marriage; (witness was then asked what that conversation was. The Commonwealth's Attorney objected to the question and the objection was sustained and exceptions taken) Mary Broden first spoke to witness about performing the marriage ceremony between Bird and herself; ceremony was not performed in Latin; two witnesses were present at the marriage witness then stated that the rules of his church, in regard to marrying a Catholic and Protestant, and that they were complied with in this case.

Re-examined: Has the license under which he married Bird and said Mary at his residence, among his church archives.

Mrs. ---- Cook testified: Lives in Washington; knows Mary Bird; her name was Mary Broden before her marriage; first saw her during the war; witnessed the marriage of Bird and Mary at McCarthy's house, Bird asked her to go to the clergyman's and she went with him; Mary Bird is now living.

Cross examined. Was first introduced to Mary as Mrs. Bird during the war; don't know where her husband was; Bird was the only man who came to Mary's house; I understood T.R. Bird to be her husband; never heard Mary called by any other name than Mrs. Bird; never heard her called "Irish Moll;" never heard any men call and enquire for "Irish Moll": witness lives four or five squares from Mrs. Bird's; Mrs. Bird owned a house on M street, in which she lived.

Mr. Cook testified. Lives in Washington; knows Thomas R. Bird and Mrs. Mary Bird; was present at the marriage of Bird and Mary at McCarthy's house; Father McCarthy performed the ceremony; they were married in January, 1868; they lived on M street, between 4th and 5th Streets in Washington, after they were married. Bird, through witnesses' wife, asked him to witness the ceremony, ...

Dr. R. R. S. Hough testified: I live in Alexandria; have lived here three years; am a minister; was such March 1st 1871; know T. R. Bird and also know Miss Henrietta Godwin; married Bird and Miss Godwin March 1, 1871 in Alexandria; married them under a license; it was produced to witness before he married them; married them according to rules of M.E. Church South; am licensed to perform marriage ceremonies.

Col. R. S. Ashby testified he lived in Alexandria; have lived here since 1849; know Thos. R. Bird and Miss Godwin; know Rev. Dr. Hough; was present at marriage of Bird and Miss Godwin, on 1st day of March 1871; Dr. Hough married them.

The Commonwealth here rested the case and the Court took a recess until 2 o'clock p.m. (*Alexandria Gazette* July 14, 1871, p.3.)

THE BIGAMY CASE - VERDICT OF THE JURY AND PRISONER SENTENCED TO THREE YEARS IN THE PENITENTIARY - EXECUTION STAYED ... At 20 minutes past 5 o'clock the jury left the Court room, and returned at 6 o'clock, to ask the Court whether or not they could, upon the evidence adduced at the trial, find that the first marriage was celebrated according to the laws of the District of Columbia. The Court instructed them that they could. Counsel for prisoner excepted.

Afterwards, at 6:35 o'clock the jury came in with a verdict of GUILTY, and fixed the term of imprisonment at 3 years in the penitentiary. (*Alexandria Gazette*, July 16, 1871, p.3.)

^^*^*^*^*^*^*^*^*^*^*^*

BIGAMIST – It was mentioned among the telegraphic news from Washington, in yesterday's *Gazette*, that a colored man named Robert Williams, formerly of Alexandria, had been arrested on the charge of bigamy. The Washington Star of that date gives the following account of the case: – "In the police court, Judge Snell, this morning, Mary Williams, a respectable colored woman, charged that Robert Williams, her husband, did feloniously marry one Henrietta A. Humphries, knowing that his former wife, Mary Williams, was living and a resident of the United States. Robert said "he didn't know; he didn't recognize himself when it was done, as he was intoxicated at the time." Mary produced her marriage certificate showing that they were married in October, 1871, in Alexandria. She brought two witnesses who were present on that occasion. Wife No. 2 testified to her marriage in January following with Williams in this city, and brought the certificate to corroborate it. The priest, Rev. Mr. Hoggenforst, of St. Joseph's Church, Capitol Hill, testified to performing the marriage ceremony, and that Robert was as sober as a judge at the time. Robert being headed off all round, the judge committed him for action of the grand jury." If all the colored men who have two living wives are to be arrested and tried as bigamists, the courts will be pretty well occupied. (*Alexandria Gazette*, April 25, 1872, p. 3.)

^^*^*^*^*^*^*^*^*^*^*^*

A "LOVE" AFFAIR – Some time ago a man about forty-five years of age, Samuel Love by name, came to this city from Washington and made the acquaintance of one Susie Ridgeway, who lives on north Fairfax street, since which time he has visited the city quite frequently. Love's visits to Alexandria caused the wife of his bosom to suspect that "things were not what they seemed to be," so she followed him a week ago to this city, with a view of finding out what was going on. She saw him enter the woman's house, and there bestow upon another woman the affection he had at the altar, sworn to lavish upon her and her alone; in her wrath, Mrs. Love determined to kill the woman who rivalled her in the love of Mr. Love, but circumstances proving unfavorable for the carrying out of her intentions, she returned after having made a note of Love's stopping place, with feelings all wrought up, to her home in Washington, there to brood over the base treatment of her false husband. Mr. Love soon followed, and was received with a happy smile by his wife, just as if nothing had happened. He explained to his love "how tedious and tasteless" were the hours he was compelled to spend in that "dull old town of Alexandria."

13

For over a week things went on lovingly with the Loves, when again Mr. Love announced to Mrs. Love that he was called to Alexandria. He came to this city this morning and went straight to the house of his fair imamorata. Mrs. Love with bitterness in her heart and a pistol in her pocket, arrived soon after. She entered the house, and then confronted, to his great astonishment, her false husband, and at the same time levelled the pistol at the head of the Ridgeway woman, declaring with flaming eyes and heroic attitude, that she would blow her brains out; but she didn't blow. Officer Arnold here arrived on the scene and marched both of the Loves off to the station house where they were locked up until this afternoon. (*Alexandria Gazette*, April 23, 1880, p3.)

THE "LOVES" AGAIN - Mrs. Love, and her husband, Samuel Love, from Washington, whose little jamboree, were noticed in yesterday's *Gazette*, were brought before the Mayor and Justice Thompson, late in the afternoon, and after a hearing of the case, all the parties were dismissed, the Ridgeway woman, upon a promise of good behaviour in the future, and the Loves, upon a promise to leave the city immediately. The costs of the case was divided up between the two women and the husband of Mrs. Love paid her share without hesitation, but Maria Ridgeway was unable to raise her portion of the cost. There stood Sam Love able and anxious to pay for her, but he knew it was dangerous to do so in the presence of his wife. So he watched his opportunity, and Mrs. Love having occasion to turn her back for a moment, he slapped the money down quickly and turned to Mrs. Love and said: "Come, dear, let's be going." Mrs. Love is a tall woman with a bass voice, and if she don't "Tan" Sammy when she gets him home, she is not the woman she looks to be. (*Alexandria Gazette*, April 24, 1880, p.3.)

^^*^*^*^*^*^*^*^*^*^*^*^*

CHARGED WITH BIGAMY - George A. Taylor, of Washington, was arrested at the Braddock House, in this city, last night, charged with bigamy, and was locked up for future examination. He was arrested in a room in which was also a young woman who had retired and who was supposed to be the wife of Taylor. Last night the father of the young woman came here from Washington and proceeding to the station house swore out a warrant against Taylor. He said Taylor had been paying attention to his daughter, but that learning that he, Taylor, was a married man, he forbade him his house. He then took his daughter out West and left her with his brother, telling him of the circumstances and requesting him not to allow to see her if he came there. Yesterday, however, he learned that Taylor and his daughter were in this city, so he came here to have him arrested. He said that he had been told that Taylor was a married man, that recently he had deserted his wife, whom he had left in destitute circumstances, and had abducted his daughter. It appears that Taylor and the young woman came here yesterday and engaged board at the Braddock House, but last night, when the couple were taken to the station house, they denied that they were married. Taylors seems to have complete con-

14

trol over the young woman, who is of frail constitution and appears to be in delicate health. (*Alexandria Gazette*, June 12, 1891, p.3)

Geo. A. Taylor, who was held on the charge of bigamy, pleaded guilty of adultery and was fined $22.10. (*Alexandria Gazette*, June 13, 1891, p.3.)

^^*^*^*^*^*^*^*^*^*^*^*^*

DECAMPED INSTANTLY – Considerable amusement was occasioned on north Fairfax street late yesterday evening by the sudden flight from a boarding house of a man and woman who had been there since last Friday. About 10 days ago the man, who is said to be George C. Sherman, a druggist, at 12th and Vermont avenue, Washington, came here with a Mrs. Guy and on Friday put up on north Fairfax street. Yesterday evening the husband of the woman made his appearance in this city unannounced and soon located the couple. He went to the station house and asked the services of Lieutenant Smith. The latter procured a search warrant and took Officer Arrington with him to the house. The couple, it is said, were in bed at the time, but before the officers reached their room they had donned their clothing and made their escape through a window and over a back fence toward the Midland depot, where it is said they took a train for the South. Nearly eveybody in the neighborhood was in the street when the excitement was going on. Mr. Guy came to this city again this afternoon to collect evidence for a suit for divorce and damages which he will institute. Sherman has returned to Washington and Mrs. Guy is at present at a house in Fairfax county a short distance from this city. (*Alexandria Gazette*, March 14, 1894, p.3.)

^^*^*^*^*^*^*^*^*^*^*^*^*

BENT ON BIGAMY – James Dickenson, a Washington machinist, who has a wife, has, according to the Washington papers, been endeavoring to add to his household by arranging to marry several other women. He is charged with bringing a young girl named Mary Ricker to this city for the purpose of marrying her, but her mother came here yesterday and with the aid of the police located the young woman and took her home. On Christmas he gave Miss Ricker a handsome cape. Dickenson, it is alleged, passed himself off as a single man, and attempted to marry several other young women, among them Lizzie Mull, Rosa Baldwin, Carrie Russell and Julia Fisher, all of Washington. Each had prepared her wedding attire and was ready to be married when Dickenson's wife appeared on the scene and frustrated the ceremony. Dickenson is from Spottsylvania county, Virginia.

P.S. Since the above was written another version of the affair is given. It is said that Dickenson's wife, who lives in this city, brought Miss Richer to her home here, with the consent of the young woman's father, in order to have her for a witness against her husband, from whom she will apply for a divorce. Miss Ricker, it is alleged, in a

15

short time will become a mother as the fruits of her intimacy with Dickenson. The young woman's father was here today and corroborated the statement made above, and says when Mr. Dickenson shall have obtained a divorce his daughter will be enabled to marry Dickenson. The injured wife, it is claimed, has no objection to this procedure. (*Alexandria Gazette*, February 1896, p.3.)

ARRESTED - Miss Richer's father changed his mind considerably after leaving Alexandria yesterday, and when he reached Washington he swore out a warrant for the arrest of James H. Dickinson, the machinist, who is alleged to have brought his daughter to this city and placed her in the home of his wife. Dickenson was later arrested on a warrant charging adultery. The girl's father says that he will prosecute Dickenson to the end, and send him to the penitentiary if possible. The accused, who has a long mustache, which he keeps carefully waxed, and large liquid blue eyes, says that he is not worried, that he has been on bad terms with his wife for two years, and that the Ricker girl knew that he was married. He denies that he made arrangements to marry the five others girls. He further says Miss Ricker, with whom he had an interview yesterday will testify in his behalf. (*Alexandria Gazette*, February 4, 1896, p. 3.)

^^*^*^*^*^*^*^*^*^*^*^*

ALLEGED MARRIAGE - The death on Tuesday of Minnie Dixon, who was thrown from a buggy in this city last week, was the text for a sensational article in a Washington Paper this morning, the writer claiming that Mr. Arthur J. Dixon, of this city, had married the deceased six years ago. She was originally Miss Minnie Mater, and, according to the writer, she has two grown daughters, the fruit of a union previous to her alliance with Dixon. The writer claims that the ceremony was performed and its legality admitted by all the parties to the affair. The long-kept secret, it is said, was only told upon the death of the woman. During the absence from this city of Mr. Dixon's mother and sister, the alleged wife on Friday last came to this city and for the first time in her six years of wedded life entered her husband's home. In the afternoon she went driving with her reputed husband and the horse becoming unmanageable ran away, throwing the woman from the carriage. She recovered sufficiently to return to Washington that night, but became unconscious on the street and had to be carried to her residence. The injuries, together with a stroke of paralysis, caused her death. (*Alexandria Gazette*, August 6, 1896, p.3)

^^*^*^*^*^*^*^*^*^*^*^*

MUCH MARRIED MAN - It was stated yesterday that A. M. Robinson, of Montgomery Couty, Maryland was here looking for his mother and sister, who, he said, left their home some time last August. They were located by the police on Prince street, where the daughter had been living with a man whom she claimed to be her husband and to whom she had borne a child. Today another woman put in her appearance and claimed she was the lawful wife of the man. The latter,

16

in the meantime, vanished, but reappeared in this city this afternoon, when he was arrested by Officer Atkinson. Wife No. 1 is still in this city and, it is said is still unprovided for. Each of the women positively avers she is the man's lawful wife. The man gave his name as C. McDonald Wilkerson, and, with the woman has been living here since last May, being mainly supported by charity. Wife No. 1 says she is from Forestville, Maryland, and today, after seeing the woman who had supplanted her, left for her home but said she would return. Wilkerson is held at the station house. *Alexandria Gazette* November 16, 1897, p.3.)

SENT TO THE WORK HOUSE – Everett McDonald Wilkinson, who was locked up at police headquarters yesterday charged with being the husband of two wives, was brought before the Mayor this morning. He was arrested on a warrant issued on the complaint of Mrs. Kate Wilkinson, of Forestville, Maryland, who arrived here yesterday. As was stated on Monday, A. M. Robinson, of Montgomery County, Maryland was here on Sunday in search of his mother and sister, who, he said, had left their home in August last. The two women were located by the police at 317 Prince street; where they were living with Wilkinson. The son returned home without his mother and sister. Both women claim to be Wilkinson's legal wife. Wilkinson after having been locked up acknowledged that Mrs. Kate Wilkinson was his wife, but denied that he had married Miss Phoebe Robinson. He had worked for the young girl's father in Maryland, and confessed that he had betrayed the confidence of his employer. He deserted his wife and with the girl he had wronged went to Occoquan, Virginia, to live. Later he secured employment at Fort Sheridan, and afterwards came to Alexandria. Wilkinson, Mrs. Robinson and her eighteen year old daughter, who is the mother of an infant of a few months old, have been mainly supported by charity since their residence in this city. The young woman confessed that she was not the wife of Wilkinson, and that she had made a contrary report to the police, hoping to shield her betrayer. Mrs. Wilkinson, the legal wife, returned to her home in Maryland yesterday evening. This morning the Mayor sent Wilkinson to the work house for thirty days under the vagrant act, and ordered the mother and daughter to leave the city. The mother stated to the Mayor this morning that she lived in Prince George's County, Maryland, and said she would go home as soon as she could get proper clothing. She also said she knew Wilkinson was a married man, but that he had told her and her daughter that he would marry the latter as soon as he could get a divorce. (*Alexandria Gazette*, November 17, 1897, p.3.)

CHAPTER THREE

Arson

The frequent occurrence of Fires recently, gives unmistakeable evidence of the presence of the daring incendiary in our midst. The peace and security of the public demand an untiring vigilance and energetic performance of duty on the part of the officers of the Corporation, whose business it is to watch over and protect the slumbering denizens in the "balmy hours of sweet repose." Thus far has mischievous villany successfully applied the torch; for it is my firm conviction, it is done by thoughtless youth for the love of frolic, and not for the purpose of malicious injury to property. How are we to remedy this evil? That is the question which has given rise to this communication, and which I trust may direct the attention of our city Fathers to the subject. It is easier to find fault with an existing law, (which I believe is faithfully executed,) than it is to project a new one that is better; therefore I enter on this task with diffidence. But to the question. How are we to remedy the evil? I answer.--First, pass a law prohibiting minors from running with the fire apparatus, and make it the duty of the Police and the Wardens to arrest, and send to the Watch House, all minors found running to, at, or coming from a fire, and if the present police force is not sufficient for the purpose, let the Mayor appoint a special Fire Police to act during a conflagration.

Secondly, reorganize the present watch system. Appoint a superintendent of the watch to remain at the Watch House, and see that every man does his duty. Two lieutenants of the watch, to make the rounds of the city, and report all delinquencies on the part of the watch, and insure their vigilance. Sixteen Watchmen, four for each Ward.

The next consideration is the effective distribution of this force, which is very important to effect the object in view. Subdivide the Wards into four parts or beats, and station a Watch Box in each. Confine each watch to his particular beat, and oblige him to make a careful round every hour. Let the watchmen meet at the Watch House at 9 o'clock. Call the roll, and the vacancies filled by substitutes (dock the delinquents and pay the substitutes) then proceed to their respective posts and watch till sunrise; return to the Watch House the roll called; and dismissed by the Captain. Appoint efficient officers, pay them well, say for Captain $1.50 per night, Lieutenants and Watch, $1.25. Adopt this plan and in my humble opinion you remedy the evil. FIREMAN (*Alexandria Gazette*, April 14, 1852, p. 2.)

19

ARSON – BE WARNED! Incendiaries are in our midst, and who knows now, where is to be the next scene of conflagration? Already have they succeeded in destroying much valuable property. It is time that the most active and energetic steps were taken. Patrols ought to be organized. Rewards should be offered for the detection of the offenders. Every citizen should be on the alert. Vigilance must be the word. Let us act and not talk. CITIZENS. (*Alexandria Gazette*, June 6, 1854, p. 3.)

^^*^*^*^*^*^*^*^*^*^*^*^*

DESTRUCTIVE FIRE – About midnight, on Sunday night last, the watchmen on duty, discovered flames bursting out from the roof of one of the brick warehouses on Union, between King and Prince streets. The alarm was immediately given, and upon repairing to the spot it was discovered that the warehouse occupied on the wharf by J.T.B. Perry & Son, and on Union Street by D.F. Hooe as a store house for flour, was on fire through all the upper story. The firemen and citizens, as usual, went to work with a zeal and determination worthy of all praise, to extinguish the flames where they originated, and to prevent them from spreading to the neighboring buildings. All their exertions could not save the adjoining warehouse occupied by S. S. Masters & Son. The whole block rented, by the merchants we have named, was destroyed, with much of their valuable contents, flour, guano, and groceries. The fine new block of warehouses, south, lately erected by Wm. N. McVeigh, and occupied by Green, Suttle & Co., Robinson & Payne, McVeigh & Chamberlain, and Wells A. Harper & Co., were in imminent danger, but were finally saved, with scarcely any damage. The warehouses north, occupied by James Dempsey and S. Shinn & Son, were also saved without any loss.

During the progress of the fire three distinct explosions occurred in the store of Messrs. Perry & Son. They arose from the bursting of a keg of gunpowder, a canister of gunpowder, and, the last, it is thought, must have been from a keg of saltpetre. No damage was done by these explosions, the roofs of the warehouses having been previously burned off, and there being a fee circulation of air.

The buildings destroyed belonged to the estate of the late John C. Vowell, and to John S. Miller, of Philadelphia. They were insured in the Potomac and Fire Insurance offices of this city, for about $7,500.

We grieve to say, that there is no doubt of this fire having been caused by an incendiary. No one connected with the occupants had been in the store since Saturday evening. It is supposed that means must have been found to enter the warehouse either through the store of the Messrs. Perry, or through a side door leading into Mr. Hooe's warehouse on Sunday night. The work was done effectually, for, when discovered, as we have said, the upper stories were in a blaze.

About 8 or 900 bushels of corn in the warehouse of S. S. Master & Son, were burned or otherwise destroyed. A quantity of guano in the lower story was injured by water. Books and papers saved. Insurance to the amount of $6,000 in the Fire Insurance office. The insurance will probably cover the loss. In the warehouse of J. T. B. Perry &

Son, a quantity of groceries were destroyed. Books and papers saved. Insured in the Potomac office to the amount of $2,300. Insurance will probably cover the loss....

We repeat our expressions of praise and thanks to the Firemen for their gallant conduct, on this, as on all similar occasions. They well deserve the encomiums that are bestowed upon them, for their zeal and efficiency. (*Alexandria Gazette*, June 6, 1854, p.3.)

^^*^*^*^*^*^*^*^*^*^*

COMMUNICATED - The incendiary burning of Mr. James Green's two warehouses, on his wharf, on Tuesday morning last, is a matter which ought to excite, at least, the vigilance of the whole community. Although the night was dark and rainy, it was a fit occasion for the midnight prowler to accomplish his fiendish purposes. The burnt warehouses were close to the Pioneer Mills, to Mr. Hooff's extensive flour store, to several large piles of lumber, to the shipping, Foundry, etc. so that the location, like the time, was just such as to effect the most damage. For a year past, there appears to have been a settled purpose to burn property on or near the wharves. The incendiaries who commenced this, seem to be amongst us. In the case of the last fire, it is said, they must have applied the match by getting inside of the building, or by putting it through a plank torn from the outside. Will nothing be done, either by the Corporation, or by individuals? I do not think the adding of two or three watchmen to the present night watch would do any good whatever. There must be some other method of ferreting out the villains, and arresting their crimes. (*Alexandria Gazette* January 11, 1855, p.3.)

^^*^*^*^*^*^*^*^*^*^*

INCENDIARIES ABOUT AGAIN - Again have the incendiaries commenced their work-interrupted for some time. About 1 o'clock A.M. yesterday morning - the time when a city is generally in deep sleep - it was discovered that fire had been communicated to three different buildings, in different situations - one was a barn containing hay, on a lot at the south end of Royal street, belonging to Mr. Stephen Shinn - another, a house on a lot near Yeate's Garden belonging to Mr. Samuel Miller - (both of these were burned down) - and another a house on Naylor's Hill, where the flames were extinguished before they made much progress. These buildings were all fired at the same time, and evidently by concert with the incendiaries. There is proof therefore, that there is a gang engaged in burning, and probably, in plunder and robbery. It is time, for our citizens to be on the alert. The loss by fires mentioned was not great, but who knows where this will end, if some detection be not made. (*Alexandria Gazette*, March 8, 1856, p.3)

^^*^*^*^*^*^*^*^*^*^*

ARSON - The first case taken up was that of the Conmonwealth vs. Thomas Parsons, charged with setting fire to the warehouse of Messrs. S. S. Masters & Son, on the night of the 5th of September last.

The evidence in the case was mainly for the prosecution, and the jury, after remaining in their room about ten minutes, returned into Court, and gave a verdict of guilty, and ascertained the prisoner,s punishment at five years' imprisonment in the penitentiary. The Court sentenced him accordingly. C. E. Stuart for prosecution; S. F. Beach for the defence. (*Alexandria Gazette*, November 9, 1858, p.3.)

^^*^*^*^*^*^*^*^*^*^*

INCENDIARY ATTEMPT - The alarm of fire last night, between half past seven and eight o'clock was caused by an incendiary attempt to burn the frame building at the corner, made by the intersection of West, Commerce and Prince streets, belonging to Mr. J. W. Atkinson, but occupied by a colored man, named John Hackley, as a shoemaker's shop. The fire was kindled in a back room, under a pile of furniture. Fortunately the flames were discovered and extinguished before the house or its contents had received any serious damage. Four young men, natives and residents of this city, were arrested by the police soon after the alarm had been sounded - (one of whom, however, Pierce Noland, managed to effect his escape) - and locked up all night in the Watch House, on suspicion of being the parties who committed the crime. The result of their examination, held this morning, is mentioned in the *Gazette*'s police report. (*Alexandria Gazette*, January 2, 1868, p.3.)

Thomas Javins, Geo. Webster, and William alias Cud Grady, arrested on the charge of setting fire to a house belonging to Mr. J. W. Atkinson, were discharged. (*Alexandria Gazette*, January 2, 1868, p.3.)

^^*^*^*^*^*^*^*^*^*^*

LATE INCENDIARY ATTEMPT - ARREST OF J. RAMMELL AND SAMUEL EHRLICH, THE PROPRIETOR AND CLERK OF THE STORE - PRELIMINARY EXAMINATION OF THE ACCUSED. The preliminary examination of J. Rammell and his clerk, Samuel Ehrlich, charged with an attempt to burn the house at the southeast corner of King and Columbus streets on the night of Sunday last, was held in the chamber of the Common Council, the Mayor's Office not being capacious enough to hold the large crowd that had assembled to hear the evidence, at six o'clock yesterday evening before Mayor Latham and Justices Uhler and May. Commonwealth's Attorney, conducted the prosecution. Col. C. E. Stuart appeared as counsel for the accused. Messrs. Brill and Eichbergh were sworn as interpreters - the prisoners not speaking the English language intelligible.

Capt. J. M. Steuart being sworn testified as follows: "Knows the accused - he kept a store on the southeast corner of King and Columbus streets - the young man is his clerk; between 12 and 2 o'clock on Sunday night a fire occurred at this store on going to the fire found the counter had been pulled out into the street, and heard that embers had been found under this counter in the store; hearing a citizen say that

22

there was no competent officer to investigate the affair, and from what he saw and heard thinking that an enquiry should be made, the statement made by Mr. Henry Stuart induced him to believe that the parties living in the house were the proper ones to be arrested, and believing so he had arrested them. When he went into the yard in rear of the store, he found that nearly everything that had been in the house except one or two mattresses and some other few things of little value had been taken out and was piled up there and saw Rammell lying on a mattress in the yard covered up - his wife saying that he had drunk some ice water and that it had made him sick. Mr. Stewart informed him that he had seen a young man come out of the store and cry fire, and had told him to stop crying fire and look after the man who was in the house; he did not suppose the value of the stock of goods at the store to be greater than $200. Mr. S. H. Janney, an insurance agent, who was present, stated that a policy of $1500 on the stock, and $500 on the furniture had been gotten out about two weeks ago. Shoe boxes and paper collar boxes seemed to constitute most of the stock; ...the house had apparently been gutted; Ehrlich had no shirt on when witness saw him; the fire originated in the store room which communicates with the other part of the house; judged the goods he found in the yard had been removed before the alarm of fire was sounded, and his reason for so judging were founded upon the narrowness of the means of exist from the store and the condition in which the goods were packed....

B. F. Price: Lives on west side of Columbus street, the windows of his bed room overlooking Rammell's yard; was waked up by his wife between one and two o'clock on Monday morning and told that she heard noises in Rammell's yard; got up and looked out of the window; saw persons in Rammell's yard removing goods from the house, about five or more minutes after he saw persons removing goods from the house into the yard he heard the cry of fire; dressed and went to his store; when he got there one half of the counter was burnt; did not go in the store until the fire was nearly out; saw in the back yard, household goods and furniture, but no store goods supposed it required ten or fifteen minutes to move the goods found in the yard from the store; among the goods in the yard were some bedroom furniture, but does not know the internal arrangements of the house, or whether any bed rooms were on the lower floor; saw . Rammell moving goods from his house into the yard before the alarm of fire; after the alarm saw him lying on a mattress in the yard apparently in pain.

Capt. J. F. Webster: Knows Rammell when he sees him; ...Rammell had two stores, one in the German building and one on the corner of King and Columbus street...examined the premises, and found in the front room, on the second floor, one bed or matress; in the next room one bedstead, stove, stand, and thinks some few paper boxes; in the next a beadstead and mattress; it appeared as if most of the things of value had been removed to the back yard...All the goods in the yard were piled up near the back fence; it would have taken two persons 15 minutes to have removed the goods found in the yard from the house if they had been properly arranged in the house....

This morning (July 20, 1870)...the accused appeared before Mayor Latham and Justices Uhler and May but by agreement of the counsel;

the further examination of witnesses was waived and the parties admitted to bail, the proprietor in the sum of $2,000 and the clerk in $1,000 for their appearance at the quarterly term of the Hustings court, next Ocotober to answer the charge. ... (*Alexandria Gazette*, July 19 & 20, 1870)

HONORABLY ACQUITTED - Mr. I. Rammell, and his clerk, Samuel Ehrlich, who have several times been examined before magistrates and once by the Court upon the charge of setting fire to the framed store house on the southeast corner of King and Columbus streets, on the night of the 17th of last July, were re-examined yesterday at the Mayor's office, in the presence of a large crowd of spectators, before Justices Beel and Beach, and after a patient hearing of all the evidence were honorably discharged. (*Alexandria Gazette*, October 28, 1870, p. 3.)

^^*^*^*^*^*^*^*^*^*^*^*^*

SUSPECTED OF INCENDIARISM - Near eleven o'clock last night Engineer Wood, of the Columbian engine, reported at the station house that a well-known young man of this city had taken a bunch of waste and had left the engine house with the intention of setting fire to a frame house on the north side of Prince street, between Alfred and Patrick.   Lieut. Smith and Officer Hall repaired to the vicinity and secreted themselves on the opposite side of the street from which position they saw the man enter the premises by the cellar, where he lighted several matches. He later emerged and re-entered the house by getting over the front fence. Lieutenant Smith hastened across the street and found the man's shoes on the pavement, near the cellar door.   The suspect had in the meantime escaped by the back way. The lieutenant and Officer Hall secreted themselves under a tree in a vacant lot on the opposite side of the street. The man soon returned in search of his shoes, but being unable to find them went to his home, about a square away.   The lieutenant then procured a light and made a thorough search of the premises, but apart from a few matches found in the cellar he could discover no evidence of an attempt at incendiarism, no waste nor oil being found as was reported this morning. The man went to the station house this morning and asked that his shoes be returned to him, he denying that he had any intention of setting fire to the house and giving as an excuse for his conduct an over-indulgence in stimulants. The man was arrested this evening and the matter will be investigated by the Police Court.   It is charged that during the night he took a five gallon can of coal oil out of the Columbia house.   The can was found later on Prince street. (*Alexandria Gazette*, August 6, 1896, p. 3.)

^^*^*^*^*^*^*^*^*^*^*^*^*

A YOUTHFUL INCENDIARY - In Washington on Saturday evening, Brook Corbett, son of Mr. F. E. Corbett, who is engaged in business here and who formerly resided in this city, tried to burn his father's house because a small amount of money had been refused him. Hard

24

work by the fire department saved the house, which is located at 92 M street northwest. The young man's mind is said to be affected, and he will be examined by the authorities. Saturday morning Brook was in a bad humor. He is just twenty-one years old, and claimed that on this account his parents should give him $100, so that he would not have to ask his mother for change every time he wished to buy anything. His parents owed the boy no money, and tried to quiet him. He said nothing more, and his mother thought the matter had ceased to trouble him. Later the house was found to be on fire. The back steps and the carpets of the rear rooms had been saturated with coal oil, and were blazing when discovered. The members of the fire department on arriving, saw that an attempt had been made to burn the house, and told Officer Carrington, who, after a few questions, arrested young Corbett. He was locked up at the station, where, during the afternoon, he talked in a rambling manner. At the house Saturday afternoon Mrs. Corbett declined to discuss the unfortunate affair, except to say that her son had been in bad health for a short time. In addition to firing the house, he broke the large front windows with stones. The damage by fire and water amounted to about $100. (*Alexandria Gazette*, March 26, 1894, p.3.)

CHAPTER FOUR

Graverobbing

GRAVE ROBBERS IN ALEXANDRIA - THEIR WORK LAST NIGHT -
The announcement on the streets this morning that grave robbers had
visited this city last night and "resurrected" several bodies from their
resting places in the cemeteries, created a profound sensation, it
being the first time that such a bold attempt at "body snatching" was
ever made in Alexandria. The bodies of two persons were taken from
their graves, but before they could be "spirited" away, the men who
came for them, were detected, when they fled, leaving the corpses
lying on the cold earth beside the graves where they had been interred.
Miss Elmira Jacobs, about 70 years of age, daughter of the late Pres-
ley Jacobs, and sister of Mrs. W. H. McKnight, of this city, after suffering for some time with an internal disease - supposed to be a tumor
- that puzzled the medical profession, died in Washington, rather suddenly, Sunday last. The remains were brought to this city Tuesday
last and interred in the Presbyterian Cemetery, of which Jerry Frazier,
colored, is sexton. The members of the family in this city never once
dreamed of the body of their deceased relative being disturbed, and it
was far from the mind of the sexton that there lived a man with a heart
so hard as to wish anything but peace to the inhabitants of the "silent
city" under his care, until last night, about ten o'clock, when Mr.
Emmanuel Webb, living at the corner of the lane leading to the grave
yards, heard the noise of a wagon proceeding up the road. Mr. Webb
is sexton of several of the grave yards, and is ever on the watch. He
regarded the circumstance as suspicious, and looking out of the window he hailed the driver of the wagon and asked him where he was
going. The man replied that he was on his way to "Vinegar Hill," but
had mistook the road. Mr. Webb informed him that he could not reach
the place he was looking for in that direction. The man drove on,
however, and Mr. Webb, watching the wagon, saw it turn into the lane
leading to St. Paul's Cemetery, on the east side of which is an
entrance to the Presbyterian yard. As soon as the wagon stopped, he,
accompanied by a colored man named John Landon, went to the first
named grave yard, and found the wagon halted at the side entrance, but
the driver was absent. He examined the wagon - a tight top vehicle,
with dark bay horse attached - and found the bottom covered with
straw. After waiting a short time the man who acted as driver came
out of the yard, followed by another man. He asked them what was
their business at a grave yard at that time of night. One of them
replied that they were on their way to "Vinegar Hill" but had lost the

27

route. In response to other questions, they responded that they lived in the country, about four miles from this city, but could not tell the name of the place, or the names of any of their neighbors; and that they were looking for a man named Harris.

Mr. Webb thinking that something was wrong, requested the colored man with him to go after a policeman, and started to walk up the lane to see if anything was disturbed. The two men then jumped into the wagon and drove off at full speed down the lane, keeping down Wilke's street until they were out of sight.

The Police authorities being informed of the matter, officers Goodrich and Pat Hayes, were sent out to the grave yard to make examination. Upon entering the Presbyterian yard, accompanied by Mr. Webb, they found the body of Miss Jacobs lying at the foot of the grave in which it had been placed last Tuesday with her hands clasped over her right shoulder, and her clothes much displaced.

The grave was filled up and there was very little, besides the body of the lady lying before the three men, to indicate that grave robbers had been at work.

Mr. B. Wheatley was then notified, and the body was removed to his establishment, where it was examined, but the only marks found upon it were two ridges around the wrist of each arms, supposed to have been caused by the rope used in drawing it out of the coffin.

Early this morning Capt. Webster, of the police force, and officer Goodrich, visited the grave yards to see if they could find anything that would lead to the detection of the criminals. In walking around they discovered foot prints in the ground, which they followed to the southwestern corner of the M. E. Church South, Cemetery, where they found the body of Sarah Jane Simms, colored daughter of Jerry Frazier, sexton of the Presbyterian Cemetery, who died last week of consumption, lying on the side of the grave in which it had been placed Monday last. Walter Daily, sexton of that ground, took charge of the body, and it was reinterred this morning.

Both the graves had been filed up, and it seemed that the bodies had been taken out of their graves by parties who had been hired by the men who came after them, for they were already for shipment.

Captain Webster picked up near the grave of the colored women a piece of tissue paper, wadded up and torn in three pieces with one part gone. It proved to be a press dispatch and what remained, being put together, read as follows: "Add Albany, New York. Owing to the scarcity--prices have gone up here; stove size Ch--ollars--for Lakawanna $50."

The two men in the wagon who were disguised, but supposed to be white, are described by Mr. Webb as being about 5 feet 8 inches high, and slender.

This afternoon Officers Goodrich and Arnold arrested Thomas Vaugn, Bab Carpenter, Chas Gaskins and Reuben Massey, colored grave diggers in the several cemeteries, on suspicion of being parties to the crime, and lodged them in the station house for examination tomorrow morning.

The law of Virginia against the robbing of graves is extremely light. It is as follows:

"If any person unlawfully disinter or displace a dead human body, or any part of a dead human body, which shall have been deposited in any vault or other burial place, he shall be confined in jail not more than one year and fined not exceeding $500."

There is but one other case of this kind known to have occurred in this city. Mr. Jas. Smith died about three years ago with brain disease, and was buried in one of the cemeteries. When the family, for some reason, decided, a short time after the interment, to remove the remains, a headless trunk was found. After ten years ago the body of a child was found in the lane leading to the grave yard, but it is supposed it was dropped there by some one who wished to bury it without going to the expense of purchasing a lot.

There is a tradition, which is well remembered, that a man named Pompagail who lived on Peyton's Point, over fifty years ago, a well known character in those days, was a professional grave robber. It is said that on one occasion, when surprised by the night watch, coming down Prince street with the body of a man in his arms, he placed it against a lamp post, and declared he would never again attempt to carry another drunken man home. (*Alexandria Gazette* January 27, 1880, p. 3.)

TRIAL OF THE GRAVEROBBERS - THREE OF THE ACCUSED SENT TO THE GRAND JURY. The excitement caused yesterday by the discovery that the bodies of Miss Elmira Jacobs, and Susan Jane Simms, the latter colored, had been removed from their graves, and the arrest of Baptist Carpenter, Reuben Massey, Thomas Vaughan, and Charles Gaskins, colored grave diggers, and Albert Butler, a colored driver for an undertaking establishment, charged with the crime, showed very little abatement to day when the examination of one of the prisoners commenced at eleven o'clock, before Mayor Smith. ... The station house up stairs and down, was crowded with anxious spectators, both white and colored. ... the first witness called was Baptist Carpenter, colored, who stated that he was a grave digger; was home on Monday night; did not go home Tuesday night till 9 o'clock; saw Butler Monday night with coffin case of Miss Simms; Butler asked him if he wanted to make some money; said he, Carpenter, could make four or five dollars between that time and Saturday night, by taking up a few bodies; that he knew a doctor in Washington who would give $2 apiece for subjects; Butler came to see him again Tuesday night on the subject, and he, the witness told him he would not do such a job for fifty dollars. ...

Mr. John G. Philips was then called and testified that he was at the Washington and Alexandria depot Tuesday night; after placing the mail in the cars, he went into the sitting room of the depot; saw there a heavy bearded, respectable looking gentleman in a much excited state; the stranger asked if there were any wagon drivers about the place; on being asked who he wanted, he stated that he was Dr. Riley, of Washington, and that a light colored man, who had promised to meet him there, had disappointed him; the man he wanted drove a wagon, and he thought he was a huckster; ...

Thomas Vaughn, a colored grave digger, was the next witness. He stated that Al Butler came to him Wednesday night and told him he would give him (Vaughn) $2 to watch while he went up to the Methodist Protestant grave yard to take up bodies; that he wanted that body, but did not say what body it was; he agreed, and went off to the fodder stack in the yard where he lived (Spring Garden, in Grave Yard lane) and Butler went on to the grave yard; this was about 8 o'clock; he did not wake up until he was scared out by the wind and the noise of the wagon...

Office Goodrich testified that he was sent to make an examination of the grave yards on the night of the robbery of the graves; that he notified Mr. Wheatley of the fact that the body of Miss Jacobs had been taken from the grave and was lying exposed in the grave yard...

Walter Daily, sexton of several of the yards, testified that his tool house was in St. Paul's Cemetery; Carpenter had access to it, but brought the key to his house about five o'clock Wednesday evening and it was not taken away again; all the dirt was taken out of the grave of the colored woman Simms, and the body was drawn out by means of a rope placed around the neck of the corpse....

At the conclusion of the testimony, the court retired for consultation and upon returning to the room, Mayor Smith said it had been decided unanimously to send the prisoner (Butler) on to the grand jury. ... After hearing other testimony Charles Haskins and Reuben Massey were discharged as there was no evidence against them, and Thos. Vaughn and Baptist Carpenter, the two who testified against Butler, were sent on to court. Bail was fixed at $250 for each of the prisoners. (*Alexandria Gazette*, January 28, 1880, p.3.)

THE GHOULS IN JAIL - FURTHER DEVELOPMENTS... Butler the leader of the gang was found to be guilty of the crime, made a further statement to officers Goodrich and Arnold. He declared that Carpenter was innocent of the crime; that he and Butler did the work of removing the bodies from their graves, for men who were to call for them from Washington; that the tools used in the work were obtained from his house; that after they had procured the bodies and placed them beside the graves for the man who were to come for them, they hid the tools in the yard of 'Spring Garden.'

Having obtained the confession from Vaughan, officers Edward Goodrich and Julian Arnold proceeded, this morning, to 'Spring Garden' in grave yard lane, where Vaughan lives, and found the picks and shovels used in the removal of the bodies and officers Coleman and Lattin visited the house of G. A. Lumpkins, colored, corner of Prince and Alfred streets where Butler boarded and found a coffin screw and pair of pants covered with mud.... (*Alexandria Gazette*, January 29, 1880, p. 3.)

^^*^*^*^*^*^*^*^*^*^*^*

WHAT DR. RILEY SAYS - The several corporation officials who went to Washington Tuesday last, on business, accidentally met Dr. Riley, of that city, who was seen in this city looking for a colored wagon driver, on the night of the recent grave robberies. The Doctor, not knowing the officials, or the other gentlemen with them, talked freely of his visit to Alexandria on the night named. He said he was here on the night of January 26th to see a colored man named Charles Chapman. Upon discovering that he was talking to Alexandria officials, he endeavored to explain away his visit, by saying that he had attended Chapman, who had been thrown from his wagon in Washington some time ago, and that he had been invited by his patient to call to see him if he ever came to Alexandria; that being in Alexandria on the night of the said 26th of January, he thought he would like to see his colored friend. It is understood Governor Holliday will be asked for a requisition on the District authorities to bring Dr. Riley to Virginia to answer the charge of being a party to the unlawful removal of two dead human bodies from their graves in the cemeteries of this city. (*Alexandria Gazette*, February 18, 1881.)

^^*^*^*^*^*^*^*^*^*^*^*

REPORTED GRAVE ROBBERY – On Thursday last Reuben Dudley, an old colored man who had been an inmate of the Alms House for some time past died and on Friday his remains were buried in Penny Hill during a severe rain storm. On Sunday evening persons who visited the cemetery noticed that Dudley's grave had the appearance of having been tampered with, and a colored man named Vernon, who works there, said he felt confident that the body had been removed. He says that on Saturday night from his home, he saw lights flitting about the spot where the old man was buried, but that he was afraid to go to the cemetery lest he, too, might be "snatched." The next morning however, he went to the grave and found it much caved in, and he now believes that the body was removed. As yet no examination into the matter has been made, but the robbery is not believed, the caving in of the grave being explained by the settling of the earth after the heavy rain. (*Alexandria Gazette*, November 26, 1889, p.3.)

CHAPTER FIVE

Hangings And Lynchings

THE EARLIEST KNOWN HANGING IN FAIRFAX COUNTY, VIRGINIA
- April 7, 1759 - Slave Tony to be hung for robbery and rape - Body
then to be hung in chains. (*Fairfax County Court Order Book*, 1756, p.
330 - Abstracted by Edith Sprouse.)

∧∧*∧*∧*∧*∧*∧*∧*∧*∧*∧*

An 18th Century Hanging

Negro Tom was charged with breaking into the storehouse of John
Pomery and stealing from thence 5 pieces of calico, 1 piece of cheek
linen, 1 hat and cash amounting to 4 shillings, the property valued at
$30.

Negro Tom pleaded NOT GUILTY to the crime and thereupon the
witnesses against him were examined. After considering the evidence
"it is the opinion of the court that he is guilty of the charge aforesaid
and that he shall be hanged by the neck until he be dead."

It is ordered that the sergeant of the town execute the said Negro
Tom on the 1st day of April between the hours of 10 in the forenoon
and 4 in the afternoon and it is ordered that the sergeant have a gallows erected in the direction of the Georgetown Road at the extremity
of the limits of the corporation.

Negro Tom, the property of John Clark, who was this day condemned to be hanged, is valued by the Court to the sum of 50 pounds,
current money which is ordered to be certified to the order of Public
accounts." (Alexandria Court of Oyer & Terminer, February 27, 1797.)

∧∧*∧*∧*∧*∧*∧*∧*∧*∧*∧*

EXECUTION OF THREE NEGROES - PRINCE WILLIAM COUNTY,
VIRGINIA, Feb. 13 ¬ The execution of three of the five murderers of
Mr. Green, the well known schoolmaster of this county, took place in a
pine grove in the immediate vicinity of this village, a little before 1
P.M. today. Up to last night the condemned (five in all) had been
receiving constant attention from our local clergy, all of them profess-
ing to be under conviction. - Last night they spent in singing hymns
and praying together. They confessed their dreadful crime some time
ago and since then have professed great penitence for it. At noon, the
three-old Nelly, aged from 65 to 70, her daughter Jane, and the eldest

33

boy, William (the two younger boys, twins, aged fifteen or sixteen, being respited) – emerged from the jail under the guard of the High Sheriff of the county, his deputies and the jailor, and, mounting a two-horse wagon, were conveyed to the place of execution, where a space of near an acre in extent had been cleared for the erection of the gallows, standing room for the spectators, etc. On the way from the jail to the gallows they were singing hymns all the time.

On arriving at the gallows, they mounted up the steps with apparent alacrity, and in conversation professed their willingness to expiate their crime, declaring that they placed their trust in Jesus, and believed that they had so repented as to have secured salvation through him. The man alone said anything on the gallows, and he only sent word by the jailor to the two respited boys, to be sure to be ready to follow them. That is, to be sure that they make their peace with God. In ten or fifteen minutes after they mounted the gallows the white caps that hung upon their necks at the back of their shrouds were drawn up over their faces, and the sheriff, cutting the fastening of the trap, launched them into eternity. The necks of the younger woman and the man are supposed to have been instantly broken.

There were perhaps a thousand persons present, a majority of whom were negroes. Such was the atrocity of the circumstances of their crime, and so much was their victim beloved by all in this section, that the negroes evinced, if anything, less sympathy for them than the whites. Half the crowd accompanied the cortege from the jail in vehicles, on horseback, and on foot. Hundreds, to get good views, climbed the pines, until they looked as though growing a crop of men and boys.

It is thought here that the respited boys will not be hung. Their old fiend of a grandmother, it will be remembered, concocted the plot and instigated the rest to the dredful deed – of beating their master's brains out, and burning his house into which they dragged his corpse to conceal their crime. – Corr. of the *Washington Star*. (*Alexandria Gazette*, February 18, 1857, p. 3.)

^^*^*^*^*^*^*^*^*^*^*^*^*

EXECUTION OF JACKSON – The Last Moments of the Condemned – He Protests, His Innocence – Remarks on the Scaffold – Death Struggle – Scenes, Incidents, etc.

The third execution which has taken place in Alexandria within the past half century, and the second which has occurred here within the past years, took place at the jail yard today: William Jackson, a colored man, convicted on the 12th of November last, in the Circuit Court for the county of Alexandria, of the murder of Mary Jackson, his wife, in the month of February, 1872. Jackson was sentenced, upon his conviction, to suffer death upon the 16th of March last. An appeal from certain rulings of the Court below having meanwhile been taken to the Court of Appeals, the execution of the sentence was deferred for a decision of that tribunal, which overruled the appeal. At the term of the Circuit Court, subsequent, the execution of the sentence was fixed for Friday, the 11th of July, whence it was respited until the 1st of August, and again, in consequence of the absence of Governor Walker from Richmond, respited until today.

Soon after his conviction and sentence he yielded to the religious influences by which he was surrounded by the colored ministers who came to visit him in prison, and by the Jail Committee of the Alexandria Young Men's Christian Assc., which bestowed especial attention upon his case. He renewed a conversion that he professed to have experienced many years ago, and has for many weary months of his imprisonment devoted to religious affairs and the matter of his salvation, by far the greater portion of his time and attention.

He has seldom been hopeful of his release from the death penalty, and never sanguine. With an unfailing pertenacity, he has declared that he was not responsibile for the death of his wife, and that he had been unjustly condemned. Quite docile in the jail, he has given his keepers less trouble than almost any one of the many prisoners who have been in their charge since his confinement, bearing, in this respect, a marked contrast with Manley, in the earlier days of his confinement in jail. He excited greatly the sympathy of a large number of persons, and multiplied attempts were made to obtain for him executive clemency, efforts which at one time, it was believed would be crowned with success, but which were destined, in the end, to be disappointed.

Jackson has been quite sleepless of late and spent on Tuesday and Wednesday the entire night in singing and praying, loud enough to be heard throughout the jail. Last evening the Christian Association Committee came in the jail about 8 o'clock, and remained with Jackson in devotional exercises until twenty minutes past nine o'clock. Soon after they left, the condemned man called Keepers Cline and Ward, and asked that the light might be put up high so that he could read. Shortly after that he called again and asked that the light be put out, saying it was his last night on earth, he had made his peace with God, and had no enemies; he believed he would take his last sleep on earth. The light was extinguished and for some time the stillness of death reigned in his cell. This silence was so unusual that the guards feared he had committed suicide, and after listening at the cell door and hearing no sound, Mr. Ward opened the door softly and crept in. Jackson was in a deep sleep, breathing easily. The door was softly closed again and the doomed man slept until 4:20 this morning, when he arose, and began again to sing and pray.

At 5 1/2 o'clock the prisoners are let into the yard for exercise. By this time Jackson had dressed and breakfasted, eating heartily. Shortly after the members of the Christian Association arrived and Jackson sat with them in the corridor and engaged in devotional exercises. The rain having begun to fall in heavy drops upon the crowd outside, the throng, mostly colored people, were admitted to the jail yard, where they stood patiently looking at the gallows and getting as close under the walls and under umbrellas as they were able, to keep themselves from the drenching showers.

Within the corridor the devotional exercises continued without intermission.

There were no tickets required; all who came were admitted, but the heavy rain prevented the undue crowding of the yard.

At 11 o'clock the following dispatch was handed to Mr. O'Neal, which cut off all hope if any had lingered until then:

RICHMOND, Aug. 15, 1873

To John B. Smoot:
The Governor declines to interfere with the execution of the law in the case of William Jackson. T. F. OWENS, Colonel and A.D.C.

At 12:5 the sheriff accompanied by the under Sheriffs, went into the corridor and bade Jackson farewell, and as it was raining outside, said all the formalities would take place in the cell.

The Sheriff then read the sentence under which the execution was ordered, with the various orders or respital and the telegram refusing interference.

At the conclusion of the reading of the sentence, and papers relating to the execution Jackson said - What is that about "cursed." I don't understand that.

The Sheriff explained that the word was not cursed but "accused" and meant any one charged with crime. Jackson then professed himself satisfied.

When the jailor's wife came in to bid Jackson farewell, she said, "good bye, I hope it will all be well with you." "God grant it, God grant it," responded Jackson....

Thence the procession moved to the gallows, the Sheriff leading and Jackson coming next. As he came out the door he bowed to some friends and wished them good bye in a loud voice.

Upon arriving on the scaffold, which was surrounded by some three hundred people with umbrellas, for it was raining hard, Jackson in a nervous high-pitched voice spoke in substance as follows:

I am going; I have nothing to keep from God. Friends here I am, and there is my child. I have nothing to keep back from God. If I had anything to keep back I would tell it to the Lord. Lord I never remember that I killed anybody. If I am a wilful murderer, I do not know it, though this gallows is to receive me. The Lord understand me. If I am a murderer, Jesus knows that I is, but I am not. Father of Heaven take charge of me; give me way into Paradise before Thy Throne. Friends, look at me. May God give you warning for Jesus sake; take a look and turn. I have no more to do with it. Gentlemen, please take warning. I am gone. Jesus I want to come to thee. O, save my soul. Please take care of me. O Lord, how near; farewell! farewell! farewell! farewell!

Jackson here took his place on the trap and as the rope was adjusted about his neck asked for a drink of water. Sometime was occupied in getting the water from the jail, the doomed man meanwhile standing upon the gallows, and praying aloud, "God forgive me; give me help in that terrible world," and other broken sentences. The water was brought and he drank; then he said, "This is nothing strange, I saw this rope Sunday night. Father in Heaven catch my soul." The cap was here adjusted and the drop fell.

The body fell with a thud at 12:24, but in a moment it became evident it had not broken the neck of the doomed man; his head moved and the limbs were convulsed for some time, and it was a full fifteen minutes before the body became still.

At 12:50 the remains were lowered, pronounced dead by Drs. Adam and Garrett; placed into the coffin, and given in the charge of Mr. Wheatly, the undertaker. At 1 o'clock the yard was clear.

The crime of which Jackson was convicted was accompanied by many circumstances, making it one of marked brutality. Jackson, who was a laborer at the brick yard near the Long Bridge, lived in that neighborhood with his wife, two families occupying one house. Early in February the wife gave birth to a child, suffering much after her delivery with childbirth fever, and being often delirious. Jackson seemed to be displeased that she occasioned him so much trouble (at least this is the statement of the witnesses for the prosecution) and on the 15th of February he came in and found her sitting up in her bed. He had previously told her that she must lie down all the time, and keep quiet, but she in her delirium paid no heed to him. On this occasion, when he found her sitting up he said, "Now, you lay down there." She paid no attention to his command, whereupon he seized a large stick of wood and struck her with such force on the head that it was afterwards discovered in the post mortem that her skull was fractured. She fell back senseless and thence forward are suffered almost continually with spasms until 2 o'clock upon the morning of the 16th of February, when she died.

During her sickness after the blow, the only exclamation made by the stricken woman was, "Oh! my head," while the only information about the matter which Jackson vouchsafed was that "she was in his way anyhow, and he rather she'd be gone." The blow was struck about ten o'clock on Thursday night, and the woman died on Friday morning about 8 o'clock.

When Jackson found she was dead, he told the woman there to cover up the remains; he bolted the door of the room and went off, saying, "Don't let the ladies know she is dead, I've no money to bury her," and he was never seen again until his arrest.

Information of her death being communicated to a neighboring magistrate, a jury of inquest was held, and Jackson arrested and carried to jail at Alexandria, where he remained until his execution.

There was much talk after the execution was over concerning a piece of paper which Jackson dropped from the scaffold just before the drop fell. It was said that this paper contained a confession. The facts about it are these:

Mr. Bernard Cline, Deputy Warden of the jail at Jackson's request wrote this morning three names, H. Thompson, and two others upon a piece of paper, and Jackson put it in his pocket. During the exercises Jackson told Mr. Hecken, of the Christian Association, that he had a paper he intended to give to Mr. Beadle, containing full information relative to his family, etc., and as Mr. Beadle was not there he (Hecken) must watch and see when he dropped it from the scaffold and pick it up. Hecken accordingly watched; the paper was dropped. Hecken picked it up and he and Mr. Bruner opened it, but it contained only three names and was evidently the same paper written in the morning by Mr. Cline. (*Alexandria Gazette*, August 15, 1873, p. 3.)

^^*^*^*^*^*^*^*^*^*^*^*^*^*^*

At a Court of Oyer & Terminer, appointed & held for the County of Fairfax, 26th May, 1792:

Present: George Giesson, James Wren, Charles Alexander, John Fitzgerald, Roger West, Gents, present.

Will, a negro man slave, the property of Jacob Fortnay of the said county, who was committed to the Gaol of this County by warrant under the hand & seal of William Herbert, Gent., and charged with Feloniously breaking and entering the Dwelling and store house of George Stovin of the Town of Alexandria, in the night time, and stealing thereout sundry silver money of the value of fifteen pounds and upwards, and being this day arraigned in open court for the said fact, pleaded Guilty, and thereupon the several witnesses against him being sworn and examined, and Consideration of the same had, The Court are of opinion that he is Guilty of the said fact. Therefore it is considered that the said Negro will go from hence to the prison, from whence he came, from thence to the place of Execution, there to be hanged by the neck til he be dead. (Signed) George Gilpin.

Will, a negro man-slave, Blacksmith, belonging to Jacob Fortnay, being this day convicted and condemned by this Court for Felony & valued at one hundred pounds, current money, which is ordered to be certified.

To His Excellency Henry Lee, Esquire, Governor of Virginia:

The petition of several of the Inhabitants of the Town of Alexandria and County of Fairfax, Humbly Sheweth That a slave named Will, belonging to Jacob Fortney of the said Town, hath been lately sentenced to suffer Death for an offence rendered Capital by the laws of the Land. That the Law appears to have two objects in view; first to prevent further Transgressions by the same person, and by the severity of the punishment often bearing no proportion to the offence, to deter others from similar practices. That whenever these ends can be answered by other means than by depriving a fellow creature of his existence in the prime of Life, the intention of the Government appears to be fulfilled, and the society in no manner to be injured. That by sending the culprit to some of the British, Spanish, French, Dutch, or Danish Settlements in the West Indies, the feelings of humanity will not be so sensibly affected, the society being relieved from an apprehension of further injury done by the same person as effectually as if the sentence was fully executed. For these considerations your Petitioners are induced to request your Excellency to grant a pardon to the said Will upon condition that He be shipped to some one of the above mentioned settlements in a reasonable time, and not be permitted to return. (The above petition was signed by one hundred eight

Alexandria and Fairfax County residents) (*Calendar of Virginia State Papers and Other Manuscripts* (Richmond, VA 1885), Vol. V. pp. 616-619.)

∧∧*∧*∧*∧*∧*∧*∧*∧*∧*∧*∧*∧*∧*

HANGED BY A MOB - Joseph McCoy, the Assailant of Little Annie Lacy, Taken from a Cell in the Station House and Hanged to a Lamp Post - Thrilling Scenes in and around Police Headquarters.

The righteous indignation of old Alexandria was aroused last night to a degree akin to that manifested in the Christmas riot of 1865, and as a result Joseph McCoy, a negro ravisher, was strung up to a lamp post, bullets sent into his body, his head split open with an axe and other indignities heaped upon his quivering remains. It was the fourth case of outrage which has occurred in this vicinity in less than a year - one in Alexandria county early last summer where a young white girl was the victim of a negro brute; one in the First ward a month or so ago when a little simpering white girl told a revolting story of gross wrong on the part of one who should have been her protector; the recent case of Lewis and Mrs. Reidel and the startling exposure made yesterday afternoon concerning McCoy and his victim.

Some gentlemen living in the southern part of the city obtained information of McCoy's conduct toward Annie Lacy, daughter of Mr. Tobias Lacy, who lives in the southern part of the city, and the information was lodged with Lieutenant Smith, who started an immediate search of the accused. Shortly before seven o'clock he found the negro in a stable on south Washington street, near the Catholic cemetery, and took him to the station house. McCoy at first flatly denied the charge, but upon being locked up he made one of the most revolting confessions ever listened to. His victim is about ten years of age, and the fiend acknowledged that the reason her sister, still younger, was not his victim also was through no fault of his. The crime had been going on for the past two weeks, and yesterday the children's condition became so serious that they were compelled to make a confession. A physician was called and a revolting exposure followed.

When the facts in the case became noised around the greatest indignation was aroused, and suggestions of summary vengence were made by numbers, but the more sober minded believed a conservative spirit would overcome the minds of all and that the law would be allowed to take its course. The result, however, showed the surmise to be erroneous. Instead of quieting down, the spirit of vengeance was growing every moment. The streets near the City Hall were swarming with people from early in the night and excited and determined groups were on corners talking angrily. At ten o'clock the Mayor undertook to cast oil on the troubled waters by advising all he met to abstain from rashness and let the law take its course, but in the face of the indignation that was manifested his admonitions were but little heeded. Crowds were in the neighborhood when the relief guard went out at ten o'clock, and at that time were becoming menacing, but the police, Chief Webster and Lieutenant Smith, who were in the station house, believed the angry waves would soon subside and the excitement quiet down. The crowd, however, kept in the vicinity and would occasionally come on the station house pavement, but attempted no violence. The officers had determined to protect the negro as long as possible, and made every preparation to resist an attack. About 12 o'clock the first decided movement toward taking McCoy from the cell was made. The front door was broken open and a number of excited men, among them Mr. Lacy, entered. The attack was successfully repulsed by the policemen and some of the ringleaders captured, but subsequently released. At this juncture Lieutenant Smith appeared at the front door and ordered the crowd to disperse. He advised them to be law-abiding citizens and to let justice take its course in the usual way. The Mayor had ordered the officers to protect the prisoner and would have called out the Alexandria Light Infantry had it been deemed necessary, but all in authority at that time believed the trouble was over, as the crowd had scattered when the officers discharged their pistols at the first attack. But the assemblage had no intention of abandoning their purpose and had repaired to a neighboring lumber yard, where a large piece of timber was procured to be used as a battering ram. At a quarter past one o'clock the mob returned with a yell, and it is believed that at least five hundred people were in the gang, and strange to say, it was impossible, in the excitement, to identify those who composed the crowd. Some were strangers and nearly all had their hats pulled down over their eyes. The station house door was smashed in a few seconds and excited men surged in immediately. The chief, lieutenant and officers Wilkinson, Atkinson, Lyles, Davis and Knight and Constable Webster were thrown aside by some and secured by others. The chief was knocked back on the steps he was descending and the lieutenant was thrown first one way and then another and finally pinioned and made helpless by half a dozen men. The chief had drawn his pistol but was prevented from using it. Officer Knight had also produced his pistol, but his arm was caught and the weapon turned against his own head. It was with greatest difficulty that he succeeded in turning the muzzle upward and prevented it from being discharged. In the meantime the crowd outside which could not gain an entrance were breaking the windows and cutting out sash in their eagerness to get at McCoy. Those inside soon demolished the door leading into the corridor and went directly to the ravisher's cell. McCoy, who had been listening to the assault, had become terribly frightened and had climbed up on the door and was secreted near the ceiling. The mob supposed they were at the wrong cell, and were about to leave for another, when one of McCoy's legs was discovered. He was pulled down with a yell and dragged to the pavement, and the mob surged toward Cameron street with him. The negro cried piteously for mercy and resisted all the way. The crowd turned down Cameron street to Lee street and on the southeast corner made rapid preparations to carry out their purpose. A rope had been procured from Mr. G. E. Price's awning, a noose was soon around McCoy's neck and in less time than it takes to tell it he was dangling from the lamp post on that corner. Bullet after bullet was sent into his body, and when he had been cut down, one of the mob used an axe on his head and blood and brains were spattered on the pavement.

40

The remains were gathered up this morning and taken to Mr. Demaine's undertaking establishment.

The affair has been the chief subject of conversation today. The fact that it is the fourth instance within less than a year where females have been shamefully treated in this vicinity has naturally aroused the righteous indignation of the community, and while all believe in law and order, the general sentiment has been that the fiend has met his just reward.

The damage to the station house will amount to about $50. The fact that no one was seriously hurt save McCoy was fortunate. The officers at the station house were roughly handled and somewhat bruised, but they suffered no material injury....

In the meantime a post mortem examination will be held. The body showed a bullet wound over the heart, a cut on the neck, a bad cut on the head and a slight burn on the body. Fire had been applied to certain parts of the negro's body.

Gov. O'Ferrall today telegraphed to Judge Norton asking him to wire him the facts in the case and then to write him the full particulars. The Governor stated that he thought it strange that a city like Alexandria, with a police force, a military company, such a lynching should have occurred.

The father of Annie Lacy took her to Dr. O'Brien yesterday, who found her to be suffering from a specific disease. A malignant growth had to be removed. The doctor asked if Mr. Lacy thought his child had been tampered with and he replied in the negative. Annie, however, subsequently admitted her relations with McCoy, when the father, fearing his other children had been victims also of the negro, questioned them and found his horrible suspicions to be real. He requested Dr. O'Brien to examine them, and he and Dr. Snowden discovered that the two other children aged 6 and 8 years, had been as unfortunate as their sister. Annie, upon whom the operation was performed, is doing well and the two other children show no ill effects from their injuries.

Captain Bryan, of the Alexandria Light Infantry, received a telegram from the Adjutant General today asking him to send an explanation concerning the apparent inactivity of the company at the time of the lynching. The captain had received no official call from the Mayor for the company, it being believed after the first assault on the station house that there would be no further trouble. When the mob returned they did so so suddenly and performed their work so expeditiously that the company could not have been formally summoned in time to have frustrated the purpose of the lynching party.

The body of McCoy has been at Demaine's establishment all day and has been visited by many inquisitive persons. So far none of his relatives have been there, however, nor has there been any claims made by them for the remains. (*Alexandria Gazette*, April 23, 1897, p. 3.)

^^*^*^*^*^*^*^*^*^*^*^*^*^*

INDECENT CONDUCT - Benj. Thomas, colored, was arrested yesterday evening by Officers Knight and Wilkinson charged with attempting to commit an assault on Lillie Clark, a little seven-year-old white girl, living at 702 north Patrick street. The Mayor directed Officer Knight to quietly arrest and confine Thomas in the station house until this morning at 9 o'clock and that officer with Policemen Wilkinson carried out the orders so well that few citizens knew of the matter. The colored people, however, early in the night began to congregate on corners and boisterously commenting on some imaginary report of a proposed lynching, caused the crowds of colored men to become larger and more boisterous towards 12 o'clock, most of the white citizens in the meantime remaining totally unaware of any excitement. The Mayor was on the streets until after 12 o'clock conversing with numbers of citizens and heard no comment or remark concerning the arrest. About 12:15 o'clock a party of colored men went to the Mayor's house and on being asked why they had come at that hour said they wanted protection for the prisoner at the station house. The Mayor told them to get off the streets and go home as they would be arrested if they did not do so, that no one was threatening the prisoner and that the colored people themselves were creating all the excitement. At one o'clock Lieutenant James Smith called on the Mayor and reported large congregations of colored men in the vicinity of the station house. He was directed to take men from the street, order the colored men to disperse, and if they refused, to arrest them and lock them up. The lieutenant promptly carried out the orders, and the disturbance was at an end. This morning, as will be seen from the police report, the parties causing the disturbance were punished. The Mayor took occasion to say that the case exhibited a most remarkable condition of affairs. A man accused of a heinous offense quietly arrested, the white citizens of the community unaware of any trouble and attempting no demonstration, and yet colored men, with most boisterous display of regard for the safety of one of their own race noisily congregate and recklessly invite a catastrophe. The trial of Thomas elicited the fact that he took indecent liberties with the little girl and the Mayor on the evidence sent the case on to the grand jury. Lillie Clark's evidence was that she was drawn into the door by Thomas, who was sitting on the indoor side of the house steps, and took indecent liberties with her, but that he committed no assault, and that she pulled away from him and informed her mother of the matter. The child was the only witness examined. After the examination of Thomas, Mayor Simpson was handling a pistol taken from one of the negroes during the night. In some manner the weapon was discharged and the ball entered the wall in the office. The report was heard in the street and it was the origin of several idle rumors heard about the city later, one to the effect that Thomas had attempted to escape and had been shot at by one of the officers. While apprehending no trouble, the Mayor has deemed it best to take all precautions against any excitement which might arise over the above affair. He, therefore, today directed Chief Webster to select four trustworthy members of the police force for duty at the jail tonight. The Mayor has supplemented these by the appointment of ten guards, who will also be stationed at the lock up during the night. Chief Webster will proceed with his men to the jail at sundown this evening and remain there until tomorrow morning and, should any ill-advised movement be made, every means will be resorted to in order to protect the prisoner. (*Alexandria Gazette*, August 8, 1899, p. 3.)

LYNCHING OF A NEGRO - Benjamin Thomas Taken from Jail and Hanged from a Lamp Post - Dragged six Squares by the Head - His Body Riddled with Bullets.

Old Alexandria was the theatre for another lynching last night, and for a time the normal quietness of the city was supplanted by intense excitement. The particulars concerning the arrest of Benjamin Thomas, the young negro man charged with attempted assault on the seven-year-old daughter of Mr. Edward Kloch (printed Clark yesterday by mistake) are fresh in the minds of all, and need no recapitulation here. The Mayor had committed the offender to jail to be brought before the grand jury at the next session of court, and preparations for his safe custody until that time had been made. Those who moved around among the people, however, could not fail to observe an undercurrent which animated numbers to entertain a desire to relieve the court from the responsibility of the case, and the more conservative endeavored to calm angry breasts by suggesting that the law, which is plain enough, would wreak its own vengeance. In some cases there was a partial acquiescence, but in many others the arguments of sober minds were controverted, and there were indications of approaching trouble. As the sun set, the number of people on the streets increased and the head-to-head conversations and the earnestness displayed showed too plainly that the matters being discussed were not intended for all ears. The Mayor had placed Chief Webster in charge of a squad of four policemen and ten guards with the responsibility of protecting the prisoner should any overt act be attempted on the part of a crowd. As the hours passed the groups of men in the streets increased and, although scattered over considerable ground, they were like fragmentary clouds floating in different quarters of the heavens designed to mingle and precipitate a storm. People grew more apprehensive every moment, and in cases people living in some quarters of the city passed the night with friends and relatives residing in other neighborhoods.

Shortly before 12 o'clock those on the streets realized that the climax had been reached and that an attempt to get possession of Thomas was imminent and the consequent excitement inevitable. By this time the crowd had closed up almost compactly, and it is believed to have numbered at least 500. One hundred women are said to have been on the streets and in the neighborhood of the organization. The march toward the jail was made almost in a double-quick, and the surging mass of humanity was, in less time than it takes to tell it, surrounding the lockup, manifesting a determination to wreak vengenance on Thomas.

The guards, at the jail, of course, knew what was coming, as the exclamations from the maddened crowd could be heard for a long distance, and every preparation was made to hold the mob at bay and protect the prisoner. The latter had been taken to the cellar and placed in a fish barrel in the hope that should the building be forced no one would think of looking in such a hiding place. The heavy pounding at the front door had announced the presence of the infuriated crowd, and upon being denied admission their frenzy was augmented a hundred fold. The battering grew fiercer and fiercer and the exclamations showed too plainly that the people had risen in their might and had become irresistible. Cries of "Burn the jail," rang out every now and then, and the situation was becoming more critical every moment. Pistol shots, too, began to emanate from the crowd and the outlook was exceedingly serious.

Mayor Simpson, who had been watching the course of events during the night, at this juncture appeared in front of the jail, and endeavored to pour oil on the troubled waters by promising to have summary justice meted out to the offender in a legal way if the crowd would disperse. He addressed the multitude in the middle of the street, from the pavement and jail steps, but his promises and admonitions had no effect whatever, and he was finally pushed from the door and a heavy and long piece of scantling which had been taken from the front of a house in course of erection on Cameron street was used as a battering ram and in a few moments the door was demolished and the crowd surged in.

To overpower the guards was the work of but a few moments, although those in the building did all they could to deter the maddened multitude from carrying out their purpose. Chief Webster's right hand was seriously injured during the conflict with the mob, who were endeavoring to obtain possession of the keys to the corridor and cells. They wrenched his pistol from his hand and eventually took the keys from the wardens and, with a yell, as many as could crowded through the passageway and made for the cells, and unlocking one caused two colored individuals who were confined in one of them to turn several shades whiter by mistaking them for Thomas. They were pulled about for some time before the excited crowd could be made to understand that they had the wrong man in custody. By this time every cell and room in the building had been invaded by the frenzied people, but the object of their search could not be found. A detachment finally invaded the cellar where every hold and corner was searched, and an attempt to turn the fish barrel aside disclosed Thomas's whereabouts. With a yell he was pulled from his hiding place and dragged upstairs.

When an attempt was made to carry him to the street Officer Wilkinson who was at the front door, undertook to rescue Thomas by drawing his pistol, and during the excitement which followed the darkey managed to break away and crawled through the crowd into the street and made his way into a house next door to the jail. The crowd surged around the officers so thickly that it was impossible for them to move. Many from the crowd on the outside had in the meantime followed Thomas to the house and recaptured him. It appears that Officer Wilkinson had exclaimed, "You have got the wrong man," which accounts probably for him getting away from the crowd temporarily. A rope was placed around his neck and under his arms and as many as could get hold of it started on a double-quick with him down St. Asaph street.

The excitement at this time was at fever heat. The negro had been thrown down by a jerk given on the rope when the start was made from the jail, and first on his back and then on his face he was pulled six squares - down St. Asaph street from Princess to King and down King to the southwest corner of Fairfax. At Cameron street Officer Wilkinson cut the rope, but it was soon tied together. When Thomas reached the spot his face and head were much lacerated by being pulled over the cobble stones and blood was flowing from his wounds. A noose was quickly made in the rope and he was pulled from his back to his feet and was soon dangling in the air from a lamp post a target for a number of pistols which were emptied into the body.

The crowd after this began to grow thinner, and after Thomas had hung for about fifteen minutes he was cut down by a policeman. It is said at this time life was not entirely extinct, although, of course, it was ebbing fast. The body was later taken to Mr. Demaine's undertaking establishment.

The streets gradually resumed their normal quiet. It was a noticeable fact that during all the excitement incident to the lynching but few colored people could be seen on the streets, although on the previous night they had swarmed about and in some instances had become menacing. In, fact it is believed by many that had they remained indoors Monday night and refrained from threats and defiance there would have been no overt act on the part of whites. But the fact that some blacks on that occasion had endeavored to bring on race troubles and had been arrested with razors and pistols in their pockets, exasperated the multitude to such a degree that the event of last night was but the natural consequence.

The lynching has, of course, been the main theme of conversation today, and there is still a wave of excitement on, which the more conservative are laboring to allay. The authorities have taken decided steps to prevent any further breach of the peace.

INQUEST - An inquest was held by Dr. Purvis, the city coroner, this morning at Mr. Demaine's undertaking establishment upon the body of Thomas. ...Dr. Jones, who had previously performed an autopsy, was the first witness. He testified that Thomas had been shot twice - once in the right chest, the ball passing through lungs and heart and the other ball entering his abdomen and penetrating his small intestine. The neck had not been broken, but the body was much bruised and covered with blood and nearly stripped of clothing. ... The jury then returned the following verdict: We, the jury, find that Benjamin Thomas came to his death at the hands of a mob unknown to the jury. Immediate cause of death being gunshot wound in heart. Thomas's body will be buried tomorrow....

Last night while the excitement was going on, Commonwealth's Attorney G. L. Boothe, Mr. S. G. Brent and others were with Mayor Simpson and did all they could to avert the lynching. (*Alexandria Gazette*, August 9, 1899, p. 3.)

CHAPTER SIX

Murders And Attempted Murders

EARLY MENTION OF MURDERS
IN
FAIRFAX COUNTY, VIRGINIA, 1749 – 1756

1749, September 26 – Special Court Session – Hayden Edward charged with murdering a Negro slave belonging to the Hon. Thomas Lee found not guilty. – (*Fairfax County Court Order Book*, 1749, p. 32)

1752, June 17 – Thomas Kelley confessed to the murder of Thomas Davis. – (*Fairfax County Court Order Book*, 1749, p. 207)

1752, November 6 – Mulberry a Negro man belonging to John Colville, Gent. was murdered by Wm. Coulter & Thomas Trammell. – (*Fairfax County Court Order Book*, 1749, p. 249.)

1752, December 7 – Negro woman Pegg murdered. Robert Colclough was acquitted of the crime. – (*Fairfax County Court Order Book*, 1749, p. 295.)

1754, September 27 – David Davis accused of "feloniously murdering" John Mears. Davis was imprisoned but later acquitted. – (*Fairfax County Court Order Book*, 1754, p. 161.)

^^*^*^*^*^*^*^*^*^*^*

ALEXANDRIA – January 4 – Last Tuesday fe'nnight, two Sailors called at a Tipling House in this Town for Grog, but being refused, they turned about to go away, when someone in the House immediately opened the Door and discharged a Gun at them, the Contents of which was lodged in the Shoulder of Thomas Handbough, Carpenter of the *Betsy* (Capt. Story) who expired soon after. A Jury of Inquest being summoned on the Body, brought in their Verdict "Wilful Murder." -- The supposed perpetrator of this horrid deed has absconded, yet it is hoped he will soon meet the just Rewards of a Murderer. (*Virginia Journal* and *Alexandria Advertiser*, January 4, 1787, p. 2.)

^^*^*^*^*^*^*^*^*^*^*

ALEXANDRIA, Jan. 27 – On Saturday last came on, in the Court of this County, the trial of Negro Moses (mentioned in this paper of last week) charged with the murder of Hezekiah Williams, his Overseer. It appeared in evidence that the deceased had, in many instances, treated with great severity the slaves under his authority, and the prisoner in particular: That he had confined him in chains several days and nights - that, on the evening when the deed was committed, he had cruelly flogged him, merely for having requested one of his fellow slaves to give him a seat in his cart to carry him to the Overseer's house, (where he was confined every night) finding great difficulty in walking, by reason of his iron spancels - that he was confined by a staple drove into the wall - that the Overseer had threatened to treat him the next morning in the manner had done his brother Bob (who died soon after his flogging, and, as had been suspected in consequence of it.) Under the impression of these denunciations, and the terrors naturally excited by them, it appears that, whilst the Overseer was asleep, in the same room where the prisoner was confined, the latter disengaged himself from his hand-cuffs, drew the staple, and, taking down the Overseer's gun, which happened to be loaded, went out as silently as possible; determined, if he could effect it, to make his escape: That the Overseer, awaking went in pursuit of him, and found him near the house, not having been able to make much progress on account of his spancels - that Moses cautioned him repeatedly to stand off, saying he should not take him, that he had a loaded gun, and would shoot him, sooner than let him take him - that Williams, disregarding these warnings, pressed on him with three dogs (said to be trained to Negro catching) till Williams almost touched the muzzle of the gun, when the other discharged it, and lodged the whole contents in his body - that, thereupon, Moses went up immediately and surrendered himself to his Master. Being asked by his master why he had committed that desperate deed, he answered, "Sir, the Overseer would have killed me, had I not killed him." It appeared from the testimony of several witnesses, who had been a long time acquainted with the prisoner, that he had always supported the character of an honest, faithful slave, and that he had always been uncommonly submissive to those in authority over him; that, being able to read and write, he had been employed by his former master as an Overseer for 16 years, during which time he had been entrusted with the sale of corn and other articles, of which he had always tendered his master a just and true account.

It was urged by the Counsel for the Prisoner - that a Master's authority over the Slave was limited - That, even by the laws of this country, he had no right to deprive his slave of life or members - That a slave, notwithstanding his degraded station, still retained some natural rights, particularly that of self preservation, which could not be taken from him by human laws, as he derived them from a source infinitely superior to all human authority - That, when a master inflicts on his slave cruel and severe punishment, which endangers the life or members of his slave, he transgresses the limits of his authority, and trespasses on the retained natural rights of the slave; and in that case the slave has the same right to defend those rights that a freeman has - That, from the character of Williams, his threats, and the cruel treatment he had received from him he had sufficient reason to believe that his life was in imminent danger - and to prevent that danger he discharged his gun at him; in doing so he was prompted by self-preservation; a principle which actuates the meanest reptile in the animal creation.

In taking the opinion of the Court, it was found that they were not unanimous. The prisoner was, of course, acquitted.

To the honour of the humanity of the inhabitants of this town and neighbourhood, it is mentioned that in no instance was ever manifested such general anxiety on a judicial question. In no instance was the Court House of Fairfax County so crowded - and never was sentence pronounced that gave more general satisfaction.

Whether that sentence be warranted by a strick construction of the law, in its utmost rigour, or not, it is sincerely hoped, that the acquittal of this slave will have the effect of impressing upon Overseers in general the propriety of treating the unhappy persons committed to their authority with mildness and humanity: And it is devoutly to be wished that the adjudication in the case of Negro Moses may establish an era from which to date the universal kindness and tenderness of masters to their unfortunate brethren: "Knowing that they also have a Master in Heaven." (*Alexandria Gazette*, January 27, 1791, p.3.)

^^*^*^*^*^*^*^*^*^*^*

Yesterday presented a scene which for savage desperation hardly has its parallel. Between 5 and 6 o'clock in the morning the family of Messrs. Korn and Wisemiller was alarmed with the cries of murder in the upper story of their dwelling, but before those who were up in the house had more than halfway ascended to the apartment whence the cries issued, they were met by a negro woman who had just breath to make them understand that her husband had attempted her life, and pointing to her throat, where there was then a razor sticking, fell dead at their feet. To complete the dreadful catastrophe, the perpetrator, immediately on the woman's setting out of the room, threw himself, head-formost, from the garret window of a three-story house to the pavement, putting a period to a life, the termination of which exhibited a frenzy not to be accounted for and a spectacle too horrid for description. The parties were upwards of 60 years of age. (*Alexandria Gazette*, January 9, 1796) (520 Prince St.)

^^*^*^*^*^*^*^*^*^*^*

HORRID MURDER - On Thursday night the 4th of this month, a most cruel murder was committed on a Spaniard or Frenchman, in the county of Prince William, in Virginia, between Hay-Market and Buckland, by two unknown persons who are either Spaniards or Portuguese. The circumstances were according to the evidence of Mr. Jeremiah Hutcheson, a respectable citizen of Fairfax, (who had come on in pursuit of the suspected persons) taken by the mayor of this place as follows:

That on Thursday came to his house three persons who appeared to him to be foreigners - they were travelling up the turnpike road - one of them could speak broken English and was the interpreter to the others, who appeared not to understand the English language. This person said that he had with him five hundred dollars in money, and about the same amount in small jewellery, consisting of gold watches, gold chains and rings, which he carried in two boxes in a small valice. He was about five feet six inches high, well made, his countenance had a lively, active appearance - he had on a blue superfine cloth coat, pantaloons of fine cloth, black worsted stockings, shoes, a fine furred hat, a fine colored cambric neckcloth, fine cambrick ruffles to his shirt, a gold watch with a gold chain which was formed by two or three gold strands - his eyes were dark and his hair very black, his face and hands were pitted with the small pox. He stated that he had come from Philadelphia and had some friends in Baltimore; that he was endeavoring to raise money for the purpose of redeeming a near relation who was a prisoner in Algiers; that he was going a short distance further with the two persons who were with him, and that he should return in a few days....

On Friday the 5th instant, the dead body of the first described person was found by means of the blood, a short distance from the road covered over in the snow and entirely naked. Near the body were found two walking sticks of hawthorn wood dyed black and much shivered, and a part of a gold chain and a razor with an ivory handle was found in the snow. The throat was cut from ear to ear, and the head gashed in eleven or more different places.

The suspected persons were seen the day before travelling in company with the murdered man, and, as they said, going to Fauquier court-house. The day after the murder the suspected persons were seen returning on the same road near Fairfax court-house, one of them having his face much scratched and endeavoring to conceal it. The same persons were traced by Mr. Hutcheson and two others down the turnpike road to Alexandria and seen by some persons in Alexandria on Saturday afternoon passing down King Street, apparently much fatigued.

A person was apprehended in this town on suspicion. He was carried before the Mayor. He proving by several respectable witnesses that he was in Alexandria before and on the day of the murder was committed and continued here ever since, was discharged.

Justice, humanity and public safety demand that all officers and others, not here but elsewhere should use their best exertions to detect and to bring to trial the perpetrators of this wicked deed. (*Alexandria Gazette*, January 12, 1816, p. 3.)

^^*^*^*^*^*^*^*^*^*^*^*^*^*

Washington, July 24, 1820 - At the last term of the Court holden for the County of Alexandria, in this District, a man by the name of William Davis was convicted of the crime of murder; and Friday next was appointed the day for his execution. On a representation, unanimously signed by the jury which convicted him, founded on evidence, posterior to the trial, of a general defect of intelligence in the person convicted, and an incapacity to discriminate clearly between right and wrong, we understand that the President of the United States has respited the execution – whether for a longer or shorter time, we know not. The object is, we presume, to keep him in confinement for some time at least, if the sentence of the law should not eventually be put in force. (Nat. Intel.) (*Alexandria Gazette*, July 25, 1820, p. 2.)

^^*^*^*^*^*^*^*^*^*^*^*

A MURDER RECALLED – The present gathering of the Grand Army of the Republic at Washington and the reduced rates which have been offered by railroad companies have brought some people to Alexandria (their old home) who have not been in this neighborhood for many years, some of whom are unknown to the present generation. Among those who have been noticed on the streets in the form of an old man who figured in a tragedy in this city over sixty-five years ago. The individual referred to is Alonzo Pelton and the tragedy recalled is the killing of George Webster, son of the late John Webster, one Saturday night in February, 1837. Webster and Pelton were youngsters at the time and previous to the fatal affray they had become involved in a difficulty over a game of bandy. Webster in company with several of his friends was on his way up King street. He was whistling at the time and had passed the northwest corner of King and Pitt streets and was in front of an alley adjoining on the east the building now occupied by Mr. B. B. Smith (505 King St.) when he encountered Pelton. The latter asked Webster if he was whistling the "dead march," and it is said made some threat which caused Webster to stop and warn him of the consequences of his insolence. Pelton, it was alleged, applied an offensive epithet to Webster once or twice and the latter returned when he was dealth a heavy blow on the head by Pelton who had taken a grape-vine club from the alley in the mean time. Webster was half dazed by the blow, and his hat having been knocked off by the blow, he was in a stooping position endeavoring to secure it and a handkerchief which was in it, when Pelton again emerged from the alley and drove a knife in his back. Webster regained his feet made his way across the street and staggered and fell on the pavement in front of the store now occupied by Mr. P. M. Bradshaw. (510 King St.) His companions, who did not know he had been stabbed until he fell, carried him to the residence of the late William Mills, on St. Asaph street, near King, and Dr. Washington was summoned, but Webster's life was ebbing fast when the doctor arrived. He soon lapsed into unconsciousness and died. Pelton was arrested and tried. The jury brought in a verdict of murder in the second degree and he was sent to the penitentiary for five years. (*Alexandria Gazette*, October 10, 1902, p. 3.)

^^*^*^*^*^*^*^*^*^*^*^*

(COMMUNICATED) The editor of the Alexandria *Gazette* is requested to state, in proof of the fact generally known and admitted, of the present wretched state of the police of the town, that an aged and respectable citizen of our town was rudely assaulted on his way home from a meeting on Sunday night, by a set of boys, and was near being seriously injured. The proper officers, after this disgraceful affair, were in vain sought for. Every night the streets are paraded by a gang

51

of vicious boys and no one to check or stop them. Last week we had an affray and murder! When will these things stop – and where are the police officers? (*Alexandria Gazette*, March 2, 1837, p. 3)

^^*^*^*^*^*^*^*^*^*^*^*

The killing of one unfortunate youth by another in this place, on Saturday the 25th, ultimo, has naturally excited attention. The lamentations and groans of the deceased youth's afflicted relatives, over his lifeless corpse, have made an impression on my mind and sympathies, which will not soon be dispelled. Such an act perpetrated by one so young, is rare in the midst of a christian community. Why should it be remarked, by persons residing fifty or a hundred miles from us, that our boys excel in depravity? To this I am not willing to agree. But, I am sorry to say, that, it is too much the practice of boys to be running about the streets, committing great irregularities. This might and ought to be remedied. The irregularities also, of the passions of boys may be remedied by restraints, fears and hopes, rewards and punishments. The way of boys is generally wrong, particularly at setting out, and often leads to ruin and death; from which it is the duty of parents, guardians and masters, to recall them. They all bring with them into the world some bent and inclination, a certain current of passions and affections, which if suffered to run its own way, will draw into it all the actions of their future life; then, "Train up a child in the way he should go; and when he is old he will not depart from it." Why are not these loud complaints and severe censures made of the boys of other cities of the United States? I answer, because they are formed to a decent and humane behaviour; corrected for immoralities whether in words or actions; and instead of running about the streets in a manner scandalous to the christian name, the are sent regularly to school, and taught improvements of the highest interest and importance, fitting them for trades, and the business of life, and to be useful to the commonwealth... (*Alexandria Gazette*, March 4, 1837, p.3.)

^^*^*^*^*^*^*^*^*^*^*^*

United States vs. Dorcas Allen. The prisoner who stands indicted for murder was led to the bar in custody of the keeper of the public jail of this county, and being thereof arraigned pleaded not guilty, and for her trial put herself upon the country, and a venire facias is awarded returnable immediately whereupon came a Jury to wit: (*Alexandria County Minute Book*, October Term 1837 – 8th day, p. 104)

The United States vs. Dorcas Allen. The prisoner who stands indicted for murder was again led to the bar, and the jury who to try the issue in this appeared in Court, and returned the following verdict: "We of the Jury find the prisoner Not Guilty" and she is ordered to be discharged from this indictment. (*Alexandria County Minute Book*, October Term 1837 – 9th day, p. 105)

Yesterday, about noon, an altercation took place between two free colored boys, between fourteen and fifteen years of age, on King street, and a fight ensued, in the course of which, one of them struck the other several times over the head with the handle of a hickory broom with which he was sweeping, causing death immediately. – The boy who killed the other has been committed to jail for further examination. As the boy is to have his trial for the offence it is not necessary or proper that we should give any of the details of the affray, which ended in this melancholy manner. (*Alexandria Gazette*, June 25, 1844, p.3.)

^^*^*^*^*^*^*^*^*^*^*^*^*

At the conclusion of the performance at the Circus, on Wednesday night, a row occurred between some boys of this place, and some of the Circus Company. It appears that when the tent was being taken down, the boys began throwing stones at the men engaged. From this a fight ensued, when one of the boys, named John Welch, was struck on the head with a swingle tree belonging to one of the wagons, causing his death in a few hours. The police officers were soon on the spot, and in conjunction with the Night Watch, arrested two of the boys and one of the men attached to the company, named Robinson, said to be the one who struck John Welch. An inquest was held on the body of the boy, yesterday morning, by Coroner C. Neale, and after a strict examination of the witnesses, rendered a verdict that the deceased came to his death from blows inflicted by an unknown person. The man suspected of the murder was taken to prison and had a trial yesterday, before the Mayor and Justice English.

After some four or five hours were spent in the examination of witnesses, and listening to the arguments of the Counsel on both sides, the case was sent on for further trial to the County Court, which will take place on Tuesday next.

The case excited considerable interest, and the Court House was densely crowded. (*Alexandria Gazette*, September 23, 1853, p.3.)

The said Austin Robinson was set to the bar in custody of the jailor of this county and charged that, he the said Austin Robinson did on the 21st day of September in the year 1853 in the County of Alexandria, assault, beat and kill one John Welsh. Sundry witnesses were examined and the prisoner by counsel heard in his defence. On consideration thereof the court is of opinion that felony had been committed but that there is not probable cause to charge the said Austin Robinson therewith and the Court doth order he be discharged. (*Alexandria County Court Order Book*, September 6, 1853, p. 140.)

^^*^*^*^*^*^*^*^*^*^*^*^*

HORRIBLE MURDER – Yesterday morning, early, the dead body of Michael Kiggin, a watchman employed at the Cotton Factory, at this place, was discovered lying in the yard of the Factory. His head was brutally mashed in, evidently by blows from a heavy stick, and he must have died immediately upon being struck. – Coroner Neale held

53

an inquest upon the body of the deceased, and the jury returned a verdict that the deceased came to his death by blows inflicted on his head by some person unknown to the jury. It was stated on the examination of the case, that a person living in the neighborhood, about three o'clock in the morning, heard loud words in the direction of the scene of the murder, and some one curse another, and, in a few minutes, saw a man running from that direction. It is probably that the murderer, entered the yard, and after a dispute, assailed his victim, and killed him with a stick of wood which he picked up near the furnace.

Kiggin, the deceased, was an Irishman by birth, about 24 years of age, and had been employed as a Watchman in the Factory, for some months past, in place of a man discharged, for inattention to his duties, K. was a sober, trustworthy man, and gave satisfaction to his employers. He lived in the neighborhood of the Factory. Some suspicions are excited, and the police have the matter in charge. They will use every effort to discover the murderer. In the meantime, a man named Arrington, has been arrested on suspicion, and committed to jail by Justice English, for examination this morning.

This murder of a quiet, and inoffensive citizen, by a prowling assassin, has, naturally created considerable feeling. It is unusual to have to record such an event as happening in the midst of this community.

It will be seen that the Mount Vernon Cotton Factory, has offered a reward of $200 for the apprehension of the murderer of Michael Kiggin, who was killed whilst employed in the discharge of his duties as a watchman at the Factory, on Thursday morning. (*Alexandria Gazette*, July 21, 1854, p. 3.)

Gaiten and William Arrington, suspected of being concerned in the murder of Michael Kiggins, late watchman at the Cotton Factory, were arrested on Friday last, and taken before Justices English and Brown for examination. Gaiten Arrington, the father, was discharged, but William Arrington, his son, was remanded to jail to await a trial before the next term of the County Court for this county. (*Alexandria Gazette*, July 31, 1854, p.3.)

Commonwealth vs. Arrington - The said Arrington charged as aforesaid was again set to the bar in the custody of the jailor of this county. Sundry other witnesses were examined, and the prisoner by counsel heard in his defence. On consideration thereof the Court is of opinion that a felony hath been committed and that there is probably cause to charge the said Arrington therewith, and doth remand him for trial in the Circuit Court of this County. (*Alexandria County Court Order Book*, August 15, 1854, p. 241.)

William Arrington who stands indicted of murder was led to the bar in the custody of the jailer and a jury to wit. .... After hearing the evidence the jury declared that the said Arrington "is not guilty of the murder as in the pleading hath alleged..." It is considered by the Court that the said Arrington be discharged of the murder. (*Alexandria*

ᕯᐱᕯᐱᕯᐱᕯᐱᕯᐱᕯᐱᕯᐱᕯᐱᕯᐱᕯᐱᕯᐱᕯ

HORRID AFFAIR - On Saturday night last, about eleven o'clock, a dreadful affair occurred in this place, which has caused no little excitement. It appears that as persons were returning from Heller's exhibition, at Liberty Hall, some difficulty occurred between Emory Crump and Joseph Bloxham, (two young men of this place) on King street, near the corner of Washington, which resulted in the interference of George W. Crump, (brother of Emory Crump) who stabbed Bloxham in the back, with a dagger, causing Bloxham's death in about fifteen minutes. After committing the deed, Crump, throwing the dagger over a fence, in a vacant lot, ran home, where, shortly afterwards, he was arrested, by officer Chipley, and carried to jail. The body of Bloxham was carried into the office of Dr. R. H. Stabler, where an inquest was held over it, by Wm. B. Price, acting as Coroner. A post mortem examination was made by Drs. R. H. Stabler and C. W. Chancellor. They described the wound as having been inflicted by a sharp, two-edged instrument, which penetrated the body, in the back, between the sixth and seventh ribs. just behind the shoulder blade, going through the lower lobe of the left lung, and also passing through the pulmonary artery, causing death in a short time, as before stated. The Coroner's jury returned a verdict that the deceased came to his death by a stab inflicted by George W. Crump, in accordance with the above facts.

Yesterday morning, Crump was brought before Justices English and Price, for examination. It was proved that as several persons were going up the street, in coming from the exhibition, the Crumps called out after Bloxham, using terms of derision, to which he replied, using epithets towards them. This continued until they reached the corner of King and Washington streets, when Bloxham, who was a cripple, walking with a crutch and cane, struck Emory Crump twice over the head with his stick. George W. Crump who was walking by the side of Bloxham, was seen to strike at him in the back. Bloxham, in the act of falling, was caught by some of his friends. He was asked what was the matter, and replied that he was cut in the back. He was asked then, who stabbed him, and he said, Bee Crump. He was then carried to Dr. Stabler's office, where he shortly afterwards expired. Crump ran, as soon as he was seen to strike, and was observed to throw something over a fence into a vacant lot close by the scene. This lot was searched on Sunday morning and a dagger with a blade a little more than eight inches long, with blood on it, was found. A number of witnesses who were present at the affray, and who came up afterwards, were examined, and all confirmed the statements given.

Officer Chipley went immediately in search of Crump, and found him at the house of his brother. Upon being told that he was charged with killing a man, he exclaimed, "My God, is he dead." He was arrested without resistance.

Bloxham lived in the West End, near the Toll Gate. Crump worked with his brother at a carpenter's shop in this place. This dreadful affray has caused deep feeling not only among the friends of the parties, but throughout the whole community. The peace and quiet of our city have seldom been disturbed by such an occurrence - a man stabbed and killed in the public streets.

After a patient hearing of all the testimony offered, the Justices in attendance directed Geo. W. Crump to be committed to jail, to wait an investigation of the case to be held before an Examining Court, which will meet on the first Monday in April next.... (*Alexandria Gazette*, March 13, 1855, p. 3.)

The Court proceeded to the examination of George W. Crump a white man charged with a felony in this that he did on the 10th day of March 1855 feloniously and of malice kill and murder one Joseph Bloxham. Sundry witnesses were examined and the prisoner by counsel heard in his defence. On consideration thereof the Court is of opinion that a felony hath been committed and that there is probable cause to charge the said Crump therewith and doth remand him for trial in the Circuit Court of this County. (*Alexandria County Court Minute Book*, April 2, 1855, p. 297)

Crump was convicted of murder in June, 1855 and sentenced to 12 years in the State penitentiary. (*Alexandria Gazette*, July 21, 1860, p. 3.)

^^*^*^*^*^*^*^*^*^*^*^*^*

SUPPOSED MURDER - An Irish woman, named Downey, was found dead in a house near the jail, yesterday morning. A coroner's inquest was held and a post mortem examination ordered; the results of which have not transpired. Downey, her husband, has been arrested and lodged in jail, to await an examination.

SUPPOSED MURDER CASE - VERDICT OF THE CORONER'S JURY - Coroner Neale held an inquest on the body of Sally Henarty, (improperly reported Downey) on Wednesday evening, and ordered a post mortem examination, which was made by Drs. M. M. Lewis and J. C. Broun, and, yesterday morning, the jury rendered a verdict, "that Sally Henarty came to her death from personal violence, committed on her person by her husband, Francis Henarty, on the night of the 7th of February 1856." Henarty is in jail, and will be examined this morning. (*Alexandria Gazette*, February 8 & 9, 1856, p. 3.)

Commonwealth vs. Henarty - The court proceeded to the examination of Francis Henarty, a white man charged with a felony. Said Henarty was set to the bar in custody of the jailor of this county and charged that he the said Henarty did on the 7th day of February in the year 1856 in the County of Alexandria feloniously and of his malice aforethought kill and murder one Sally Henarty. Sundry witnesses were examined and the prisoner by his counsel heard in his defence. Upon consideration whereof the court is of opinion that the felony aforesaid has been committed and that there is probable cause to charge the said Henarty therewith. And the court doth remand him for trial to the next term of the Circuit Court of this County and the said Henarty was remanded to jail. (*Alexandria County Court Order Minute Book*, March 3, 1856, p. 28)

Francis Henarty who stands committed upon a charge of murder to the jail of the county and the Grand Jury having failed to find a bill of indictment against him the court doth order that he be discharged from custody. (*Alexandria Circuit Court Common Law Order Book*, May 19, 1856, Vol. I, p. 135.)

∧∧*∧*∧*∧*∧*∧*∧*∧*∧*∧*∧*∧*

CHARGE OF MURDER – An inquest was held on Sunday last, by Coroner Neale, on the body of a man named Wm. Howard, found dead on the public road, in Alexandria County, near the residence of Anthony R. Frazier. Dr. M. M. Lewis examined the body and found five stabs inflicted on it, with a sharp instrument, supposed to be a knife, and which wounds had caused death. Two of the stabs were in the chest; and one of them had penetrated the heart. The verdict of the jury was, that "the deceased Wm. Howard came to his death from wounds inflicted on his person on the evening of the 14th inst., by his brother Samuel Howard." Samuel Howard has been arrested, on this charge, and commited to the jail of the county. He will be examined before Justice Hunter, this morning, at 10 o'clock.

The Howards were residents of this county, and had had some previous difficulty, it is said. Before the Coroner's inquest, Noah Drummond testified that Samuel Howard came to his house on the evening of the 14th, and pulled out the identical knife which was produced before the jury, and remarked that he had bought it, to keep off Mr. Frazier's folks – repeating the expression, and flourishing the knife. He then left in the direction where the body was found. He had on then the same shirt that he wore when arrested, now bloody, but then free from blood. – Another witness saw Wm. Howard lying, on the evening of the 14th, on the side of the road, apparently drunk and insensible. – James Jones testified that on the 15th he went to the room of Samuel Howard (the prisoner) and found at the foot of his bed, a bloody hat, and a small bundle and under him a bloody shirt and knife, with blood on his pantaloons and shoes. The prisoner asked witness, – "Is he dead." Witness answered, he was. Prisoner then asked, "Will this hang me?" He then asked if it was his brother – and added – "Will they take me to Alexandria? This is Sunday, they will not take me on Sunday."

An account of the affair is, that William Howard, interfered in a fight between Samuel Howard and a negro man, and that Samuel Howard stabbed his brother in the affray.

The *Washington Star* of yesterday, giving an account of the murder says:

"Samuel Howard bore enmity to Mr. Frasier and his employees and servants, which he was in the habit of expressing when he was intoxicated. Leaving the toll gate he proceeded down the road to where his brother lay sleeping, and awakened him. On doing so, the latter at first endeavored to make him go away; but finally got up and proceeded with him some distance, perhaps half a mile further down the road, where the altercation ensued, in which the murderer stabbed his victim some five or six times in the back and side, one wound at least penetrating his heart, and probably producing death instantly. The murderer not long afterwards, bloodied over, with sleeves rolled up and knife in hand, went up to the buggy of Mr. McLean, lumber dealer in this city, who resides near where the crime was perpetrated, and was about entering his gate when thus accosted. Mr. McL., knowing his bad character, motioned him away menacingly. His crime only became known by the discovery of the corpse of his victim yesterday morning by persons passing over the road. Suspicion was instantly fastened on Sam'l Howard, and he was promptly sought for at his home four miles further up in the country; and was found there in bed, his bloody shirt and knife being discovered under the bed.

Both these men are said to have been engaged in the riotous conduct that took place at the recent county election at the Alexandria county precinct, wherein many outrages were perpetrated by them and other such characters from the neighborhood and this city. (*Alexandria Gazette*, June 17, 1856, p.3)

CIRCUIT COURT – Second Day – The case of the Commonwealth, vs. Samuel Howard, on an indictment for murder, was taken up, and after a trial, the jury rendered a verdict of manslaughter in the second degree; and the prisoner was sentenced to five years imprisonment in the Penitentiary. ... (*Alexandria Gazette*, November 13, 1856, p. 2.)

^^*^*^*^*^*^*^*^*^*^*^*^*

DEATH OF DAVID HUME, ESQ.
    "None knew him but to love him,
    None named him but to praise."

We are called upon this morning to chronicle an event that has cast a deep gloom over our community, the death of David Hume, Esq. who was killed in Washington, on Saturday morning last, by Dodridge C. Lee, of Loudoun County, a clerk in the Pension Office. Our Washington correspondent sends us the following account of the sad affair.

MURDER IN WASHINGTON – WASHINGTON, Feb. 28 – David Hume, Esq. of Alexandria, was shot this morning, at the Pension Office, by D. C. Lee, a clerk in that office. The circumstances of the case are briefly these. In the great crowd at the Presidents Levee, last evening, Lee missed his pocket book and turning around, accused Mr. Hume of stealing it. This morning, Mr. Hume proceeded to the Pension Office, accompanied by Mr. Walker, the reading clerk of the House, and asked a retraction from Lee, which the latter refused to make. Mr. Hume, thereupon, struck him several blows with his cane, when Lee drew a pistol and fired. Mr. Hume iustantly fell and died in less than five minutes. The greatest excitement was occasioned at

58

the Pension Office, and hundreds rushed into the building. The coroner was sent for, and will investigate the latter. Mr. Lee immediately surrendered himself to the officers of the law.

Other statements as to the affair are, that Lee not only accused Mr. Hume of picking his pocket last evening, but slapped his face, and that the parties were separated by their families. Another informant says that Mr. Hume did not strike Mr. Lee this morning, but merely raised his cane, as if intending to do so. Mr. Hume was shot through the heart, and the bleeding from the wound was almost wholly internal. The Coroner's inquest will develop all the facts in the case.

...Solomon G. Heaton saw the transaction last night at the President's levee; was passing towards the East room with a lady and near the doorway of the President's reception room, came in the rear of Col. Lee; noticed that he had one or two ladies with him; stood there for a moment, the crowd being so great could not pass; a gentleman coming from the reception room met them and seemed to be trying to pass us and go out; deceased was this gentleman; Col. Lee stood rather facing deceased and while in that position saw Col. Lee put his hand on his pantaloons pocket; he then spoke to deceased, and at the same moment stepped up to him and collared him saying, "You have my pocket book"; could not say if deceased had a lady with him or not; Col. Lee remarked further that he should not let him go until he gave up the pocket book; and the Colonel then called for assistance, turning his head towards witness; deceased did not reply immediately, but looked surprised, his first reply, that witness heard, was: "For what reason do you make this charge?" Mr. Lee did not seem particularly excited; Lee said: "Sir, I felt your hand in my pocket and saw you take it out;" deceased replied that he had not taken the pocket-book, and seemed surprised at the charge, and immediately enquired of Col. Lee his name; Col. Lee gave his name and turning to witness said here is a gentleman who knows me; Col. Lee still retained his hold upon his coat during this conversation; witness said to deceased that he knew Col. Lee; deceased began to get a little excited manifesting some feeling, and said to Col. Lee, "Come, go with me"; witness then passed Col. Lee, and that is all he saw of the occurrence then; came up to the office about 9 this morning, to room adjoining; soon after came into this room; found Col. Lee; made inquiry how the affair terminated last night; he was relating the circumstances; the chief clerk, Mr. Cole, of the Pension Office, opened the door; came in, and inquired if Col. Lee was in; immediately two gentlemen came into the room; Colonel Lee was standing by his desk at the time; two or three other gentlemen were in the room; recognized deceased as one of the gentlemen who entered; Colonel Lee passed towards the door from his desk advancing somewhat towards the gentlemen or in the direction of the door; thinks deceased remarked "you are the gentleman I met last night at the President's, and accused me of taking your pocket book," enquiring at the same time if he recognized him; Col. Lee replied that he did recognize him distinctly; they entered into conversation, and deceased undertook to explain why he should not be accused of committing an act of that kind; remarked that he had lived an upright man for forty-five years and had probably given away more money than Col. Lee was worth, and asked what motive he could have in picking his pocket – also if he still reiterated his charge; Col. Lee answered that he did reiterate his charge; they stood facing eaeh other at that time, deceased had a black cane with a bent handle in his hand; (a cane was identified by witness as the one) deceased struck Lee over the head as many as three times; Col. Lee retreated, deceased at same time striking him with cane; heard report of pistol; afterwards saw the pistol in hands of Col. Lee; deceased fell over and exclaimed that he was a dead man; Colonel Lee stood leaning forward at the time he fired, with his back towards the deceased; thinks he must have reached his hand around and fired under his arm. Col. Lee told witness this morning that after witness left him at the levee a gentleman touched him and said "You have mistaken your man," telling him who deceased was. That he was a Mr. Hume of Alexandria.

Several other witnesses were examined and the jury brought in a verdict that deceased came to his death from the effect of a pistol ball from a pistol in then hands of Doddridge C. Lee, which caused his death in less than ten minutes.

Drs. Storrow and Berry made an examination of the body, and testified to the effect, that the ball entered the abodomen one inch from the medium line and three inches below the umbilicus, passing inwards and downwards, causing death by hemorrhage, and probably by pressure on the spinal cord.

The body was brought to this city on Saturday afternoon, in charge of the committee, appointed at the meeting of the Merchants, and was to have been conveyed to Orange Court House, yesterday morning.

A dispatch received on Saturday night, stated that Lee was still in custody; his friends endeavoring to ascertain if bail would be taken for his appearance.

Mr. Hume was an honorable, high toned gentleman, and possessed the esteem and confidence of all who knew him. He had been a resident merchant of this city for several years. Immediately after the receipt of the intelligence of his death, by telegraph, numbers of our citizens, could be seen congregated at various points, with the deepest melancholy depicted upon their countenances, talking over the sad event. Every evidence was shown of the love and respect entertained for the man by our citizens. He has left four interesting children to mourn his untimely end. (*Alexandria Gazette*, March 2, 1857, p. 3.)

VERDICT – Washington, March 29 – The case was given to the jury at five and half o'clock, yesterday. The Court resumed its session this morning at half past ten. ...The judge said, that yesterday, he refused the prayers of the counsel for the prosecution on the ground that there was no evidence whatever, showing that Lee designed to provoke Hume to strike him. In reply to an inquiry of one of the jurors, the judge said the case should rest on the point, whether Lee could have retreated further, before shooting, or whether he had reason to apprehend personal bodily injury from the force and rapidity of blows. He said Hume went to Lee's place of business – Lee said nothing except reply to questions propounded by Hume. ... The jury returned and reappeared a half hour afterwards, with verdict "NOT GUILTY." Lee was discharged, and the court adjourned. .. (*Alexandria Gazette*, March 31, 1857, p. 2)

^^*^*^*^*^*^*^*^*^*^*^*

MURDER AT FISHTOWN – An inquest was held yesterday morning, by Coroner Neale on the body of James Clark, who was killed on Sunday night, at Fish Town, by George Goodrich. From the evidence taken before the Coroner, it appears that Clark and Goodrich, were in the booth of Walter Carroll, and were apparently friendly – nor was there any reason to apprehend that Goodrich intended to attack Clark. The two men had been wrestling, in a playful manner, and Clark had taken his seat, when Goodrich drew a knife and rushed upon him, stabbing him in the abdomen, from the effects of which he died in a few moments. The jury brought in a verdict that the deceased came to his death from wounds inflicted with a knife, by George Goodrich. Goodrich was arrested and taken to jail, to await an examination before the next County Court. (*Alexandria Gazette*, April 14, 1857, p.3.)

CIRCUIT COURT – The case of the Commonwealth, vs. George Goodrich, indicted for the murder of James Clarke, was tried yesterday. A number of witnesses were examined; and the case submitted to the jury without argument. The jury brought in a verdict of murder in the second degree, and ascertained the term of his confinement in the penitentiary, to be eighteen years. – Goodrich was remanded to jail to await the sentence of the Court, which will necessarily be before its adjournment. (*Alexandria Gazette*, May 26, 1857, p.3)

^^*^*^*^*^*^*^*^*^*^*^*

INVESTIGATION OF THE SUNDAY SCHOOL HOMICIDE IN ALEXANDRIA COUNTY, VIRGINIA – The regular monthly term of the Alexandria County Court commenced on Monday morning. After disposing of considerable business which was brought up, the case of Manvil Austin, charged with killing James H. Burch, on the 28th day of June last, was taken up.

Turner Dixon, esq., Presiding Justice; Charles E. Stuart, for the prosecution, and Francis L. Smith for defence.
The prisoner was brought into Court. He is about sixteen years of age; of good size; with a mild blue eye, and a countenance indicating great natural intelligence.
...That the difficulty which led to the death of Burch originated in a quarrel between the defendent and two small boys; that there had been a picnic, at which Austin had cut a grape vine which the boys were using as a jumping pole or hoop; and that at some previous time these same boys had had a difficulty about a swing with which Austin interfered; that on the day of occurrence, being Sunday, Austin went to the church prepared with a pistol; that Jas. H. Burch was there, not as one of the party who had quarreled with Austin, but stopping near by as a spectator; that he was called upon to prevent the affray between the

61

boys; that he jumped off his horse for this purpose; and that Austin not only shot him once but followed this up, firing two fatal shots after he had resisted the attack on him successfully. If the party implicated should be proven to have acted upon motives of deadly animosity, and with the malignant purpose to take life, then he should receive at the hands of the Court that punishment which the laws of his country provide for the preservation of the peace and welfare of the Commonwealth.

Mr. Smith for the defence.... He expected to show that on the day previous to the affray, these persecutors had uttered threats and abuse towards the prisoner to justify him in procuring the means of defence, that he had done so, and on the fatal morning had gone to the church, when he met the two boys who commenced the assault upon him, coming together for that preconcerted purpose, and challenged him to fight; he refused and requested them to go away; saying "let me alone, I have no difficulty with you," at that time Burch entered into the affair, and aided them to carry out their fell purpose; Austin, seeing the difficulty and danger of his position, fled towards the sanctuary where he had right of all places to expect safety – the church – but was pursued thither by his tormentors, and when overpowered and trodden down, by their multiplied and united assaults, as a last resort drew his weapon and fired upon them; that goaded to desperation by the cowardly and infamous wretches who knew no mercy, and pressed to the wall, he drew his pistol in the spirit of desperation and defended himself, firing again and again upon them; the first shot being insufficient to deter his assailants, he had repeated the discharge until his deadly opposer was dead; that this did not end the conflict, but his opposers wresting the pistol from his graps, he fled, they pursuing and firing upon him as he fled.

Mr. Smith concluded by stating that he put the whole thing upon the broad ground of self defence on the part of the prisoner, and held that the court had full power to draw the line of distinction between murder and manslaughter; the principal question would be whether the prisoner had reason to believe that his life was in peril, or that he was in danger of enormous bodily harm before he drew the trigger. (*Alexandria Gazette*, July 8, 1857, p. 3.)

THE CASE OF AUSTIN – ... the Court ordered the discharge of the prisoner from arrest. His acquittal was received with expressions of satisfaction by the auditors... (This incident transpired at the Episcopal Sunday School situated at Balls Cross Roads.) (*Alexandria Gazette*, July 9, 1857, p. 3.)

^^*^*^*^*^*^*^*^*^*^*^*^*

CONVICTION FOR MURDER – We stated yesterday, that a negro woman, named Jenny, slave of Mr. Bazil Hall of this county, was convicted of the murder of Mrs. Elizabeth Hall, (wife of Mr. Bazil Hall,) and condemned to be hung on the 26th of next month. The following is the testimony in the case taken before the Court:

Dr. Wunder sworn - Three weeks ago, yesterday, (Sunday) I was called to see Mrs. Hall; she was burned from the knee up the back, and also in front, pretty much to a crisp; she was in much pain, sick at stomach and throwing up blood; don't think the flame went down her throat, but the burning outside caused it; I was called in at 3 o'clock, P.M. Sunday; she died about 1 o'clock that night; I remained with her until 10 o'clock that night; she dying when I left; I apprised her of her condition; she knew she must die, and appeared reconciled; she requested Mr. Hall to take good care of her children after she was gone, and write to her sisters. After that the deposition was taken. I applied remedies externally and internally; they relieved her pains; she said, "Doctor, I am burnt to death." When the deposition was given, she thought she must die; thinks her remarks about her children were after her deposition ... Mrs. Hall was in good health, I suppose, up to the time she was burned; she was pregnant at the time; I asked the question and she told me so; I am satisfied that her death was caused by the burning.

H. W. Febrey sworn - I was at church that day; was informed that Mrs. Hall had been thrown in the fire, and requested to go over. When I got there I met Mr. Hall in the yard and went with him into the kitchen; I asked if Mrs. Hall was badly burned; he said she was; he then showed me some fragments of burnt clothing, and the fire upon which she was thrown, and the bench upon which she was sitting when the attack was made upon her...; she evinced no anger or vindictive feelings; she seemed calm at the time. I, as Justice of the Peace took her deposition in writing, and read it over to her ... she said it was correct and authorized me to sign it, to be used after her death.

The deposition was here produced by witness, and read as follows:

"I told Jenny to go to the spring, and Salina to hurry about dinner, that it was late. I laid myself back on the bench upon which I was sitting, and fell into a dose. When I roused up, I asked Jenny where was Salina, and she said she had sent her to the spring. I asked her why she had sent her to the spring contrary to my orders? She gave me some of her insolence, and I slapped her in the mouth. She then took a piece of pine board, and put it in the fire. I told her that was wrong, as she knew I wanted the ashes saved to make lye, that I was having nothing but hard wood burned. She then took it out of the fire. She again put it in the fire. I told her to take the board out of the fire again. She then caught me and put my head between her knees, and pushed me in the fire. I begged and plead with her not to do me so; my clothes were all in flames. Jenny ran out and shut the door, and held it so that I could not get out. I tore off my clothes as best I could. She again came in and threw me in the fire the second time. I again begged and pleaded with her not to do me so; if she would not, I would not have her whipped, I would get her master to set her free, and I would give her all the money that I had. She again went out and held the door. I got the fire out as best as I could. I tried to get out of the door, but could not. I then thought of the windows. (She had put all of her children in the other room, and tied the door.) I bursted the door open, and ran to the window, and in attempting to get out she heard me, and came in and caught me, and pulled me back, and in doing so I fell in the cradle on her child. I told her she would kill her child. She

63

took it by the arms and threw it on the bed, or back in the cradle, I know not which. She drew me back to the fire, and threw me in the third time. She also caught up her child's clothes, and the clothes that I had torn off, and held them over the fire. When they were all in flames, she held them on my head. She again went out at the door and held it. I ran to it and pulled it over, and in doing so it fell in a tub that was sitting under it with some persimmons in it. I first put my head in it as far as I could, for my hair was all on fire; I then sat down in it. I again ran to the window and succeeded in getting out, and got on the stile. She ran and caught me by the leg and arms, and struggled hard to drag me back. I partially succeeded in getting loose; she then caught me by the arms and around the neck. In struggling I got loose and got over the stile, and hallored murder as loud as I could. I started to run but did not get far before I fell. She then saw the servant man William, and called to him and told him to run here for mistress was almost burned to death. She then told him to run for his master. I begged him not, for I was afraid if he left me she would murder me. While I was pleading with him, my son came, and I told him to go for his father, and he did so. ELIZABETH HALL. This deposition taken before me, in my County, this 13th day of December 1857. H. W. Febrey, J.P. ...

Jenny is a woman of about 30 years of age. She plead not guilty and was very little affected when the sentence of death was pronounced upon her. She has a very young child which has been taken home. She has made no confession and stoutly denies that she committed the murder. (*Alexandria Gazette*, January 6, 1858, p. 3.)

...Jenny was sentenced to be hanged on the 26th of February next, between the hours of 10 and 2 o'clock. (Alexandria County).

EXECUTION – The negro woman Jenny, convicted of the murder of Mrs. Hall in this county, was hung yesterday according to the sentence in the jail yard, at twelve and a half o'clock. She made no confession. There were but few persons within the enclosure, but a large crowd, many from Washington and the County, were congregated outside the walls. (*Alexandria Gazette*, February 27, 1858, p. 3.)

^^*^*^*^*^*^*^*^*^*^*^*

MURDER – An inquisition was taken on Wednesday last, by Justice Summers, in the absence of the Coroner, at the house of Daniel Joice, No. 131 Queen Street, upon the view of the body of Catharine Ages, a free colored woman; and the jury rendered a verdict "that the deceased came to her death by blows inflicted with a chair by her husband, Wm. Ages, a free negro. The blows were inflicted several weeks ago, and she died on Wednesday morning. Ages on hearing of her death, fled, and the last seen of him he was going up the Little River turnpike. He had threatened his wife's life on several occasions previously. (*Alexandria Gazette*, June 25, 1858, p. 3.)

WIFE MURDER - John Murphy was arrested on Thursday night, by the Watch, on the charge of murdering his wife, Margaret Murphy, and on yesterday was taken before Justice Price, who committed him to jail to await a further examination.

Coroner Neale yesterday held an inquisition over the body of the woman, and the jury returned the following verdict: "That the deceased, Margaret Murphy, came to her death by a wound inflicted on her neck, on the night of the 1st instant, by her husband, John Murphy." From the evidence before the Coroner, it appears that on Wednesday night, Mrs. Murphy was picked up in the street in an intoxicated condition, and carried home, whereupon her husband became very abusive; words passed between them, and he inflicted a severe wound upon her neck with some sharp instrument. She lingered until Thursday night, when she died from the effects of the wound. The parties have lived very unhappily together. The murder was committed on the alley, on the west side of Pitt, between Cameron and Queen streets. (*Alexandria Gazette*, December 4, 1858, p. 3.)

CIRCUIT COURT THIRD DAY - In the case of the Commonwealth vs. John Murphy, a nolle prosequi was entered, as witnesses could not be procured. (*Alexandria Gazette*, November 17, 1859, p.3.)

^^*^*^*^*^*^*^*^*^*^*^*

A MURDER CASE - On Tuesday evening last a fight occurred on Union street, in this city, between Wm. King and Joseph Riley, both sailors, who arrived here on the same morning, in the ship *Charles Ward*, from the Chincha Islands. In this affray bcth men were considerably bruised and battered, and Riley charges that he was struck with a slingshot in the hands of King, knocking out several of his teeth.

Early yesterday morning, Riley called at the boarding house of Eli Petty, and inquired for King; and learning that he was in the yard, in the rear of the house, went through the house into the yard, and stabbed King with a sheath knife, in the upper part of the left breast, from which wound King died in about forty-five minutes.

An inquest was held on the body of the deceased, at 10 o'clock yesterday morning, by Coroner Chancellor, and a post mortem examination made by Drs. Lewis and Chancellor. The jury, after the facts were stated, returned the following verdict: - "That the deceased, Wm. King, came to his death, from a wound inflicted in his chest, by a knife in the hands of Joseph Riley."

Both King and Riley shipped on board the *Charles Ward*, at Callao. King was an Irishman by birth, and Riley, and Englishman - hailing from Liverpool. King, on the ship's papers is put down as a citizen of the U.S. The deceased was about 35 or 38 years of age.

Immediately after Riley had stabbed King, he went on the ship, changed his clothing, and then came ashore, and meeting the officer in pursuit of him, gave himself up, without resistance or trouble. The captain states that King was turbulent man, and had been quarrelling

65

with Riley almost the whole voyage and that he considered Riley a quiet, and peaceable sailor.

Yesterday afternoon, Riley was brought before Justice Price for examination.

Various witnesses were examined, and the facts brought out as above stated. The prisoner himself made a statement, acknowledging that he stabbed the deceased – but that he previously received great provocation, had been subjected to great insult, and that he did not intend to kill the deceased when he stabbed him. It appears that in cutting at King, the prisoner, when his arm was seized by King, cut himself severely on the right thigh, from which he was quite lame. The history of the matter as given by Riley, created considerable sympathy in his favor, in the Magistrate's Office. Justice Price after a full hearing of the case, committed the prisoner to jail for his trial before the Court, the 1st Monday in September. (*Alexandria Gazette*, August 18, 1859, p.3.)

Joseph Riley, charged with the murder of William King, (both sailors on board the ship Charles Ward, lying at this port at the time, and the particulars of which have been already published) in August last was arraigned, found guilty, and sentenced to eight years confinement in the Penitentiary. (*Alexandria Gazette*, November 17, 1859, p.3.)

^^*^*^*^*^*^*^*^*^*^*^*

SHOOTING AFFAIR – Yesterday evening, between 5 and 6 o'clock, Buck Rye was shot at Fishtown, by a man named Thomas Penn. A witness of the affair says that he saw the two men sitting on a boat, on the fish wharf, apparently quarreling, when Penn drew a knife, and made threats against Rye, and chased him; when they both entered their respective houses near, and appeared again almost simultaneously, each with a gun. Rye made no attempt to discharge his, and was in the act of entering his house again, when Penn shot him; the load, duck shot, taking effect about the left hip and thigh, and a few striking Rye's mother, who was near. Rye, it is thought, is badly wounded. Penn at last accounts was not arrested. (*Alexandria Gazette*, November 2, 1859, p.3.)

CORONER'S INQUEST – Coroner Chancellor held an inquest on Sunday, on the body of Wm. H. Rye, who was shot some two weeks since by Thomas Penn. ...A post mortem examination was made by Drs. Lewis and Chancellor, and after hearing the evidence in the case, the jury rendered a verdict: "That the deceased came to his death from the effects of a gun shot wound received at the hands of Thomas Penn."

Rye was in indigent circumstances and the Coroner's jury generously contributed a sufficient amount to defray the expenses of his burial.

Penn was arrested at the time of the shooting, and had an examination before the County Court, when, from want of sufficient evidence, he was discharged. Upon the rendering of the verdict of the Coroner's jury on Sunday, he was rearrested by Officer Padgett, and committed to jail by the Coroner to await an examination on the charge of murder before the County Court. (*Alexandria Gazette*, November 15, 1859, p.3.)

^^*^*^*^*^*^*^*^*^*^*^*^*

HOMICIDE – Yesterday morning about 11 o'clock, John E. Monroe and Wm. Howard, who had fought on the 8th inst., when Howard was severely beaten by Monroe, met in the road leading from the Little River Turnpike to the Theological Seminary, about half a mile from Padgett's tollgate, and renewed the fight, and while both were down, Monroe, who was on top, was shot through the heart by a ball from a pistol in the hands of Howard, and expired in less than five minutes.

A coroner's jury was summoned, and the evidence elicited was to the following effect, viz: – That a warrant had been obtained by Howard against Monroe, for the beating on the 8th inst. and that yesterday was the day set for the trial. Both the parties met at Catts' Hotel, West End, where the trial was to have taken place before Justice Padgett; but Monroe objecting to having Padgett sit on the case, Justice Daniel Kincheloe, who happened to be present, was proposed, but was objected to by Howard, when Justice Kincheloe continued the case, and Howard left for home; and Monroe, by taking another road, got into the road that Howard was travelling, and waited for him, and on his approach, pulled him off his horse and got him down, and while down, Howard discharged three barrels of a revolver at him, one only taking effect near the heart, killing him in a few minutes.

Two young men, named Howard, who witnessed the affray, gave the evidence upon which the jury rendered the following verdict: – "That Joseph E. Monroe came to his death by a ball from a pistol in the hands of William Howard, which, in our opinion, was used in self-defence."

The body of the deceased was brought to the residence of his brother, Harrison L. Monroe, in this city, from whence the funeral will take place this morning.

Howard gave himself up to the authorities, but on the rendition of the above verdict, was discharged. (*Alexandria Gazette*, March 29, 1860, p.3.)

^^*^*^*^*^*^*^*^*^*^*^*^*

A MYSTERIOUS AFFAIR – The late William Ingle – It will be remembered that William Ingle, a former well known resident of this city, disappeared very suddenly some years ago, and that the strictest search afforded no clue to show whether he had been fouly dealt with or whether he had absented himself voluntarily from his old haunts. A day or two since a singular discovery was made by some fishermen at the mouth of Accoteek creek, near Fredericksburg, Virginia, and in the immediate neighborhood of a farm owned by Mr. Ingle, which promises to throw some light upon the cause of his disappearance. A strong wind had laid the flats bare, and the fishermen saw projecting from the mud, the upper portion of a wooden box, some six feet in length. On opening it the remains of a man of short statue was found enclosed, and from all the circumstances it was supposed that they might be those of Mr. Ingle. An inquest was held yesterday, but the remains were so far gone in decomposition that the jury could arrive at no conclusion beyond the fact that they were those of a man. The indications were that the person thus disposed of had been murdered and buried at low-water to some depth in the mud, and that in the course of time the box had worked up to the surface. – *Washington Star* in the *Alexandria Gazette*, November 29, 1860, p. 3.

^^*^*^*^*^*^*^*^*^*^*^*

CRIMINAL RECORD – The criminal docket of our Courts is usually very small, and compares favorably in this respect with the docket of any Court in this vicinity. Since the creation of the Circuit Court of this county, in 1847, upon retrocession of Alexandria to the Commonwealth of Virginia, there have been convicted, sentenced, and imprisoned in the State penitentiary, but twenty white persons. Nearly all those convicted, were for the lightest grade of felonies. Four of those sentenced had been convicted of murder, one of arson, and one of burglary.

Of those convicted there are now in the penitentiary ten prisoners who have not yet served out their time. These are as follows: G. W. Crump, convicted in June, 1855 of murder, sentenced to twelve years; Wm. Birch, convicted in May, 1856, of burglary, sentenced to eight years; Sam. Howard, convicted in November, 1856, of murder, sentenced to five years; Geo. Goodrick, convicted in May, 1857, of murder, sentenced to eighteen years; Thos. Parsons, convicted in November, 1858 of arson, sentenced to five years; Benj. Waller, convicted of grand larceny, in November, 1858, sentenced to three and one-half years; Martha Daniels, convicted of larceny, in May, 1859, sentenced to two years; Caroline Chichester, convicted of larceny, in May, 1859, sentenced to one year; Jos. Riley, convicted at the November term, 1859, of murder, sentenced to eight years; and Mich. Bergen, convicted at the May term 1860, of larceny, and sentenced for one year.

This includes only the white convicts. The County Court have sentenced a number of negroes to the penitentiary, during the same time, who have not yet finished out the terms for which they were imprisoned. (*Alexandria Gazette*, July 21, 1860, p.3.)

^^*^*^*^*^*^*^*^*^*^*^*

KILLED – A Difficulty occurred in an old frame building, on the corner of Duke and Water streets, last night about nine o'clock, between the occupants – some contrabands – and some white boys. The boys were driven out of the house, and one of the negro men followed them to the corner, when another fracas took place, in which the negro received a wound from a large knife in the right groin, from which he died in a few moments. A coroner's inquest was held on the body this morning by W. L. Penn, acting coroner, when the circumstances stated above

68

were elicited. The jury were adjourned, to meet this afternoon at two o'clock. John Goodrich, a lad of about eighteen years, was arrested this morning, and confined, on suspicion of having committed the deed. (*Alexandria Gazette*, November 28, 1862 p.2.)

The Court proceeded to the examination of George W. Goodrich, charged with a Felonious Homicide, the prisoner was set to the bar in custody of the Jailor of this County, charged with the murder of Joseph Hyde, col. in the night of the 27th day of November 1862. Sundry witnesses were examined Whereupon the Court is of the opinion that there is probable cause to believe the said George W. Goodrich, guilty of the Homicide aforesaid and they do order that he be remanded to the jail of this county for his trial therefore at the next term of the Circuit Court. (*Alexandria County Court Order Minute Book*, January 5, 1863, p. 18)

^^*^*^*^*^*^*^*^*^*^*

Yesterday evening, about six o'clock, a soldier named James Scotten, of Company G, 4th regiment, Delaware Volunteers was murdered, in the tunnel, under Wilkes street, between Fairfax and Water streets. He was stabbed in the back of the neck five times, one cut severing the jugular and making a considerable incision in the windpipe, and one entering the spinal column, from the effects of which he died in a few moments, as Jos. Wood, who was near and was attracted by the groans, quickly repaired to the spot, but upon reaching it found life extinct. Scotten it was said, entered the tunnel at about the time above mentioned, in company with another soldier. John Rush, of Company G, 72d regiment New York Volunteers has been arrested upon suspicion of having committed the crime, and lodged in jail to await an examination. The body of the murdered man was taken to the Washington Street Hospial (Hallowell's building) where a post mortem examination was held by Surgeons Bentley, Elliott and Caruthers, the evidence to be used before the Coroners Inquest which will be held tomorrow morning at 9 o'clock, a preliminary inquisition, only having been held this morning by W. L. Penn, acting coroner. Scotten had yesterday received four months pay, but had only a small amount of money about him at the time. (*Alexandria Gazette*, March 12, 1864, p. 2.)

The Court proceeded to the examination of John Rush a white man charged with a felony, the said Rush, was set to the Bar in the custody of the Jailor of this County and charged that he did on the 11th day of March 1864 in the County of Alexandria, cut, stab and kill one James H. Scotten. Sundry witnesses were examined and the prisoner by Counsel heard in his defence. Upon consideration whereof the Court is of the opinion that the Felony aforesaid has been committed but that there is not probable cause to charge the said John Rush, therewith and the Court doth order that the said John Rush be discharged from custody if detained for no other cause. (*Alexandria County Court Order Minute Book*, April 8, 1864, p. 152.)

THE WAR BEGUN IN EARNEST - BRUTAL ASSASSINATION OF COL. ELLSWORTH IN ALEXANDRIA - ...Thus quiet possession was taken of that part of Alexandria in the name of the United States by the portion of the troops immediately commanded by Col. Ellsworth.

...Proceeding up town, Col. Ellsworth saw a Secession flag waving over the Marshall House, kept by James Jackson, a well known secessionist. Instantly entering the house, with four or five of his men, Col. Ellsworth proceeded to the house-top, tore down the flag, and trampled it under foot.

In descending the stairs the party were encountered by the keeper of the house, double-barrel gun in hand. He raised the gun to shoot the foremost Zouave, who knocked aside his aim, when Jackson instantly turned it upon Ellsworth, and firing, discharged the load of one barrel into the heart of the gallant officer, who fell dead upon the stairs. Jackson as quickly snapped the other barrel at a Zouave standing next to Col. Ellsworth, where private Brownell, another of the Zouaves, accompanying Ellsworth to take down the flag, discharged the contents of his musket into Jackson's brain, bayoneting his body as he fell, pinning it to the steps....

The news of the assassination of Col. E. E. Ellsworth reached this city at an early hour this morning, and created much excitement here. (Washington, D.C.) (*Evening Star*, May 24, 1861, p. 2.)

...The Virginia forces under Col. Terrett having evacuated this place (Alexandria) the invaders of course met with no resistance; but the frowns of the citizens gave unerring indication of their feelings, in view of this infringement upon their rights and when it was announced that Ellsworth (the Col first named) had been killed whilst endeavouring to carry off a Confederate flag from the "Marshall House" (S.E. Corner of King and Pitt Streets) which he had entered whilst the proprietor was asleep - a general expression of joy was manifested by our most quiet citizens at this result. The history of this flag will long be remembered by our people, especially in view of the tragic event with which it is now associated. The proprietor of the Marshall House, Jas. W. Jackson, heartily sympathising with the South in the unnatural contest to which she had been forced by the unscrupulous citizens of the North - had procured a Confederate Flag and placed it upon his building, avowing that whoever should attempt to remove it, would have to pass over his dead body, and the sequel shows this melancholy fulfillment of this pledge, as he fell mortally wounded in its defence, but not till he had accomplished the death of him who dared thus to invade the sanctity of his home. This is a sad day for Alexandria, and whatever may be the issue of this contest this unprecedented move upon the part of a Republican President, will ever linger in the minds of citizens while memory lasts: for, independent of the regrets expressed at the death of the brave and patriotic Jackson, the usurpations of power indicated by this movement, causes the hearts of freemen to shrink with dread from the contemplation of the future history of our beloved country. (*Diary of Henry Whittington*, Friday May 24, 1861 - Alexandria Library, Lloyd House) (Col. Ellsworth had previously served as a law clerk in Abraham Lincoln's

law office in Springfield, Illinois.   Upon Ellsworth's death his body
was taken to the White House where it lay in state. Thereafter President and Mrs. Lincoln accompanied the remains to the funeral train for
Ellsworth's last trip home to New York.)

^^*^*^*^*^*^*^*^*^*^*^*

RECOUNTER – A recounter occurred this morning at the intersection
of Royal and Cameron streets between Major Henry T. Dixon of
Fauquier and Dr. T. Clay Maddux, in which the former was shot and it
is thought mortally wounded. The Major was picked up and taken to a
room in the City Hotel, and the Dr. immediately to the magistrates'
Office, where an examination was conducted by Justice Beach.

Tazwell Grisby sworn: –   Was standing talking to Maddux; saw
Dixon walk up Cameron street, on north side, from towardsMansion
House to Cooney's corner; had my back to City Hotel; Maddux was
facing me, when I saw Dixon crossing the street, and said to the Doctor there is Dixon and stepped aside; saw Dixon run his hand in his
pocket, and both fired about the same time; Maddux had his back to
Dixon as Dixon approached; Maddux and myself were standing on the
flagging between the City Hotel and Market House; Dixon fired once;
Maddux two shots; Dixon was standing still when he drew his pistol
from under his coat; the Doctor drew his pistol as soon as he saw
Dixon; Dixon fell and said I'm killed, I walked up to Dixon who said
he was a dead man; and I then went for a doctor. Dixon called to see
me this morning; during the conversation which ensued between us
Dixon said that Maddux was not in the habit of walking the streets as
usual; I thought that Dixon was hunting for Maddux....
    John Taylor sworn – was standing in front of the Eldorado House;
saw Dr.   Maddox and Mr. Grigsby standing half way between City
Hotel and Market House; saw Dixon walk up Cameron street, from
Fairfax; as he passed up he looked over towards Maddux whose back
was towards the Market House; had heard of a prior difficulty between
Maddux and Dixon; Dixon crossed from the N.E. corner of Royal and
Cameron towards the Market House on the flagging and passed out of
sight on Royal street behind the corner of the Market House when I
heard a shot; I think Dixon fired first from the report; was certain that
Dixon was going to attack Maddux; Dixon in walking up the street had
several times put his hand under his coat; the Market House kept
Dixon out of my sight for a minute; next time I saw him he was lying
on the pavement; Maddux was in my sight all the time and I saw him
when he fired; Dixon was watching Maddux as he walked up Cameron
street and could have gotten out of Maddux's sight had he chose.
    The following is Major Dixon's deposition taken before J. L. Dyson,
a Justice of the Peace of this County.
    I am conscious of my situation; my statement is made under the
impression that I am near my end; at the time of the shooting I was
walking along Royal Street in this city; Dr. Maddox saw me as I was
walking along Royal street and shot me before I drew my pistol; I was
passing away from him at the time; I shot at him after he shot me; I
was in this city because I had business at the War Department and

was temporarily stopping here; Dr. Maddox fired at me twice; I had not started to draw my pistol before he shot me; he had fired once before I started to draw my pistol; I carried my pistol on my left side, in my holster; he sought me once before in the Mansion House and spat in my face while I was sitting in a chair without my knowing he was present; I had not seen him prior since 1857; this was about ten days or two weeks ago; not a word was said before he shot me.

MAJOR HENRY T. DIXON (who had the rencounter with Dr. T. C. Maddux) died this morning from the effects of the wounds he received. He had the best surgical assistance, but all efforts to save his life were unavailing. Maj. Dixon resided for many years in Fauquier county, and was extensively known in this place, and all the outlying country. He was appointed a Paymaster in the army, shortly after the late war came on, and has lived in Washington, ever since. A post mortem examination and inquest on the body was had this afternoon. (*Alexandria Gazette*, November 11, 1865, p. 3.)

...On Saturday morning, at six minutes before five, Maj. Dixon, after passing a night of intense suffering died. A coroner's jury was summoned to hold an inquest upon the body at ten o'clock that morning, but in consequence of the absence of a relation of the Major, who wished to be present at the post mortem examination, it was adjourned, to meet that evening at half-past two o'clock, at the City Hotel, when the post mortem would be concluded.

At a little after two o'clock that evening, the Major's body being laid out on a dissecting board, in a room in the City Hotel, a post mortem examination was made of it by Drs. Stewart, Lewis, Chancellor and Barnes in the presence of Mayor Ware...the reporters for the newspapers, and several other citizens. Two black and bloody holes – line shots they were – were seen in the right side of the body, about one inch apart, and about an inch and a half above the top of the right hip bone.

These openings being examined, and probed, an incision was made in the abdomen along the middle, extending from the pit to the rim of the stomach. The fat revealed by this incision was almost an inch thick; that portion of it about two inches above the navel was discolored by black blood, and immediately under this the Surgeon's knife grated upon the slug which was lying beneath the tough tendinous expansion of the abdominal muscles. An incision was then made from this point transversely across the stomach to the external wounds, and the course of the ball making the lower opening traced through the liver which was lacerated and discolored, to the point at which it was found. The transverse incision was then continued, until it reached almost to the back bone, and the course of the ball making the upper wound pursued through the centre of the right kidney until it was found imbedded in one of the lower bones of the spinal column. The coroner and his jury, who were waiting down stairs, were then sent for, and they, having examined the body, as it then lay, proceeded to the Mayor's Office... That all the jurors had to do was to make a verdict, defining when, how, and by whom the deceased came to his death, and that the defence was willing to concede that he was killed by bullets shot at him by Dr. Maddux. The coroner then ordered constable Chipley to immediately arrest Maddux, and bring him to the Mayor's Office .... (*Alexandria Gazette*, November 13, 1865, p.3.)

THE DIXON AND MADDUX CASE - This morning, at the appointed hour the above case came up for examination ... The examination took place in the Council Chamber.

Dr. W. D. Stewart was the first witness examined; he deposed as follows: ...first two shots were in my rear; upon the second shot turned and saw a man with his face to the City Hotel, with his pistol levelled; then I heard the third shot; cannot precisely identify Maddox as the man who fired the third shot...all the shots were rapid, the second and third almost simultaneous. ...Dixon asked me who I was? told him I was a physician; ...examined his wounds, and asked him who shot him; he said, Tom Maddux, Dr. T. C. Maddux...did not see Dixon with a pistol; he had on a blue blouse coat, unbuttoned, with pair of navy pants; he fell near the curb stone. Dr. Maddux was ten or twelve feet from the curb, on the west side of Royal street...removed a portion of his clothing, examined his wounds and had him carried to the City Hotel; was with him from the time he was wounded until death; Dixon was a large fleshy man; the shots entered the body on the right side; the lower one about four inches from the spine with a direction inwards and forwards, passing through the right lobe of the liver and lodging a little to the left of the middle line; the ball came out higher than it entered; the course of the ball was nearly directly through; found the ball below the skin; upper ball entered about the same distance from the spine...passing through and nearly dividing the right kidney, would necessarily have fallen immediately from the upper wound, as paralysis ensued; either of the wounds would have caused death; could not tell from what I saw or heard who fired the first shot;...Dixon was conscious of his condition, had no hopes of recovery;...Dixon drank about two gills of brandy before making his deposition; Dixon asked for Judge Underwood as soon as he was carried to his room; he was shot with a conical ball, which is superior to a round ball - it goes more direct;...The Commonwealth's Attorney here moved a continuance of the trial until this evening;

Albert Mitchell being called was sworn and testified: Was introduced to Dr. Maddux about two weeks ago, at the residence of Mrs. Bodkin; at that time, while I was sitting by the stove, in the parlour, I saw Dr. Maddux show a revolver; when the pistol was shown Mr. Bernard, who was in the room, remarked to Maddux, "you go prepared for skirmishers;" Maddux replied, "yes, since the trouble at the Mansion house, and if there is to be any more shooting I'll have a hand in it ..." (*Alexandria Gazette*, November 15, 1865, p. 2.)

...The examination of this case was resumed...Capt. J. P. L. Westcott testified: on the evening of the shooting I called for the second time at the City Hotel to see the wounded man; the first time I called Col. McClure informed me that the Doctor requested that no one might be admitted into the room: On entering the room saw a gentleman lying upon the bed apparently in great distress; as I approached I saw Dr. Stuart near the head of the bed; the first words I distinguished were "good Dr. - please gentlemen rub my leg; at that time Dr. Stuart and one other gentlemen beside myself were present in the room; seeing that I could be of service, I got over the foot of the bed, rubbed his leg, and continued with him during the night, doing what I could to relieve his sufferings; a good deal of conversation took place after that; Dixon presented a remarkable degree of fortitude, and was in possession of all his faculties except when temporarily under the influence of choloroform; he recognized his friends, I was absent from the room during the night for about fifteen minutes; when I came back I inferred a minister had been sent for from the Major or some one else, asking if the minister had come; soon after, the minister arrived, and after a brief conversation with the Major, some one present desired to know if he had any objection to being prayed for, he said "no, make your prayer short and do not pray loud"; then a friend came in whom he recognized, and to whom he said "tell ----- I love her," and then mentioning two other names, said "give my love to them," he then said, "gentlemen I call you to witness I am not afraid to die; I have wiped out the stain on my honor; I had rather lay here as I am than to have lived with that stain on my character; but it's hard to die by the hand of the villain, Maddux...

THE CONCLUSION OF THE DIXON AND MADDUX CASE - ACQUITTAL OF MADDUX - This case, which has occupied considerable attention for the last six days, was concluded about eight o'clock yesterday evening. All the evidence having been adduced on Wednesday...the Commonwealth's Attorney reviewed the testimony, asked that the accused be sent on for trial before the Court. Mr. Whittlesey, assistant prosecutor followed, and contended that the case should not only be sent on, but that the prisoner should not be admitted to bail. The defence was opened by Col. M. D. Ball, who summed up the evidence to show that his client acted solely on the defensive. He was followed by Col. Charles E. Stuart, and demanded the immediate and unconditional discharge of the accused. Gen'l Wells, assistant counsel for the prosecution, closed the case, and having referred the matter to the Justice, awaited his decision. Justice Beach then said, that after having heard the sworn testimony of responsible witnesses and listened patiently to the arguments of the learned counsel, he was perfectly satisfied that Dr. Maddux was justified in shooting Major Dixon, and that he should consequently order his immediate release. (*Alexandria Gazette*, November 17, 1865, p. 3)

^^*^*^*^*^*^*^*^*^*^*^*^*

ATTEMPTED MURDER - The Court proceeded to the examination of Patrick Wood and Spencer Lee, negroes who were set to the bar in custody of the jailor of this County and charged that they did on the night of the 6th day of June 1866 in the said County, burglariously and feloniously enter the dwelling house of one James Mertaugh and that Patrick Wood did feloniously and maliciously shoot Mary Mertaugh with intent to maim, disfigures or kill the said Mary Mertaugh, and the said Patrick Wood and Spencer Lee did feloniously take steal and carry away therefrom sixteen dollars in United States currency of the value of sixteen dollars, one dalaine dress of the value of seven dollars, two sun shades of the value of five dollars. One silk apron of the value of two dollars, four dresses of the value of fifteen dollars, three under garments of the value one dollar and twenty five cents, one silk cloak of the value of five dollars, four pillow slips of the value of two dollars, six towels of the value of one dollars and fifty cents, one clock of the value of two dollars, three chickens of the value of one dollar and fifty cents, one childs sack of the value of one dollar and on apron of the value of fifty cents of the goods and chattels of said James Murtaugh. Sundry witnesses were examined and the prisoners by counsel heard in their defence. Upon consideration whereof the Court is of opinion that the felony aforesaid has been committed and that there is probable cause to charge the said Wood and Lee therewith and doth remand them to the next term of the Circuit Court of this County to be tried therefore... (*Alexandria County Court Order Minute Book*, July 2, 1866, p. 601)

Patrick Lee and Spencer Wood stand indicted separatedly of burglary. The defendants were led to the bar and pleaded not guilty whereupon a jury came to wit. Both Lee and Wood were acquitted of the charges. (*Alexandria Circuit Court Common Law Order Book*, November 15, 1866, Volume 2, p. 350.)

^‡^*‡*^‡*^*‡*^*‡*^*‡*^*‡*^*‡*^*

ARREST OF THE MURDERERS OF THE LATE WILLIAM LYLES, ESQ. – $1,179 of the Money recovered. The whole of the stolen money will be recovered.

Yesterday morning, while the Cashiers of the Farmers' Bank of the Bank of the Old Dominion were in conversation together, at the Bank of the Old Dominion, a negro man, named William Plaiter, offered, at the counter of that Bank, for sale a ten dollar note of the Bank's issue, and for which he was paid $5 in currency. He stated at the time that he had several hundred dollars of the same sort of money which he wished to dispose of. As the Cashier of the Bank of the Old Dominion had been informed, about a month ago, by Mr. Lyles that he had a considerable amount of Old Dominion money, together with other Virginia money, the statement of the negro, and his subsequent behavior – for he was watched afterwards – excited suspicion, and this morning, when he offered $100 in Old Dominion notes at that Bank for sale, he was arrested by officers Davis and Webster, of the City Police. When brought before the Mayor for examination, his statements were so contradictory that he was confined for further examination; while other negroes, named by him, were immediately arrested. A negro blacksmith, named Morton, whose shop is on Fairfax street, near King, was arrested and confined, because Plaiter said Morton had some Virginia money; he was, however, immediately released, as no evidence was against him. Ellen Monroe, a negro woman who lives on Gibbon street, between Columbus and Alfred, was arrested, because Plaiter said she had given him the $100 he offered for sale at the bank this morning. At her examination she denied having given him any money, nor did she know he had any. In her house under the bed, was found $1,039 in Virginia Farmers' Bank money.

Henry Lucket and Thomas Davis, two negro men, seen with Plaiter yesterday, were arrested and confined. In Plaiter's house, which is near Smith's Old Foundry, were found two gold eagles and such articles of clothing, stolen from Mr. Lyles' house at the time of the murder, as leaves no doubt of the guilt of the party.

The examination, conducted by the Mayor, with marked ability, at his office, this evening, resulted in clearly establishing the identity of the murderers.

Of the parties arrested up to this time, Wm. Plaiter is a large negro, about thirty years old who came to this city since the war, from Pennsylvania; Thomas Davis, a man about twenty-two or three, who belonged to Colonel Jenkins, of Prince George's county, Md., and who came to this city in 1862; Henry Lucket, about the age of Davis, belonged to the Rev. Mr. Blackwell, of Warrenton, and came here in 1861; and ---- Jones, also a negro, the former carriage driver of Mr. Lyles. A negro, named --- Richards, the remaining one, escaped this evening from the officers who were on his track.

The five wretches - one is yet at large - left this city late Saturday evening last, in a row boat, borrowed from Mr. Richard Warder. They first went to the Maryland shore, near the Bluff, then crossed to the Virginia side of the Spring, where one of the party cut a fishing pole, for appearance sake. Towards night they recrossed the river, and entering Piscataway Creek, landed near Mr. Lyles's residence; then going to the house, they asked for work, upon being told to go to the negro quarters and wait until morning, they went off, and did not return until they came to perpetrate, and but too successfully carry out their villinous design. (*Alexandria Gazette*, July 17, 1866, p.3.)

SHORT HISTORY OF THE MURDERERS - The stolen Money Recovered Up to Date.

William Plaiter, Thomas Davis, William Henry Jones and Henry Luckett, the four negro men arrested in this city yesterday, by officers Davis, Padgett and Webster, by order of the Mayor, upon information furnished him by Messrs. Lambert and Marbury, the Cashiers of the Bank of the Old Dominion and Farmers' Bank, of this city, for murdering the late William Lyles, Esq., and robbing his wife, are now safely confined in separate cells in the County jail, awaiting a requisition for their rendition to the Sheriff of Prince George's county, Maryland - who is now in this city - from the Governor of that State. Three of them, Plaiter, Jones and Davis have acknowledged complicity in the murder and robbery but assert that Henry Richardson, who is yet at large, was the only one of the party armed with a pistol and is the actual murderer.

From the evidence, bearing upon the case, educed by the Mayor in his critical and searching examinations up to this time, the following facts have been elicited. Jones, who was intimately acquainted with his former master's premises, and was aware that Mr. Lyles had a consideralbe amount of money, among which was a lot of specie,

76

locked up in his secretary, imparted his information to Davis, whose old master lived but a short distance from Mr. Lyles'; the secret was then made known to Plaiter, Richardson and Luckett, and the five together, hatched the plot which has resulted so fatally.

Plaiter, on Friday evening last, hired, for fifty cents, from Mrs. Richard Warder, the boat of her husband; in this boat Plaiter, Davis, Jones, and Richardson started for the scene of their villany, but returned in a short time, because Luckett had not met his engagement, and they were afraid he had not proven true. On Saturday evening, however, the whole five were on hand at the appointed time, and started from the ship yard, in the same boat they had the evening before. Going directly across to Susquehanna Creek, and then coasting down the Maryland shore past Fort Foot, where they stopped and got some water, they went as far as the point of the bluff, from which point they recrossed the river to Johnston's Spring, where Plaiter cut a fishing pole. Waiting at this Spring till nearly dark they again took to their boat and crossed the river to the mouth of Piscataway creek, up which they rowed until opposite Mr. Lyles house, when they pulled into the shore and landed. It was now quite dark. The five then went to within a hundred yards of Mr. Lyles' residence, which consisted of a log shanty, containing a single room - his family mansion having been destroyed by fire during the war - and hailing the house, were answered by Mr. Lyles, who asked what they wanted. They responded they were looking for work. Mr. Lyles then told them to go to the negro quarters and wait until morning, when, as he had some meadow land he wanted cleared, he would see them and let them know whether they would suit him as laborers. They went to the quarters as directed and waited there until about midnight, at which hour they proceeded to the immediate vicinity of the house, and, unitedly, rushing against the door, burst it open, and four of the five - for Jones, afraid of being recognized, remained on the outside - immediately entering, commenced shooting at Mr. Lyles, who had sprung from his bed as the door fell in. The door, upon being burst open, fell upon a little negro girl, the only occupant of the room except Mr. Lyles and his wife - who was sleeping upon the floor - and she, screaming in her freight, ran out across the yard - one of the party crying out "shoot the d--d b--h." The first ball fired pierced the head of the bedstead, the second went into the wall of the house, but the third, fired close to the head of the murdered man, for his face was blackened with powder, entered his left check, just under the eye and passed through his brain. He fell instantly - never spoke after he was shot - and was caught in his fall between the bed post and the wall of the house, where he was found the next morning by the neighbors who assembled there at the cries of his wife, with a pistol grasped in his hand and hid by his night shirt. After murdering Mr. Lyles, Davis attempted to strike a match, but not being able to ignite one, Plaiter took Mrs. Lyles by the wrist, and dragged her with him to the negro quarters, where he compelled her to procure him a lamp. He then led her back to the house, but as soon as the key of the secretary, which was lying upon its top, was found, Plaiter released her, and rushing with the others to the open drawers they commenced an indiscriminate plunder of their contents. Mrs. Lyles availed herself of this opportunity to escape, so instantly running out of the house, she hid herself behind a large walnut tree in the yard, where she remained watching the murderers until they left, screening herself by gliding around the body of the tree, so as to keep it between herself and them, as they went off. After ransacking the house, and selecting what articles, besides the money – the amount of which stolen was about $2000 – they wanted, among which were a ham, a hat that belonged to Mr. Lyles, blankets, counter-paines, underclothing and a clock, they left the scene of their hellish plot, returned to their boat, and arrived in this city about sun rise on Sunday morning.

Mrs. Lyles remained about the yard of the house until day light when, as is stated above, her cries called some neighbors to her assistance. Mr. Lyles was buried on Monday evening last – his remains being escorted to their final resting place in the family grave yard by a large number of the citizens of Prince George's county. His death, but especially the manner of it, has occasioned considerable excitement in the neighborhood of Piscataway, where many assert that no man's life is safe, who is known to own anything of value, while the country, throughout its length and bredth, is daily and nightly prowled over by armed squads of vagabond negroes.

William Plaiter is a large, muscular and well formed negro, of a dark copper color. He is twenty-eight years old, and is about five feet ten inches high – has a smooth face, and has his woolly hair cut short. He came to this city in 1862 from Chester County, Pennsylvania, where he was born and raised. Shortly after his arrival here he married a negro woman named Iza Wansa – a former slave, who came here from Fauquier county, Virginia, after the breaking out of the war – by whom he has had two children, both now dead, and with whom he lived, when arrested, in a shanty on Gibbon between Fairfax and Royal streets. He says the last job of work he had was one in the neighborhood of White's Ferry, in Loudoun county, Virginia, where he was engaged as a harvest hand; but his statements are so contradictory, and his memory, good up to this time – has so failed him since his arrest, that no confidence can be placed in what he says. In his house were found a clock, some socks, and some bed clothing which belonged to Mr. Lyles, besides two gold twenty dollar pieces.

Henry Luckett is a stout and thick set negro, about twenty-two or -three years of age, and five feet four inches high. His hair, like Plaiter's is cut close to his head, nor has he any beard. He formerly was a slave of the Rev. Mr. Blackwell, of Warrenton, from which place he came to this city in 1861, and married here a negro woman named Sarah Gaskins, who belonged to a gentleman residing near Markham Station, on the Manassas Gap Railroad. With his wife and one child he was living in a house on Duke street, between Water and Union at the time of his arrest. He was employed as a porter in the ship chandler store of D. R. Wilson & Co., at Prince street dock. He is a well spoken negro, and is anxious for the return of his employer, who is out of the city.

Upon his person was found a $20 note in Virginia money.

Thomas Davis is of a light copper color, with no beard. He is about nineteen years old, and is near five feet five inches high. He is unmarried, and was previous to the war, the slave of Col. Jenkins, of

Piscataway, Maryland. He lived at the time of his arrest on Gibbon street, between Water and Union. Since his arrest he has become exceedingly drowsy - sleeping, apparently, all the time, when not engaged by some one in conversation, and even interrupting his answers to questions by frequent and prolonged yawnings. In the house in which his sweet heart lived, in rear of Fairfax street, between Wilkes and Gibbon, was found a sum of money - some specie and some Virginia money - which he had left there, saying, when he left it, "that if he did not call for it again soon she could have it."

Wm. Henry Jones, is a real negro, black as jet, with small yellow eyes. The little hair he has on his head is short and woolly. His height is about five feet, ten inches, and his age is in the neighborhood of twenty-six years. He is not married, and lives in a shanty at the corner of Water and Gibbon streets. He formerly belonged to Mr. Lyles, the murdered gentleman, and is said to have been his carriage driver, though this last statement he denies. He last worked with a Mr. Ball at White's Ferry, Loudoun Co. - (where Plaiter was employed, though he says he does not know for whom he worked and that he was engaged in the harvest field) - who was unloading coal boats there.

Henry Richardson is a light brown colored negro, about five feet eight inches high, delicately made and between twenty-five and thirty years of age. He came from Maryland, and lived in one of Seaton's houses on South Washington street. He was seen yesterday evening by one of the police officers, but managed to escape, and he, it is said, is the one who fired the shot that killed Mr. Lyles.

He had on when last seen a pair of light colored pants and a straw hat. In his house were found thirty dollars in Virginia money, and a hat which belonged to Mr. Lyles.

The police are on the track of Richardson and hopes are entertained that he will be speedily captured. Between $1,400 and $1,500 of the money has been recovered. (*Alexandria Gazette*, July 18, 1866, p. 3.)

^^*^*^*^*^*^*^*^*^*^*^*

HORRIBLE TRAGEDY IN WASHINGTON - DEATH OF AN ALEXANDRIAN - About two o'clock yesterday afternoon the citizens of the Fourth Ward, residing in the vicinity of Sixth and K streets, were startled at the sounds of pistol-shots in house No. 223 Sixth Street west, next to the corner of K Street north. A few moments after a man attired in a drab suit, was observed to leave the house and proceed rapidly down Sixth Street toward the avenue. Cries of murder were heard, and, upon entering the house, the neighbors were shocked to see lying on the floor of a room in the second story the body of Thomas S. Smoot, with the blood and gore oozing from two pistol shot wounds in the head. Inquiry led to the development of the following facts:

Henry Johnson, a butcher, about forty-four years of age, whose place of business and residence is in Georgetown, learning that his wife was in the habit of stopping at a house on Sixth Street, had for some time past suspected an improper intimacy on her part with Mr.

79

Thomas Smoot, who was formerly in his employ. He watched the premises, and yesterday afternoon, knowing the room, and that Smoot and his wife were there together, entered the house and went to their room, where he found Smoot lying in the bed, his wife sitting on the edge of the bed and holding Smoot's hand. Without a moments warning, he deliberately fired three pistol shots at Smoot, two of which took effect in his head, and death ensued about twenty minutes after.

Mr. Johnson left the house and proceeded to the Central Guard house, where he delivered himself up, and also gave up the revolver, stating to the officer that he had shot a man whom he had found in bed with his wife. The neighborhood of the tragedy was at once alarmed, and physicians were sent for, and a messenger ran to the Seventh Precinct Station and informed Lieutenant Eckloff that a man had been murdered in a house on Sixth street. This officer proceeded to the premises and found Smoot lying upon the floor with pants and shirt on and the blood gushing from the wounds received. Drs. Bowen, Behrend and Duhanel were in attendance, and endeavoring to ascertain the nature of the wounds inflicted, but Smoot lived but twenty minutes after the shots were fired.

The room where this shocking tragedy took place is about seven feet in width and as many in length, and was over the hall entrance to the building. When Johnson entered the room Smoot raised himself up from the bed, when the shots were fired, one taking effect just over the right corner of the right eye and the other on the left side of the lower jaw.

Coroner Woodward was summoned to hold an inquest. Various witnesses were examined before the jury who testified that Smoot under the name of Johnson, and passing as the husband of Mrs. J. had been occupying a room in the house where the killing took place for five or six months – that Mrs. J. herself always represented Smoot as her husband, saying that she had been married before, but she had left her first husband on account of ill treatment, etc. The jury returned the following verdict: "That the said Thomas Smoot came to his death in the city of Washington, on the 20th day of June, 1867, by means of a pistol shot discharged by Henry Johnson."

Henry Johnson's statement at the station house is substantially as follows:

That Thomas Smoot has been in his employ as a butcher for some time, and that he had assisted him in various ways in business; that the intimacy between Smoot and his wife had often attracted his attention, but he never had suspected anything criminal in their acquaintance until recently. He had accidentally discovered their place of meeting at the house on Sixth Street, and that yesterday he was satisfied that his more recent suspicions were correct from evidence which he saw while watching the window.

He knew that Smoot was in the room, and shortly after two o'clock he saw his wife enter the house, and then saw her in the same room where Smoot was. There was no hindrance to his entering the house, he passed up stairs, and on opening the door found his wife sitting on the edge of the bed, and Smoot had been lying down, but arose at the surprise, and reached toward the bureau, when he fired the fatal shots.

Mr. Smoot, our reporter was informed, was thirty-five years of age,

and his wife and four children reside in Alexandria. He served as a
sergeant in the 17th Virginia infantry, Confederate army. His brother
arrived here last evening, and at the conclusion of the Coroner's inquest took charge of the body, which was taken to Alexandria for interment.

Mrs. Johnson left the house as soon as Smoot was shot, and has not
since been heard from. It does not appear that her husband offered her
any violence, or that he ever spoke to her from the time that he entered the room until they separated at the door of the house. She is
reported to be a large woman, with coarse features, large nose, and
black hair. She has three children – a daughter married who is a
widow, and two boys aged nine and eleven years. Henry Johnson is a
mild pleasant looking man, with sandy complexion and light blue
eyes, and shows but little of the resolution in his features that has
marked the premediated homicide.

The affair created great excitement throughout the city. – Nat. Intel.

Mr. Smoot's body was brought to this city on the eight o'clock boat
this morning, conveyed in a hearse to the residence of his wife, on the
corner of Wilkes and Pitt street, and will be buried tomorrow.
(*Alexandria Gazette*, June 21, 1867, p.3.)

HENRY JOHNSON, charged with the murder of Thomas Smoot, on
Thursday last, was brought from jail in Washington, on Saturday on a
writ of habeas corpus, issued by Judge Wylie, the object being to effect his discharge on bail, if possible. Owing to the absence of two
very important witnesses, the case was postponed until this morning
at 10 o'clock, and the prisoner was remanded to jail until that time.
(*Alexandria Gazette*, June 24, 1867, p.3.)

^^*^*^*^*^*^*^*^*^*^*^*^*

MISSING U.S. SOLDIER MURDERED OFF JONES POINT – DEAD
BODY IDENTIFIED – MURDERERS IN CUSTODY

A coroner's inquest was held this morning in the county jail upon
the dead body of the man found near Glymont, Maryland on Monday,
the 30th ult. ...The body was identified as that of Edward Devlin, a
soldier belonging to Co. E, 4th U.S. Artillery, who has been missing
since the night of Thursday, the 7th of last November, at which time
his command was stationed at Fort Foot, just below this city, on the
Maryland Shore. The body was laid out on the bricks in the jail yard,
and presented a horrible appearance, the whole front of the neck and
lower part of the face, as well as part of the right hand, having been
eaten by wild animals during the night after it was found, when it was
allowed to remain unburied, and a large jagged opening existing in the
right side, through which the ends of the ribs and a lobe of the liver
protruded. The post mortem examination having been conducted by
Drs. French and Gibson, the jury were invited into the Sheriff's office,
where the witnesses were examined, and the following evidence was
elicited:

SERGEANT DRISCOL: Identified the body lying in the yard as that of Edward Devlin, who with Thomas Perry, Philip Karney, and B. F. Adams, of the 4th U.S. Artillery, visited Alexandria, as a detailed boats crew, on the evening of November last, from Fort Foot. On the night of that day, between nine and ten o'clock – the moon at the time shining brightly – was ordered by the Colonel commanding the fort to take an inventory of the effects of Edward Devlin, reported drowned. On his way to the company's quarters met Thos. Perry, who had on a shirt and a blouse, and who, in answer to a question as to what had become of Devlin, responded in a wild and incoherent manner that he had been drowned; on returning from the quarters went to the wharf to which the boat usually was tied, but not finding it there hallooed to another soldier to go down to the point a short distance off, and see whether it was there or not. As he hallooed, Perry, who was standing on the bank above the shore, gave a yell, and started off at full speed for the point, jumped into the boat before any one else had got there, threw the rudder overboard, and commenced sculling the boat rapidly out into the river, hallooing to those on the beach that if they wanted to find Devlin they must follow him. When seen sculling the boat by witness he had removed his shirt and blouse. Witness then, in another boat, searched the river between the fort and Alexandria, in which city he learned that Devlin, in company with Perry, Karney, and Adams, had started for the Fort, and that of the four, Karney alone seemed under the influence of liquor. Witness had never known Devlin to be off duty from the effects of liquor. The next morning witness examined the boat which Perry had set adrift, and found clotted blood in its stern, blood stains on its seats, and the prints of bloody hands on the gunwale on which was also tufts of bloody hair thought by witness to be that of Devlin's head. One of the boat's oars was broken – a part gone and blood stains on the remainder.

LIEUT. CHESTER: ...Examined the boat the morning after. Devlin was murdered – found blood on its stern and a broken oar – the blade and part of the handle gone; there were blood stains on the remainder. Devlin's absence was thus accounted for to him by the three men who had been with him. When near Jones' Point, Devlin, who with Karney and Adams had the oars, while Perry had charge of the rudder, in attempting to change his seat accidentally fell overboard, and was drowned, and that ten minutes after, the oar was broken and the blood in the boat occasioned by the striking of Karney over the head by Perry, in order to keep him quiet and prevent his upsetting the boat in his efforts to jump overboard after Devlin.

ANN R. GREENWOOD: Lives near Battery Rodgers. On the night of the 7th of November, about half past eight o'clock, heard a noise on the river, and going to her door to see if there was not a disturbance at the Light House, on Jones Point, saw a boat near the buoy, off the Point, and the voice of a man coming from it crying out don't drown me; I've been a good soldier and fought for my country like a man. The next morning witness heard that a soldier had been murdered and supposed the murdered man was the one she had heard in treating for his life....

All the witnesses having been examined the Coroners' Jury retired to another room and in a short time rendered the following verdict:

We, the Jurors find that the deceased, Edward Devlin, a soldier from Fort Foot, of Company E, on the way to the Fort from Alexandria, came to his death by violence at the hands of Thomas Perry, Benjamin Adams and Phillip Kearney. J. Roxbury, Foreman. *Alexandria Gazette*, January 9, 1868, p.3.

^^*^*^*^*^*^*^*^*^*^*^*

MURDER - Late on Sunday night last, three colored men entered the house of Patrick Gafney, who lived on the farm of Mr. W. N. Brown, between this city and Washington, close to the turnpike, while he was absent, and asked the colored boy, they found there, to furnish them with lights, with which to search the house. The boy having no lights, they, by means of matches, ransacked the premises, and stole a bag of bacon. Gafney returned while they were there, and they attacked him in his yard, knocking him down, searching him, and when leaving him striking him on the head with a heavy club, while one of them presented a pistol to his breast, but the noise of an approaching wagon on the road alarmed them, and they ran off. After they had left, the wounded man managed to reach the house of his brother, who lives on an adjoining farm, and stating that he had been murdered, was put to bed, and died the following day. A coroner's inquest was held upon the body this morning, and a verdict rendered in accordance with the above stated facts. The murderers remain as yet unknown, though the colored boy at the house says he can recognize them if he sees them again.

Mr. Gafney was a quiet, hard-working, industrious man, who stayed always home, and never molested anybody, and his death is much regretted by his neighbors. (*Alexandria Gazette*, May 5, 1868, p. 3.)

ARREST OF SUPPOSED MURDERERS - Yesterday evening Sheriff Steuart, assisted officers Edelin and Burnett, and night-watchman Williams, succeeded in arresting and lodging in the county jail, without much difficulty, owing to the manner in which the preliminary arrangements were carried out. Timothy O'Connor, white, and Edward Brown, James Bailey and Jinny Bailey, his wife and Alfred Lynn, colored, on a warrant issued by Justice Beach, at the instance of James Gafney, a brother of the deceased, charged with being concerned in the murder of Patrick Gafney... All the parties, but Lynn, who was taken in the city, were arrested in Alexandria county; O'Connor, on the Washington Turnpike, while driving his milk cart to this city; Bailey, at the bone factory, near Four Mile Run; Brown at O'Connor's house, back of Mr. Thomas Swann's estate; and Bailey's wife, at Dr. King's brick yard, between this city and Washington. As the latter had two children, both infants, who had to accompany her O'Connor's milk-cart was pressed into service to bring them to the jail.

A colored boy who lived with O'Connor was also arrested, but at the instance of O'Connor's wife, is detained as a witness for the defence.

The colored boy who lived with the murdered man, and who saw him killed, is also held in the jail as a witness for the Commonwealth, and, it is stated, has already recognized some of the arrested parties.

It is said that O'Connor, who was convicted of stock stealing in Fairfax county, and sentenced to the penitentiary for ten years, but was pardoned after a limited confinement by the late Governor Pierpoint, had had a difficulty with the deceased about the lease of a piece of land. Lynn lived with the deceased at one time and had had been accused by him on two different occasions of thieving.

A heavy grape vine club, smeared with blood and matted hair, was found near the scene of the murder, and was the instrument of death. ... (*Alexandria Gazette*, May 8, 1868, p. 3.)

EXAMINATION OF SUPPOSED MURDERERS – Timothy O'Connell, white, and Edward Brown, Alfred Lane and James Bailey and his wife Jenny, colored, arrested on Friday last, charged with the murder of Patrick Gafney, were examined at the jail yesterday evening before Justices Beach, Summers and Colton. Three witnesses, James Gafney, a brother of the deceased, and two small colored boys Henry Mason and Frank Carter, were sworn, but as the evidence elicited from them did not criminate O'Connell, he was held in the sum of $500 security, half his own recognizance and half on a bond of Anthony Dugan, for his reappearance...The evidence adduced against the colored parties, was also slight, but as the Commonwealth's Attorney was not present and as it was supposed that other developments would be made at the Monday examination, they were recommitted until that day. ... (*Alexandria Gazette*, May 9, 1868, p. 3.)

TRIAL OF SUPPOSED MURDERERS – The Magistrate's office, in the Market House building, was crowded yesterday evening by spectators of the trial there, before Justices Beach, Summers, and Colton, of Timothy O'Connell, white, and Edward Brown, James Bailey, and Alfred Lane, colored, who had been arrested, charged with the murder of the late Patrick Gaffney. The Commonwealth was represented by her attorney, Westel Willonghby; O'Connell was defended by D. I. Smoot; and the colored man by Chas. E. Snarf. The only evidence educed from the witnesses that tended to criminate any of the parties was a statement by a little colored boy named Henry Mason that he recognized Alfred Lane as one of the men who assaulted the deceased. It was proved by other witnesses, however, that the accused was in this city at the time the assault was committed. The examination was somewhat prolonged, and at its conclusion all the parties were discharged but Lane, who was bailed in the sum of $300 for his appearance at Court – Robert Williams, colored, going his security. (*Alexandria Gazette*, May 13, 1868, p.3.)

COUNTY COURT – After the close of the *Gazette*'s report of the proceedings of the County Court yesterday evening, the jury in the case of the Commonwealth against Alfred Lane, colored, charged with the murder of Patrick Gafney, on the farm of Mr. Wm. N. Brown, between this city and Washington, returned a verdict of not guilty. The prisoner, who had been led to believe that a white jury would certainly convict him, on account of his color, was very much excited when the court discharged him, and manifested his feelings by giving three cheers for the whole Southern people; and when he went out of the court room was profuse in his denunciation of those who had impressed him with the belief that he would not be accorded a fair trail. (*Alexandria Gazette*, August 5, 1868, p.3.)

^^*^*^*^*^*^*^*^*^*^*^*^*

FATAL ACCIDENT - About six o'clock yesterday evening, John Stone, about twelve or thirteen years of age, son of the widow Stone, who lives on the corner of Water and Duke Streets, was accidentally shot on the wharf at the oyster dock by another boy, named Samuel Blackburn, a little older than himself, who was on board the sloop of Capt. Jas. Smith. A party of boys, among them little Stone, were on the wharf near where the sloop was lying, firing a pistol. Blackburn told them if they did not go away he would shoot them, and went into the cabin of the sloop and brought out a double barreled shot gun loaded with No. 4 shot, the breech of which he pointed at them. One of the boys with a stone drove him back into the cabin, in going down the steps of which, after he had reversed the position of the gun, it was accidentally discharged, the contents entering the lower part of Stone's abdomen - he standing on the wharf a few yards off. He was at once carried to his mother's house, where he died at half-past nine o'clock. Young Blackburn was arrested soon after the shooting, and tried before Justice Moore and discharged, but after Stone's death he was re-arrested and confined in the Watch House all night. A coroner's inquest was held this morning upon the body of the deceased, and a verdict of accidental death by shooting rendered, and Blackburn again discharged.

The dead child is represented to have been a good boy, and his mother has the sympathies of the community.

Several other boys were struck by scattering shot when the gun was discharged, but their injuries were not of a serious character. (*Alexandria Gazette*, November 11, 1868, p.3.)

^^*^*^*^*^*^*^*^*^*^*^*^*

COLORED CHILD KILLED - Yesterday evening about 7 o'clock a notorious character named James Boswell, while walking up the east side of West street between King and Cameron, saw two little colored girls walking down on the opposite side of the street, on their way to the pump for water, and remarking, "well, I'll kill a nigger," picked up a brick bat and threw it at them. His aim was fatal. The brick struck one of them on the head, and mashed in her skull. She was picked up and taken to the house of a colored woman named Robinson with whom she was living, on Payne between Queen and Princess Streets where she died about two hours afterwards.

She was an orphan child and was named Martha French. Boswell, after throwing the brick, walked down King street and was soon arrested and committed to jail for further examination. He and some of his brothers have been a terror to the community for a long time past, and how they have managed to escape punishment up to this time is a mystery. It is to be hoped that after this, his latest feat, he will be prevented from committing any further depredations. (*Alexandria Gazette*, July 5, 1870, p. 3.)

...Dr. D. M. French being sworn, said that upon an examination of the child he found the skull badly fractured, and a portion of the bone driven through the membranes of the brain and imbeded in the substance of the brain, the pressure of the broken bone, and the hemorrhage attending it in the substance of the brain, caused death....

Boswell was examined at the Mayor's office this morning before Justice Bell and Mayor Latham, and was fully committed to jail for his appearance at the next term of the Hustings Court to answer to the charge of murder. (*Alexandria Gazette*, July 6, 1870, p.3.)

THE BOSWELL CASE – The Court of Appeals, sitting at Richmond, yesterday, rendered a decision in the case of James Boswell, who was convicted at the December term of the Corporation Court of this city, of murder in the second degree and sentenced to eleven years in the penitentiary. The Court reversed the judgment of the Corporation Court, and granted Boswell a new trial. The counsel in the case were, for Boswell, Brent & Wattles, Francis L. Smith, Jr. and S. Chapman Neale. For the Commonwealth, James C. Taylor, Attorney General and David L. Smoot. (*Alexandria Gazette*, April 19, 1871, p.3; May 4, 1871, p.3.)

^^*^*^*^*^*^*^*^*^*^*^*^*^*^*

EXECUTION OF MANLEY. The sentence of the law on conviction of willful murder was executed in the jail yard of this city at noon to day upon Charles Manley, who killed John Monroe, in July last.

THE CRIME – The crime of which Manley stood convicted was one of unusual atrocity. It was proven on his trial, which took place in the Corporation Court on the 14th of January last, that on the night of the 5th of July, 1872, John Monroe, an old Scotsman, who travelled about this section of country, in the vocation of mending clocks, was sitting by the side of the spring, in the valley which extends from St. Asaph street to Royal in the midst of the colored suburb known as "Petersburg." The night was starlit and sultry, and it is supposed that Monroe, after refreshing his thirst at the spring, had sat down to rest and fallen asleep beside it. He wore a plain silver watch and carried a small box containing the tools used in his calling. The shanty of a colored man named Payne is situated a short distance from the spring, and from there three men: Manley and Samuel Payne and Lewis Payne came down upon Monroe, who was heard to cry that he had no money, and to beg them not to murder him. He was, however, beaten most terribly, his head bruised, and his abdomen mashed with large stones, and then, under the supposition that he was dead, thrown into a neighboring ditch, from which he managed to crawl during the night, and on the edge of which he was found in the morning, and carried to his boarding house on West street. He lingered there in great pain, but in full possession of his senses and able to give an account of the assault upon him, until the evening, about 7 o'clock, when he died.

THE ARREST - The two Paynes made off during the night, but the father-in-law of Manley having had his suspicions aroused, communicated them to Police Lieut. Smith who came upon Manley while he was asleep and found upon him the watch, hat and boots of Monroe, all of which his victim identified before his death.

MANLEY'S STATEMENT - Yesterday a journalist met Manley at his request in the old debtor's room at the jail. Manley appeared to be in excellent health, but a nervous tremor possessed every portion of his body. At that time he made the following statement of his own relations to the murder:

I was born at Arcola, Loudoun County, Virginia, and worked on a farm until the war. During the war I served in Capt. Pollard's company of Col. Holman's District of Columbia colored regiment. I cannot write but can read a little. Since the war I have been working about and was married about a year ago in a house about a hundred yards from the spot where Monroe was killed. Since then I've been working about and was employed until the day of the homicide, upon Capt. McMaster's canal boat, Gen. Elmore. The boat came here the morning on the day after the fourth of July. I was spreeing about all that day with the Paynes' and that night left Mr. Payne's cabin with Lewis and Samuel Payne, and went down by the spring, going to Mr. Gray's, to get whiskey. We came upon two men at the spring lying down; Same Payne told them to get up, and one got up and ran away. I went ahead a few yards, but heard a noise, and looking back I saw Sam Payne strike at the man with a stick. Lewis Payne cut at him with a razor, but I said "dont' cut the man;" ran back and knocked Lewis Payne's arm. The razor cut the man's vest pocket off. If you get the vest you can see that the pocket is cut away. The wound in the man's head was given when they struck him with the corner of the tin box in which he carried his tools. There was but ten cents in the box with the tools. They took the ten cents, but left the box on the side of the hill. Sam Payne gave me the watch to keep until morning. He said he would come and wake me up early, and we'd all go to Georgetown. Then I went up to the Payne's house. What I said about "holding my head up," was a saying we had - "I'll hold up my head if my belly drags the ground," but I left out the last part, because there were women there.

HIS LAST REQUEST - Just as the gentleman was about to leave the room, Manley asked him to remain, and told him tb be witness, that if his (Manley's) wife married again, he wanted Mr. Cline to have his child....

IN THE MORNING - As early as nine o'clock a few persons gathered in the vicinity of the jail. The crowd slowly grew and at noon the vicinity was densely populated, most of the crowd outside being colored persons. The enclosure of the jail where the scaffold was erected was filled very shortly after the door was opened. Few house tops afford a view of the jail yard, and even these few were not filled, but some trees that were supposed to give some inkling of the proceedings within the walls, had climbers. There were none on the jail wall.

There had been much desire expressed to witness the execution, and the City Sargeant issued tickets allowing a number of persons to come within the jail walls, so that by 11 o'clock quite a large crowd had assembled within the enclosure. There is no military adult organization in the city and a detachment of the Relief Hook and Ladder Co. and others were summoned as a posse comitatus by the Town Sargeant. R. M. Latham commanded the posse, which were armed with the Austrian bayonet rifles of the St. John's cadets.

At an early hour Manley rose and dressed as ordinary, and during the morning there occurred from time to time the meetings and partings with relatives and friends which give on such occasions almost a foretaste of the agony of death. His wife brought his child, a slightly babe, and sat by his side while the hours of the morning passed away. His mother was also at his side. He breakfasted heartily, and soon afterwards talked awhile to his wife. His parting with many of his friends was extremely touching but the tenderness he displayed bidding farewell to keeper Cline's little children, who had been unusually kind to him, was of a nature so totally different from his whole past life, as shown by testimony and common reputation, as to excite much feeling.

About 9 his spiritual advisers were admitted into the narrow corridor in which he sat. His wife holding her child sat along side of him. ...In the corridor - a narrow passage 16 by 4 feet the meeting took place, its accompaniments being of the simplest character, but it dealth a solemn reality that impressed its earnestness upon all who were present. At the end of the corridor was hung a printed placard inscribed, "I believe in God my Father and in Jesus Christ my Saviour and in the Holy Spirit who comforts me and leads me to all truth." ... At 11:53 the accused requested all present to withdraw that he might have an interview with his wife. All left the corridor.

ON THE SCAFFOLD - At 12:10 the guard fell in line, and Revs. Marshall, Cook, Parker and Madden, all colored, went upon the scaffold with the condemned man. Manley walked with as firm a step as any of the guards.

The City Sargeant read the sentence of the court condemning the prisoner to be hung by the neck until he be dead on the 28th day of March. ...The ministers now left the scaffold, the City Sargeant and Messrs. Cline and Ward alone remaining upon it. Manley asked to kiss his child, but his mother had left with it for home.

Manley with his hands pinioned then came to the west side of the scaffold. He was dressed in a black suit. He appeared to be but little agitated and spoke as follows:

MANLEY'S WORDS ON THE SCAFFOLD - After some words in a low voice which were understood to be a wish to see his child again, he said that he wanted to say a few words to his friends - here his voice became clearer. He continued: "Whiskey, I will say, has been the death of me, but Christ has power to save me after death. I hope to meet you all in heaven, which I've got a hope of. I hope it will not be long before I will be there. I am not afraid to die. I blame nobody but – whiskey. You all see what whiskey has brought me to. Take my advice on the scaffold and leave it alone. The Christian Association have been as kind as brothers to me; if it was not for them tonight, you would have seen me make my bed in hell. I thank God that I've got to die in his mercy. Mr. Cline and his family have been more than brothers to me. All farewell I am going home to Jesus."

THE EXECUTION – He stood upright on the drop without a sign of emotion, and while the City Sergeant Steuart placed the noose around his neck, said "don't bury me until tomorrow." The cap was drawn over his face, and at 12:38, the sentence of the law was executed. He upon whom it fell died instantly. At 1:02 Dr. T. I. Adam, assisted by Dr. T. S. West made the necessary examination and shortly after, the remains of Manley were placed in a plain pine coffin that had been set beside the scaffold before the execution.

THE END – In a short time the large gate of the jail yard was opened and the crowd, some 700 in number, passed out and separated. The lesson which the law designs had been taught. (*Alexandria Gazette*, March 28, 1873, p. 3.)

...But in one instance, at least, the lesson fell on deaf ears, as a negro, who witnessed Manley's execution, went to Washington the same night and killed Frank Hahn, a cattle drover, and was hanged for the crime. (*Alexandria Gazette*, March 28, 1893, p.3.)

^^*^*^*^*^*^*^*^*^*^*^*^*

CORONER'S INQUEST – Henry Jones, who was cut during an affray at Petty's restaurant last Saturday afternoon, and has lain there ever since, died at 11 o'clock last night. His body was removed two hours afterward to the residence of his father, Capt. Ezekiel Jones on south Lee Street, where Coroner Samuel Beach held an inquest upon it at 10 o'clock this morning.

Dr. Brown, George Petty, Lewis Petty, Jos. McCann, West Makeley and U. M. Monroe were examined as witnesses, and the purport of their evidence was that Jones died from the effects of the wounds that had been inflicted upon him; that Jones had accused Beach of trying to create a difficulty between the two of the party who were in Petty's restaurant; that Beach had denied the charge; that Jones called Beach a d--d liar; that Beach responded by calling him a G--d d--d liar; that Jones then struck him, and that Beach then, in spite of the efforts of Capt. Eli Petty, who endeavored to separate them, inflicted the wound which proved mortal.

The verdict of the jury, of which E. E. Downham was foreman, was that Henry C. Jones came to his death from cuts iuflicted by a knife in the hands of Silas Beach, on the 28th ult. at Eli Petty's restaurant.

Beach, who is in jail, having been committed to await the result of

Jones' wounds, was brought before Justice May at the jail this afternoon and his counsel, Col. Stuart, waiving an examination, was fully committed for his appearance at Court to answer the charge of murder... (*Alexandria Gazette*, April 2, 1874, p.3.)

VERDICT - ...Silas Beach who stands charged with murder was led to the bar in the custody of the jailor of this city ... thereafter arraigned and arrogantly pleaded not guilty. Thereupon came a jury to wit: ... After having heard the evidence the jury returned to Court with the following verdict: "We the Jury find the prisoner GUILTY of the crime of murder in the second degree. And fix the term of his imprisonment in the State Penitentiary for the term of 15 years." Silas Beach appealed for but was denied a new trial. He was sentenced to fifteen years in the Virginia State Penitentiary at Richmond. (*Alexandria Corporation Ccurt Minute Book*: Vol. 2, Monday 13 July 1874, p. 342.)

^^*^*^*^*^*^*^*^*^*^*^*^*^*

MURDER - A man named Samuel Eichelberger, steersman of the canal boat *M. M. Lewis*, was shot and killed, last night, in a house of ill-fame on Union, between Cameron and Queen Streets, by a woman named Nettie Green, the proprietress. The deceased was a young, single man, whose home was in Hancock, Maryland, to which place his body was forwarded this afternoon. He was shot between ten and eleven o'clock, the ball entering his left temple, and being found in the post mortem examination held this morning by Drs. French and Chancellor near the base of the brain. He never spoke after he was shot. He lay at the house in which he was shot about an hour, when he was taken to the station house, where he died about three o'clock this morning. A corner's inquest was held upon the body when it lay in the station house, about half past seven o'clock, by Justice Padgett, the verdict of the jury, of which W. H. Smith was foreman, being that the deceased came to his death from a pistol shot fired by Nettie Green. Nettie Green, who was arrested soon after the shooting and carried to the station house, was examined at 11 o'clock, this morning, before Mayor Kemper, the Commonwealth's Attorney, Mr. Johnson, being present, when the following evidence was elicited:

...John Fergurson, colored, testified that he was playing the fiddle for the dancers, when he saw Eichelberger throw a tumbler full of water in Miss Nettie's face; Nettie ordered him out of the door; he stood against the door; one of the bystanders caught hold of Miss Nettie, but she jerked loose; the deceased had then gotten outside of the door, and Nettie was standing in the door; he was coming towards her, when she jumped back and fired the pistol; she had tried to put him out five or six times; after firing, she said "I told him to stop and he would not;" the deceased was standing just outside the door when shot....

Chas. R. Murray testified - Was passing and stopped at the door; Eichelberger went up to the bar and claimed a drink; Nettie sat him out a glass of water; he threw the water in her face; saw her put her hand in her bosom, and saw deceased pushed out of the door; heard her

90

say "I will shoot you," deceased then went inside the door again and immediately after heard the pistol shot, and saw the deceased fall; did not see the person who fired the pistol because he (witness) had left the door; deceased was very drunk at the time....

Keyser testified - Went into the house about 10 p.m. and had a dance and a drink; Nettie came up to him and said, "I am going to kill that s--n of a b--h; saw her fire, and picked up the wounded man; saw none of the previous quarrel; did not see the revolver but heard the report; she said "somebody gave me the revolver to shoot him," and said he had smashed a tumbler over her head and she could not stand it any longer....

Capt. James Webster testified - Was at the W. & O. depot when he heard of the murder and came to the station house and afterwards went to Nettie Greene's house and found her under arrest; ordered her to be taken to the station house; which was done; heard her say that she had shot the man; got her keys from her and went up stairs to hunt for the pistol; Mr. Byrd and Officer Crump went with him, and found a pistol in the washstand; Byrd said that he had a pistol, a seven shooter, in the stand, and that one load was out; the pistol he found had two loads out; Nettie said that deceased had kicked her and struck her; she said that a man had handed her the pistol and told her to shoot the s--n of a b--t.

The accused was then committed to jail for the action of the Corporation Court.

The prisoner came here during the war, and has been living in houses of ill-repute ever since - sometimes as a boarder - but for a year or two past as proprietress of the house in which the shooting took place, and which is known as the "Do drop in." She is about forty years old, and though a blond, is by no means good looking. She says she came here from New York, and that she is the daughter of Joseph Green, a sadler, who was born and raised in this city, and was the son of Nelson Green, but that he left here when quite a young man. To a reporter for the *Gazette*, who saw her through the iron door of the cell she occupied in the station house, she said the man went into the street and got a stone, which he threw at her and struck her; that he then threw a tumbler and the water it contained at her, which struck her in the breast; that he then, when she went to the door to call a policeman, advanced towards her with his fists doubled up, struck her and kicked her, and that then she went behind the bar and got the pistol, and as he advanced towards her again she shot him. When the reporter saw her she was reclining on the bench in the cell, her head resting on pillows against the wall, and her untasted breakfast on a waiter at her feet. She complained of being unwell; said the man she shot had hurt her, and when asked what she thought would be done with her said she didn't know and didn't care much. (*Alexandria Gazette*, September 21, 1874, p. 2.)

THE LATE MURDER - Nettie Green, the woman committed to jail yesterday for the murder of Samuel Eichelberger, is in comfortable quarters, and is kept supplied by her friends with such articles as she desires. She is unwell and complains of having been hurt by the man she killed. Dr. Gibson, physician to the jail, examined her this morning and found a bruise on her left thigh and an abrasion on the lower part of the abdomen, as though the toe of the boot or shoe which may have made the bruise had glanced upward. The report that rocks had been found in the pockets of the dead man, when his clothing was removed at the undertaker's, is incorrect. (*Alexandria Gazette*, September 23, 1874, p. 3.)

...Nettie Green...has recovered her health and apparently her spirits – has a good appetite, which is satisfied through the attentions of friends, by whom she is also kept supplied with weekly pictorial newspapers of which she is a constant reader. Dr. Chancellor makes the following statement about the wounds on her person, said by some to have been inflicted by the man she killed, and by others to have been produced since the murder:

"Was called to see Nettie Green in Police station, Monday night; made examination; found the cuticle removed from the abdomen in several places, an inch or an inch and a half above Poupart's ligament; made a second examination Tuesday morning at 8 o'clock with same results; upon a third examination made in jail this morning, in presence of Dr. Gibson, found same evidences of injury above the groin, with contusion and without abraision of thigh; cannot say what instrument was used in inflicting the wound. (*Alexandria Gazette*, September 24, 1874, p. 3.)

VERDICT IN THE TRIAL OF LOUISA TREMAINE ALIAS NETTIE GREEN – The defendant pleaded "not guilty" and after a trial the jury returned the following verdict: "We the jury find the prisoner Louisa Tremaine alias Nettie Green guilty of murder in the second degree and fix her term of confinement at seven years in the penitentiary." The prisoner then by her counsel moved that the court set aside the said verdict and grant her a new trial. The Court overruled her plea and she was sentenced to the state penitentiary in Richmond, Virginia, for seven years. (*Alexandria Corporation Court Minute Book*: Vol. 2, October 16, 1874, p. 424, 495.)

^^*^*^*^*^*^*^*^*^*^*^*^*

AN ALEXANDRIAN KILLED – About 11 o'clock last night Louis Karcher shot and killed J. W. Grimes, son of Mr. James Grimes, or this city, whom he found in his wife's bedroom, in a house in Washington.

Karcher and Mrs. Karcher were arrested and locked up at the Eighth precinct station. In appearance Mrs. K. is rather portly and about 32 years of age, of dark complexion and dark hair and eyes.. Her maiden name was Molly Herfurth. The police state that she bears an unenviable reputation. Karcher is about 58 years old, some 5 feet 8 inches tall. The weapon used was a 32 calibre Smith & Wesson revolver.

Karcher was employed at the United States coast survey as draughtsman, and was considered to be a man not inclined to fits of temper. Karcher, it seems, was asleep in an adjoining room and his wife's room was on the north side. Karcher heard a noise in her room like the tread of a man's foot, and listening heard a man's voice. He went to her door and asked for admittance, which was refused. He then forced the door open with a hatchet. Effecting an entrance he found Grimes in a closet where Mrs. Karcher had locked him up, and murdered him at once. The dead man received three shots, all of which took effect.

The scene of the murder is a two story building at the corner of Seventh street and South Carolina avenue southeast. The tragedy occurred in Mrs. Karcher's bedroom on the second floor. The murdered man lay on his back, with his feet toward the closet. His coat and one of his shoes were off and his clothing presented a "messed up" appearance. His collar and hat were found on the floor alongside a bottle of whisky. Mrs. Karcher's underclothing was scattered about the room and the bedding was disturbed. Grimes's shirt front was dyed red with blood from the wounds on his body, while a stream of blood trickled down from his mouth and a ghastly wound on the face. One wound was in the right corner of the mouth. Bloody finger-prints were impressed on the door frame and wall. The door was battered where Karcher tried to force his way in, and the room presented a ghastly appearance.

The murdered man was about five feet eight inches tall, of good appearnce, about 36 years old, dark complexioned, dark mustache, hair, and eyes. He resided at 743 Eight street southeast, opposite Odd Fellows Hall. He leaves a wife and several children. For some time he had been a sewing machine agent.

...Mrs. Karcher, it is said, has been rather loose of morals of late. Her reputation is bad. She was arrested, and locked up at the eighth precinct several days ago on a charge of profanity. An inquest was held today over Grimes's remains, after which they were brought here for interment.

It is said that Karcher has on several occasion previous to this driven men from his house who were there for the same purpose that Grimes was. On this occasion he was not so moderate. It is stated that Mrs. Karcher was under the influence of liquor when arrested.

The unfortunate victim of Karcher's wrath was well-known in this city, where he was born and reared. He was for a number of years a huckster in the market here, and previous to his removal to Washington kept a green grocery on the north side of King street, between Washington and St. Asaph. He married an Alexandria lady (a Miss Robey) about fifteen years ago. (*Alexandria Gazette*, March 28, 1884, p. 3.)

∧∧*∧*∧*∧*∧*∧*∧*∧*∧*

MURDEROUS ASSAULT - A month or so ago a colored man named Thomas Jackson, living in an alley between Fayette and Henry streets, was arrested at the instance of his wife for brutal treatment, and not having the wherewithal to pay the fine assessed against him was sent to the chain gang for a certain number of days. Jackson served out his time on the gang, but his wife, somewhat embittered by the treatment received at his hands refused to live with him after his release, which determination greatly exasperated Jackson. Last evening, between seven and eight o'clock, he repaired to the house occupied by his wife, and by entreaties and threats endeavored to persuade her to live with him again, but finding her inexorable in her former determination, he suddenly drew a murderous lookiug knife from under his coat and made a cut at the woman's throat. His wife, upon seeing the knive, involuntarily threw her right hand up in order to shield her neck and at the same time ward off the fatal steel, and received severe cuts on her arm and hand. The negro undismayed at the blood thus shed, made another "swipe" for the woman's throat, the blade entering some distance below the right ear, causing a copious flow of blood. The outcries of the terrified woman then grew so loud that her brutal husband deemed it necessary for him to take to flight, which he did in the direction of Shuter's Hill. Mr. Samuel Garnett, who happened to be in the locality at the time, noticed the direction Jackson had taken, and informed Lieutenant Smith, who had by that time appeared on the scene. The latter immediately entered a buggy with Mr. Garnett, and in a short time the couple came up with Jackson, who by that time had arrived near the late residence of Jefferson Tacey, deceased. Lieut. Smith jumped from the buggy and gave chase, running Jackson about a mile, finally capturing him. Jackson submitted to arrest and was conducted to this city and locked up in the station house. The examination of the case was fixed for this morning, but the injuries the woman received prevented her appearance, and Jackson was remanded to jail till Saturday, to which time the trial was postponed. The injuries sustained by the unfortunate woman, though of a serious nature, are not necessarily fatal. She was attended by Dr. O'Brien, who was summoned soon after the cutting. (*Alexandria Gazette*, July 8, 1885, p.3.)

THE ASSAULT CASE – Virginia Jackson, the colored woman who was cut in the neck and hands by her husband, Thomas Jackson, on the night of the 7th instant, as has been heretofore published, being able to appear at the Mayor's office this morning, the case was called for a hearing. Several witnesses testified that Jackson came home in an apparently good humor, but in a short time assaulted his wife, threw her down and while on her prostrate form cut her several times with a knife. Jackson was sent on for the action of the grand jury, which meets on Monday next.... *Alexandria Gazette*, July 11, 1885, p.3.)

VERDICT – Commonwealth vs. Thomas Jackson – Charged with felonious and malicious stabbing and cutting with intent to maim and disfigure and kill. – The defendant was led to the bar and and after a trial the jury rendered the following verdict: "We the jury find the prisoner guilty...and assess his term of imprisonment at nine months in the City jail and a fine of $5.00. (*Alexandria Corporation Court Minute Book*, Vol. 6, October 12, 1885, p. 428.

^^*^*^*^*^*^*^*^*^*^*^*^*

NEGRO DESPERADO KILLED – Between six and seven o'clock Saturday evening, Fannie Chapman, a mulatto woman, who has often figured in the police court of the city, applied at the station house for a warrant for the arrest of James (alias ("Toot") Henderson, also colored, and who, too, has been the defendant in several cases before

the Mayor's and magistrates' courts of late. According to her statement Henderson, who, it seems had been living with her for some
time, came to her residence, on the southeast corner of Pitt and
Princess streets, early in the evening in a half-drunken condition, and
stretched himself upon the floor. The woman ordered him out, a
command Henderson seemed loth to obey, and his quandammistress
becoming more positive in her request for him to vacate the premises,
Henderson arose from the floor and drawing a pistol said, with an imprecation of some sort, "I'll fix you before I go," and snapped the pistol at her until one barrel was discharged, the ball passing in close
proximity to her head. The woman fled panic-stricken into the street
attired in but one garment, a "Mother-Hubbard" robe, and meeting an
acquaintance obtained the loan of an apron, upon donning which she
repaired to the station house and swore out a warrant against Henderson. Capt. Webster, of the police force, dispatched officer Bettice to
the locality of the alleged attempted murder, with directions to
"shadow the culprit until he (Webster) attended to some business at
the station house, after which he would join him. Henderson had in
the meantime left the house of his former paramour and had gone to
another place in the neighborhood. Capt. W. shortly afterward appeared on the scene, and with officer Bettice "blockaded" both the
front and back doors to prevent Henderson's escape. The latter, upon
learning that the police were on his track, managed to escape through
the back way of the house, and started to run through the weeds on the
hill east of the valley running through "Petersburg," when he was
seized by office Bettice, but suddenly pulled away from him. He was
closely followed by the officers, and the course of his flight having
been turned by officer Bettice, who had "headed him off," Henderson
passed very swiftly within a few feet of Capt. Webster. The latter,
aware of the ferocity of the man with whom he had to deal, drew his
pistol, a self-cocking weapon, with the full determination of shooting
him should he make any murderous demonstration. As Henderson approached the Captain the latter noticed his arm was raised, but it
being nearly dark, he was unable to see either knife or pistol in his
hand. The pursued was that time within about five feet of his pursuer,
and the latter called upon Henderson to halt. Henderson cast some
imprecation on the Captain, paid no attention to the challenge and
soon lengthened the distance between himself and Captain Webster
about thirty feet, when the latter's pistol was accidentally discharged,
the hammer having been raised in the excitement and the ball striking
Henderson in the back passed through his body, making a track through
the heart in its transit. Henderson upon being shot jumped about two
feet from the ground and made a dive into a ditch. Officer Bettice
immediately ran to the ditch and discovered that the man was fatally
shot, and in a few seconds he was dead. Henderson's body was subsequently taken from the place where he had fallen and conveyed a
short distance south, and in a short time several hundred people had
assembled around the body, including the majority of the colored residents of the neighborhood. Among the number was Fannie Chapman,
who had sworn out the warrant for the arrest of the deceased, and who
sobbed and expressed all sorts of regrets that she had been the in-
direct cause of her quandam admirer's sudden exit from the mundane

sphere. Upon the news of the shooting being nosed around the crowd grew in bulk every minute until Mr. B. Wheatley's undertaker's wagon arrived, in which Henderson's body was placed and taken to Mr. W.'s establishment. Capt. Webster had in the mean time given himself up, and was bailed for his appearance today. ...The body was subsequently removed to the house of the deceased's mother, Maria Henderson, on Pitt street, between Princess and Oronoko Streets, where it was viewed all day yesterday by a curious throng. Captain Webster avers that he had no intention of shooting Henderson at the time his pistol was discharged, but that he had fully made up his mind to do so before the miscreant passed him had he discovered that he was armed, knowing him to have been a desperate character, and with the full knowledge of the fact that he had previously attempted to kill his paramour. Failing, however, to see any weapon in Henderson's hands, the Captain believed Henderson would become entangled in the weeds in his flight, when his capture could be easily effected. But in the first excitement the officer had undoubtedly cocked his pistol, and the hammer still being up the weapon was discharged unintentionally, with the fatal result narrated above. Henderson was a thick set man, about twenty five years of age, and is said to have been born here; though some assert he first saw the light of day in Petersburg. He has for some time been regarded as a desperado, having in an affray with another colored man named Dan. Nelson some months ago nearly severed the latter's head from his body by a murderous "swipe" with a butcher's knife. Nelson's throat was cut from one ear to the other, but fortunately not deep enough to sever the jugular vein. The deceased, in company with one Dan. Blandheim, an equally vicious character, went on an excursion to Leesburg recently and while in the latter place started a row, in which a colored man was dangerously cut. The identical pistol that was discharged at the Chapman woman, it is said, figured in this fracas. Blandheim, Henderson's "chum," it will be remembered, was charged at one time with having robbed a cattle dealer.

...They Mayor then stated that after the shooting Capt. Webster had come to him and he had put him under bond for his appearance today. He knew Capt. W. to be a faithful officer and from his knowledge of him and from the evidence did not believe that he intended to kill the man. Henderson he knew to be a desperate character, and was the only man since he had been Mayor who had been insolent and offensive in his office. He regarded the shooting as an unfortunate affair, but must discharge the prisoner. Capt. Webster was thereupon discharged.

The accidental (and from all the testimony it was certainly unintentional) killing of Henderson has afforded some papers further north a theme for comment, the verdict being styled "curious," extraordinary," etc. Of course it is obvious to all that this is an other attempt to manufacture party capital at the North by implying that negroes are shot down in the South on all sorts of pretexts. Persons acquainted with the facts connected with the killing of Henderson, or those willing to listen to reason, can see nothing in the action of Capt. Webster unwarrantable or unnecessary. He was elected a member of the police force twenty years ago, and has been Captain since its reorganization in 1870. He has ever shown himself to be a patient and forbearing officer, having often been placed in circumstances where both his valor and patience have been subjected to severe tests. The assertion that he would unnecessarily hurt any one is repudiated by all who know him, and that Saturday night's fatal act was unintentional is a fact incontrovertible. (*Alexandria Gazette*, August 16, 1886, p.3.)

＊∧＊∧＊∧＊∧＊∧＊∧＊∧＊∧＊∧＊∧＊

MURDER OF OFFICER ARNOLD - The city was thrown into an unusual state of excitement at an early hour yesterday morning by the report which rapidly spread that Policeman Julian Arnold had been shot and killed by a burglar whom he had attempted to arrest during the night. When it was subsequently learned that a pair of desperadoes had been engaged in the foul work and that one (John Curran, an ex-Alexandrian) had been captured and was in the station house the populace became still further incensed, and talk of anticipating the law's delay by lynching the prisoner were freely expressed. The fact that a conservator of the peace - the protector of life and property - had been ruthlessly assassinated at midnight by a human fiend who preys upon the fruits of others' toils, was justly regarded as a crime of the deepest dye, and numbers thought the expiation should be immediately made. Cooler heads, however, succeeded in bringing the excited to the plane of consideration, but throughout the day and long into the night the murder was the principal theme of conversation and groups of persons could be seen at all times discussing the matter. The spot upon which Mr. Arnold fell in the discharge of his duty was visited by throngs during the day. A stick had been placed where his life's blood had flowed, and the clotted gore when viewed added fire to the flame for vengeance which had already been kindled....

At ten o'clock last Saturday night Police Julian Arnold and Joseph Martin went on duty, and a circus company having performed on the old fair grounds, upper end of King street, the two officers proceeded to that neighborhood, supposing many persons would be in the locality, and that their presence would be necessary until the troupe had packed up and the crowd dispersed. Upon arriving at their objective point they fulfilled their mission, saw the departure of the circus people and their outfit and the gradual dwindling away and final dissipation of the assemblage which had been brought together. In the meantime the officers had their suspicions aroused by the conduct of two strange white men who still loitered around the vicinity and who invariably shrank from the policemen's sight and whom it was impossible to get near a light. It therefore seemed probable that some house they intended burglarizing had been marked, and they were only awaiting the time when the policemen should proceed on their beat and the streets become deserted to carry out their purpose. Indeed, from their movements it appeared that they had their eyes on Mr. Sefer Blouse's premises, at least the officers so divined their purpose and when that gentleman (at about 12 o'clock) closed his house (1414 King St.)

Messrs. Frank Roberts and Ernest I. Padgett proceeded down the street together on their way home. The parties whom Messrs. Arnold and Martin had been shadowing were lost sight of by this time, and the two officers started down the north side of King Street to West - one square from the circus grounds - upon reaching the corner called to Roberts and Padgett to stop as they had something to say to them. Upon approaching, Mr. Arnold told them they had been following two men for some time who seemed on mischief bent, and had lost sight of them, but believed they were somewhere in or about the circus grounds. He then directed Mr. Roberts to go back to Mr. Blouse's with officer Martin and apprize him of the fact that burglars were about to enter his house while he (Arnold) and Padgett would enter the circus grounds upon the east and search for the suspected parties. Messrs. Martin and Roberts went back to Blouse's and carried out their instructions, while Arnold and Padgett proceeded in their search. Before entering the grounds Arnold handed his club to his companion, telling him to use it if necessary, while he would depend upon his pistol in case of emergency. The two soon reached the grounds and entered the ring made by the circusmen, when to their amazement they stumbled over the two men they had been looking for. They were lying down against the side of the ring. Arnold charged them with acting suspicious and to consider themselves under arrest. At this juncture one of the men arose, drew a pistol and fired at the officer, inflicting a mortal wound, while the latter, in death's throes returned the fire and emptied two chambers of his revolver at him, though, so far as known, without effect, as the murderer after firing fled. Padgett, upon realizing the terrible tragedy which had been enacted knocked the other man down with his billy, and, supposing him sufficiently disabled, ran to the assistance of Arnold, calling at the same time, "Police! help! murder!" The man whom he had knocked down, however, soon recovered his feet and uttering some horrid imprecation ran upon his assailant with the ferocity of a maddened beast, when a terrible struggle took place - the desperado, bent on revenge, and breathing out threatenings and slaughter, while Padgett, knowing his life depended on the issue of the conflict, fought with all the desperation natural to man when in danger of his life. The latter says the man to whom he found himself bound in deadly embrace drew a pistol and endeavored to place the muzzle to his head, which attempt he frustrated, and though the weapon was discharged several times, only one shot touched him and that made but a slight abrasion on the side of his head. Upon hearing Padgett's cries Officer Martin, who was at Blouse's in company with Roberts (who is a readyman) hurried to the scene of the conflict, and upon seeing what was going on struck the man who was struggling with Padgett a heavy blow on the head with his stick, which caused him to relinquish his hold, and submit to arrest. A. W. Henderson, who had been attracted to the spot, appeared on the scene and testifies that he too, grappled with the man who attacked Padgett. Henderson, upon the arrival of Martin, took Arnold's pistol from his hand, and was with difficulty prevented from shooting the man who was then under arrest. The party who had shot Policeman Arnold, or who it is thought shot him - for Padgett at first supposed his assailant was the murderer - fled, and though he was pursued, succeeded in eluding his followers. Martin proceeded to the station house with his prisoner and Arnold, in a dying condition, was conveyed to Mr. Blouse's restaurant, where Dr. Powell soon arrived. Upon examining the wound the physician pronounced it mortal, and the dying man's wife was sent for. When the sorrow stricken lady arrived her husband was in a dazed condition and about semi-conscious, his life slowly ebbing away, and after lingering for about and hour and a half he breathed his last at fifteen minutes past two o'clock. ...

During the fusilade, about seven or eight shots having been fired according to some and less in the opinion of others, Mr. Blouse was struck by a chance shot on the left hip, which, however, only inflicted an insignificant flesh wound.

The grounds were searched for the pistol Padgett averred his assailant fired at him (none having been found on the prisoner) though without success.

Shortly after Mr. Arnold's death his remains were conveyed to Mr. Wheatley's undertaker's establishment and yesterday morning Dr. Powell summoned a coroner's jury:

An autopsy was made by Doctors O'Brien and Ashby, which showed the pistol used in the killing of Mr. Arnold was of a large calibre, about 44; also that the course of the bullet was entirely through the body, perforating the stomach, touching the liver and kidneys and severing a large vein in its passage.

...The body of the unfortunate Mr. Arnold was dressed later and throughout a greater portion of the day numbers viewed it at Mr. Wheatley's. It was finally conveyed to the late residence of the deceased.

John Curran is one of four brothers, who have figured in frequent robberies. The names of his brothers are William alias "Cockey" Curran, a pick-pocket, Ed. and Tom Curran. Tom and John have long had the reputation of being ready "shooters". John Curran, alias John McCuen, was arrested in Washington March 9, 1879, for picking the pocket of a Miss Newberry of valuable diamond ring. He was then 18 years of age. The case against him was dismissed at the time, as the lady failed to prosecute him. The ring was recovered. Subsequently he was arrested for burglary in Baltimore and served a term in the Baltimore penitentiary for his crime. He robbed the paymaster of the Chesapeake and Ohio canal at Cumberland, Md., and served ten years in the state penitentiary. His picture is in the "rogue's gallery" at police headquarters in Washington. He was raised here and was always a source of trouble to the police. The greater portion of his youth was spent in jail or workhouse. Capt. Webster, who was a constable before the days of the present police force, entered on his duties on April 1, 1866, and his first arrest was the boy John Curran, who was wanted for a petty theft. The family lived in a small house opposite Jamieson's foundry on Royal street, between Wilkes and Gibbon, and the boys were natural born rascals, following their thievish inclinations when mere children. At that time there was quite a gang of juvenile thieves in Alexandria, the Currans being prominent among them. Two of the boys joined the District regiment stationed here during the war, having been induced to become soldiers by the large bounty. At the close of the war Alexandria proved too contracted for them, and in order to drive their profession with profit they sought larger fields....

Mr. Arnold was an Alexandrian by birth and when a mere boy received his baptism of fire in the Stonewall Jackson brigade, with which he served throughout the war. He had been on the police force sixteen years and previous to its organization was a night watchman. He was a very efficient officer, of great courage and strength. He was 40 years of age, five feet seven inches in height, and weighed about 170 pounds. He was three times married, his third wife being left to mourn his sudden end. Four children survive him. ... When informed of his fatal wounding his wife, to whom he had been married less than a year, was thrown into a paroxism of grief. Her condition previously had been critical and upon realizing her early widowhood her grief was heartrending. She is now quite ill. The funeral took place today at 4 p.m. from St. Mary's Church..... (*Alexandria Gazette*, May 16, 1887, p.3.)

THE EXAMINATION OF JOHN CURRAN - ...Mayor Smoot said he was convinced from the evidence that the prisoner should be sent to jail to await the action of the grand jury, and so remanded Curran. (*Alexandria Gazette*, May 19, 1887, p. 3.)

THE CURRAN TRIAL - The trial of John Curran, indicted with Billy Williams for the murder of Officer Arnold was continued in the Corporation Court this morning.

The first witness was Dr. O'Brien. He testified to attending Arnold before his death. He examined Mr. Padgett, who had a wound on the right side of his head; saw it was a bullet wound; there was no mark of powder nor burn on his face. The powder would have been shown on his face if the pistol had been close to him, and it would have burned the side of his face.

Mr. Dan Patterson said that on the night of the shooting, between 11 and 12 o'clock, he was in Blouse's to collect for hauling goods for the circus; when he left Blouse's he came out with the man and woman of the circus; the time was about 20 minutes to 12; Arnold wanted some one to go over on the commons; said he mentioned Lanham and Tyler's names, but didn't know what his object was in seeking of the two. Roberts, Padgett and Martin were in Blouse's house as he passed the window; told Arnold not to go over after Tyler and Lanham.

Sam Gassenheimer remembered seeing Curran on the day of the killing; prisoner said a suit of clothes would come to him by express that day which did come and prisoner put them on; later Curran came back to him, put on his old suit and said he would go across the bridge; this was about 10:30 p.m.; Curran had been drinking; this was in Washington.

Chas. Ross said Curran was with him at the south end of the Long Bridge until 6 o'clock p.m. on the day in question; then left for Washington, promising to return on the 11:37 train.

W. G. Lanham was in Blouse's between 11 and 12 o'clock and was arrested by Martin; met Arnold who told Martin he had no right to arrest him as he, Martin, was as drunk as witness was.

...E. D. Soper said he knew Arnold; he once came to his house and drew a pistol on Henry Parsons without any provocation whatsoever. He was a very passionate man....

John Curran, the prisoner, then took the stand gave his version of the affair. Said he lived in Washington and on the day of the killing walked across the Long bridge and stayed at a house on the south side till dark; went back to Washington and later took a train to come back to the house, but fell asleep and did not wake till he reached this city when he was aroused by a man and a woman who sat near him; came on down the street and went to the circus ground where he was attracted by the lights; talked to some people on the ground; took a drink when three men, whom he did not know, said they would take a drink with him; shortly afterwards Padgett and another man came towards him in the ring, and without saying anything about arrest told him to throw up his hands; Padgett then said, "If you put your hands down I will hit you"; told Padgett he could search him if he was looking for anything; he then heard a shot and immediately Padgett struck him on the head and almost stunned him; when he recovered, Padgett was over him searching him; did not know how many shots were fired; had done nothing to provoke the assault nor did he put his hands towards his hip pocket; had not carried a pistol for three years; said Henderson had put a pistol in his face when he grabbed it and Officer Martin told Henderson not to hurt him; Padgett told the men when they came up to hit him as he was the man who had done the shooting when he begged them not to kill him as he had done nothing. He then told how he was taken to the station house; ... he knew Billy Williams but was positive he was not one of the men on the grounds on the night of the shooting. When shown the photograph of Williams said it looked something like him but he would not swear it was him;...

This evening Wm. Curran, a brother of the prisoner, took the stand and exhibited the bloody clothes worn by his brother the night of his arrest. ... (*Alexandria Gazette*, October 15, 1887, p. 3.)

CURRAN ACQUITTED - ...The jury then took took their places in the box, and through the foreman Dr. Kloman, handed in their verdict of "not guilty." Curran, who stands indicted for a felonious assault on Mr. E. I. Padgett still remained in the custody of Sergt. Smith, and after a colloquy between the Commonwealth's attorney and Judge Meade it was agreed that his trial for this offense should be set for Friday next. ...It is the general opinion that Messrs. Marbury and .Johnson made as strong a case as it was possible for the Commonwealth, but that the evidence to convict Curran of the murder was not sufficient. (*Alexandria Gazette* October 17, 1887, p. 3.)

Billy Williams was later apprehended and tried for the murder of Policeman Arnold in July 1888. On the 16th of that month the jury found him guilty in the second degree and sentenced him to five years in the penitentiary. (*Alexandria Gazette* July 13,14, 16, 1888, p.3.)

^^*^*^*^*^*^*^*^*^*^*

MURDER IN THE COUNTY - As stated in the *Gazette*, during a row between two young colored men, named Robert Pinn and John Carroll, on Friday morning, near Arlington, the latter was shot through the breast and instantly killed. It is not known whether or not the shooting was accidental or intentional. The only witnesses were some children and their statements are so confused that Commonwealth's Attorney Clements, of the county, is still investigating the matter. As far as can be learned the two young men were good friends, and on Friday morning they were seen talking earnestly together. Suddenly a pistol shot was heard, and the next instant two little colored boys, who were playing near by, saw Pinn attempting to raise Carroll from the ground, protesting that he did not intend shooting him.

Another version of the affair is that Pinn starting for work Friday morning, missed his whip, and thinking that Carroll had it, went to the latter's house. Carroll had the whip and gave it up without any harsh words passing between them. The young men then got to chiding each other about the amount of money they had in their pockets. Pinn offering to bet Carroll that he could not show a quarter. The latter then asserted that Pinn could not produce a cent, which the latter did and the refusal to look at the coin caused Pinn to draw the revolver and shoot Carroll. When the alarm was given some of the neighbors hurried to the spot and found the lifeless body of Carroll stretched on the ground with a bullet through his breast, but Pinn had disappeared. Carroll and Pinn were both about eighteen years of age and were employed at the brick yards near Arlington. The body of Carroll was taken to his home in West Washington. (*Alexandria Gazette*, October 17, 1887, p.3.)

^^*^*^*^*^*^*^*^*^*^*^*^*

MURDER REVEALED BY A DREAM – Until yesterday Nancy Mills, a well known colored woman of the Bailey's Cross Roads' neighborhood, in Fairfax county, had been missing for some time past and her absence gave rise to much alarm among her friends. It appears that last Monday she had a difficulty with a colored man named Stephen Cross and threatened to warrant him. Suspicion resting upon Cross a warrant was issued on Saturday for his apprehension and placed in the hands of a constable who, with a posse, started immediately to make the arrest. Cross, in the meantime, had fortified himself in his house and barricaded the doors and as the posse came up opened fire on them from a window. The fire was returned and a fusillade kept up for some time during which three of the attacking party were slightly wounded. Cross's ammunition having given out he surrendered, when the posse entered the house and ordering the desperado to hold up his hands, arrested him and took him to Fairfax C. H. where they placed him safely in jail. A few nights since an old colored preacher in that neighborhood dreamed that the woman was dead and was buried in a manure heap near the house of Stephen Cross, who lived near Barcroft's mill. Yesterday he made known his dream, and upon search being made the body of the woman was discovered under the manure with her throat cut from ear to ear. The discovery of the body caused the wildest excitement.

102

It has been learned that after the quarrel on Monday Cross killed the woman and dragged her body into some bushes where he hid it. That night he took it to a ravine near by intending to bury it. He partially dug two graves but becoming alarmed went off but later returned with his wagon into which he placed it and hauled it to the manure pile, back of his barn where he covered it up. When found the woman's head was crushed, beside her throat being cut. Had her body been found before Cross was taken to jail on Saturday he would probably have been lynched.

Nancy Mills, the murdered woman, formerly belonged to Mrs. A. M. Fitzhugh, of this city, and for some years after the war lived with old aunt Nancy Franklin near the cemeteries. (*Alexandria Gazette*, January 21, 1889, p. 3.)

^^*^*^*^*^*^*^*^*^*^*^*

FATAL AFFRAY - About five o'clock yesterday evening Frank Scarce and John Wright, two young colored men, who with others had been participating in Christmas stimulants, began "skylarking" on Queen street, between Fayette and Henry, during which Scarce shoved Wright, but whether in a playful or menacing way is not apparent. The two immediately clinched and rolled in the street, but soon separated and regained their feet, only, however, to grapple again with the same results. They once more relaxed hold on each other and separated when Scarce drew a pistol and fired at Wright, the ball striking the later in the left temple, inflicting what proved a mortal wound. Scarce was later arrested in the fourth ward by officers, Hayes and Jones. The injured man, was taken to his home on Queen street, where he was attended by Dr. Klipstein, and about ten o'clock this morning expired. Scarce was taken before the Mayor this morning, and after the evidence of several witnesses had been taken, he was remanded to jail to await the result of Wright's wound. The latter, however, died before Scarce reached the jail door. Scarce says that he shot Wright for the reason that if he hadn't Wright would have shot or cut him. Both men were natives of this city. Scarce of late had been employed in Washington but for several years previous had been employed as driver in this city. Scarce's remains were taken to Mr. Demaine's undertaking establishment shortly after his death, and Dr. Purvis, coroner, held an inquest. ...The ball was found in the left side of the posterior lobe of the brain. (*Alexandria Gazette*, December 27, 1890, p.3.)

VERDICT - ...The prisoner was arraigned and pleaded "not guilty". After the jury heard the evidence they presented the following verdict: "We the jury find the prisoner "not guilty"... The prisoner was then discharged from custody. ... (*Alexandria Corporation Court Minute Book*, Vol. 9, April 21, 1891, p. 114.)

^^*^*^*^*^*^*^*^*^*^*^*

A TRAGEDY IN THE STREET - George S. Smith Shot and Killed by Jeff Phillips. Last night about half-past nine o'clock three pistol shots in rapid succession startled everybody in the vicinity of the City Hall and brought conversations to an abrupt termination. In a few minutes people were seen running from all points of the compass toward the corner of Cameron and Royal streets, where Jeff Phillips, who has all his life borne an unsavory reputation, stood with a smoking pistol in his hand, while on the opposite side of the street, in a doorway stood George S. Smith, with his life's blood oozing out and dying. Phillips, who made no attempt to escape, was secured and his victim taken to a neighboring public house, where, within half an hour's time, he expired.

The origins of the difficulty dates back several weeks, and, as is so often the case, a woman, whose reputation is as unsavory as that of the assassin, figures in it. It seems that for some time past the victim of the tragedy had allowed his infatuation for a woman named Capitola Crossman, more commonly known as "Cappie," to seriously disturb his domestic relations, and after a scene in which he figured, he left the city for a few days, the woman disappearing a day or two later. An amicable reconciliation, however, had taken place between himself and his family. Phillips was also enamoured by the blandishments of the women and was a familiar visitor at her house and last Sunday night, while in the tolls of the green-eyed monster Jealousy, struck his inamorats. Mr. Smith was considerably angered by such an ungallant act, and upon his recommendation a warrant was issued and Phillips was arrested, taken before Justice Beach and fined.

Both men being fired with jealousy, the affair of the warrant made more bitter blood between them, and on Tuesday Smith had a game which was being conducted by Phillips at the driving park in the county stopped. Thus relations stood between the two men yesterday when Smith, with a friend, approached Phillips in the El Dorado House for the purpose of negotiating an amicable settlement, saying to him in substance, that he was not desirous of harboring further resentment, and was willing to let by-gones be by-gones and become friends again. They shook hands and parted with pleasant expressions, Phillips remarking "George, I have got no bad feelings against you," and all parties took a sociable drink and they did not see each other until their meeting last night. The two men parted, however, as the sequel proved, with the trouble between them merely gilded over - so far as Phillips, at least, was concerned.

It was about half-past nine o'clock last night when Phillips was sitting in the doorway of the El Dorado House (319 Cameron Street) in conversation with Mr. Samuel Orison, when he saw Smith, who had just left a saloon on the west side of Royal street with Mr. Zoro Hill, stop at the southeast corner of Royal and Cameron streets.

Phillips brought the conversation to an abrupt termination by arising and walking toward the two men. As he passed his victim he exclaimed, "George Smith!" and whisking out a pistol fired at him. Smith upon realizing that he was about to be killed, ran toward the northwest corner, and as he fled, and while under the electric light Phillips fired two more shots in rapid succession, both taking effect. The report of the pistol produced the greatest consternation among the people who were seated in front of their doors, and the wounded man ran towards the front door of Mr. John Harlow's residence. (202 North Royal Street) The members of the family, who were seated around the door, became panic-stricken and fled precipitately, supposing the man who had so unceremonously come among them was doing the shooting. Smith closed and fastened the front door and and remained standing in the vestibule till his brother, Lieut. Smith came, when he said: "My God, Jim, I am shot, Jeff Phillips did it for nothing." By this time other officers had made their appearance, and Phillips, with the pistol in his hand, was found standing on the opposite corner. He was quickly hustled off to the station house, apparently in no wise disconcerted over his deed. Lieut. Smith, of the police force, was among the first attracted to the spot by the report of the pistol, but was totally ignorant of the fact that his brother was the victim of the tragedy, and upon approaching him and discovering his identity and realizing that he was dying, his grief and lamentations were piteous and caused numbers to turn away in sorrow. The dying man was taken from the vestibule and borne to Mr. F. Schwab's saloon, a few doors south (132 North Royal Street) and Dr. Jones summoned, but by the time the physician arrived the vital spark had fled. Members of the family of the deceased had also arrived, among them a sister, whom he recognized, and his estimable mother, now an aged lady, whose locks have been bleached by the snows of many winters, and who is now called upon to bear a crushing sorrow in the advanced evening of her life. Her grief, as may be supposed, was poignant, and her presence elicited the heartfelt sympathy of all spectators.

The livid pallor soon settled upon the features of the dead man, and the glassy eye, half-opened mouth and bloody clothing told another sad story of the allurements of a frail woman and the train of evils which to often follow in her wake.

Upon the news of the shooting being noised about much exasperation was produced and there were some threats of executing summary punishment on the assasin.

The body was then taken to Mr. Smith's late residence, on St. Asaph street. (222 North St. Asaph Street)....

Mayor Strauss this morning had Phillips arraigned before him, but the latter waived examination and was sent on to the grand jury. ...

The victim of the tragedy was a son of the late Lieutenant John L. Smith and was forty-two years of age. During his life he had engaged in various occupations, some it is said, savoring of a sporting nature, but was of an open and frank disposition and popular among his acquaintances, and his untimely end is a source of regret among all who knew him. He was at one time City Bill Poster, and at another Lieutenant of the Capitol police force. Of late he had conducted the wood and coal business in this city. He leaves a wife and one child. ...Two or three years ago he was shot and dangerously wounded by Frank DeLea, who claimed that he had been duped by him in a game of cards.

Phillips was seen in his cell in jail by a reporter of the Gazette this morning. ...He said, however, that he had been informed that Smith had threatened to kill him on sight and that when he passed Smith his first impulse was to shoot quickly. He declared that he did not know who Smith was till he was in the act of passing him on the corner and that when he left Mr. Orrison he did not know Smith was anywhere about. (*Alexandria Gazette*, July 23, 1891, p.3.)

VERDICT – ...Shortly before 10 o'clock this morning the court was notified by the Deputy Sergeant having the jury in charge that a verdict had been reached and the Judge apprised of the fact. The jury then entered the room. ...The clerk having taken his place at his desk, to the usual querry, "Have the jury agreed upon a verdict?" he was handed the following, which he read:

"We, the jury find the prisoner guilty of murder in the first degree – T. L. Chase, foreman.

...The trial of Phillips for the killing of George S. Smith on the night of the 22d of last July, has doubtless excited more interest in Alexandria and caused more excitement than any similar case in the past half century. Every day the prisoner was placed in the dock the room was packed until this morning the room has been packed to overflowing. ...But few supposed that a verdict for the extreme penalty of the law would be rendered.... (*Alexandria Gazette*, January 19, 1892, p. 2.)

RETRIAL OF JEFF PHILLIPS – Jefferson Phillips Convicted of Murder in the Second Degree – To Go to the Penitentiary for Eight Years – A Midnight Tribunal – Yells and Exclamations in the Court Room – The Place Crowded to Suffocation. The trial of Jefferson Phillips for the killing of George S. Smith on the night of July, 1891, ceased its weary course between 11 and 12 o'clock last Saturday night by the jury bringing in a verdict of murder in the second degree and fixing the term of imprisonment of the accused at eight years in the penitentiary....

It has been nearly two years since Phillips killed Smith and the courts have been nineteen months in disposing of the case. He has had four trials altogether – one in the police court, one in the Court of Appeals and two in the Corporation Court with four postponements of the case in the latter tribunal. The last trail began on Monday and dragged its slow course along until last night when, like all sublunary things, it had to come to an end....

Phillips looked much brighter, was more cheerful and evidently felt relieved from the mental strain under which he had labored since his sentence of death had been changed for a verdict of eight years in the penitentiary. (*Alexandria Gazette*, May 15, 1893, p. 2.)

JEFF PHILLIPS PARDONED – It is customary on the beginning of a year for the Governor to exercise executive clemency to some inmate of the penitentiary by granting him a pardon. This year an Alexandrian – Jeff. Phillips – has been the recipient of this favor. ...He has been confined in the jail and penitentiary four and a half years. His pardon was granted on account of failing health, it being supposed that he is suffering with consumption. (*Alex. Gazette*, January 2, 1896, p.3.)

PROBABLE WIFE MURDER – Shortly after nine o'clock last night the neighborhood of south Lee street was startled by two pistol shots and cries of murder. People ran from all directions toward Little Zion Church (Lee Street), the locality from which the cries emanated and found that a young colored woman generally known as Lon Taylor, but said to be married to Turner Gaines, had been shot and probably mortally wounded by her husband. From what could be learned it appears that the domestic peace of the couple has been ruptured at intervals for some time and during the past two weeks there had been a sort of separation between them, the wife intending to go to Washington today for the purpose of entering into service. This determination on the part of his wife angered Gaines, and he formed a resolution to kill her in order to frustrate the carrying out of her programme. A rehearsal for an exhibition of some kind was in progress in the Little Zion Church last night, and the building was well filled with colored people, among the number being Gaines' wife. He procured a pistol and repaired to the church, muttering as he went along that he would meet his better half "on ice," etc. Upon arriving at the building he sought his wife and after a short parley, drew the pistol and fired at her, but, strange to say, neither the woman nor any one else in the crowd was hurt. The greatest excitement followed and the woman who was the object of his murderous passion ran into the street until she reached the old Battery Rodgers pump at the corner of Lee and Jefferson streets, where Gaines caught her, and taking her by the right hand and drawing her arm out straight he pointed the weapon at her breast and pulled the trigger. A cry of anguish followed the report of the pistol, and the woman struggled with a bullet in her right lung. The cries of murder which proceeded from the frightened people who had gathered and the blowing of whistles produced intense excitement and alarm. The wounded woman staggered toward the house of a relative, about a square off, but fell, and a number of people soon gathered around her, and while the kindly disposed were endeavoring to examine the wound the red-handed murderer forced himself through the crowd and cooly asked his wife if she was much hurt. Neighbors finally conveyed her to the house of her aunt, near the corner of Lee and Franklin streets, and in a few minutes the police arrived and a physician was summoned. Dr. Herndon answered the call and upon reaching the house made an examination of the wound, and from his diagnosis it appeared that the ball had entered the right side of the chest and into the lung, where it had lodged, making a very dangerous wound, from the effects of which she will, in all probability, finally die. The woman when taken into the house was in a profuse perspiration, with her pulse beating very fast, but upon the arrival of Doctor Herndon she had grown cold and her flesh clammy. Throughout the night she suffered considerably. Gaines, after leaving his wife, proceeded up the street, and in passing a house where some colored people were standing he asked them "what they had to do with this," and became so menacing that the crowd ran in the house and locked the door. Mr. George Craven who lives in the neighborhood and who happened to be near the scene of the shooting determined that the would be murderer should not escape and followed close upon his heels. Gaines, however, proceeded to the sta-

107

tion house and gave himself up, and this morning was brought before Mayor Strauss, who continued the case. The would be uxorcide is a low set mulatto and is said to be vicious and prone to shooting and cutting. When asked last night why he attempted to kill his wife, he made the unsatisfactory response that he "did it for cause."

This morning Doctors Herndon, Purvis and Jamieson made a further examination of the wound made by the pistol shot and succeeded in locating the ball near the spinal column, it having passed entirely through the lung. The injured woman was not so well as at the first examination, and while her wound may not necessarily be mortal, her condition is critical. (*Alexandria Gazette*, August 27, 1891, p. 3.)

IN A CRITICAL CONDITION - Lou Gaines, the colored woman who was shot on south Lee Street on Wednesday night by her husband, Turner Gaines, continues in a critical condition, with but slight chance of her recovery. (*Alexandria Gazette*, August 28, 1891, p. 3.)

IMPROVING - Lou Gaines, the colored woman who was shot by her husband on south Lee street last Wednesday, and who, it was supposed, was fatally injured, is now believed to be in a fair way of recovery. Drs. Herndon, Purvis and Jamieson have removed the bullet, which, after passing through the lung, embedded itself in the back near the spinal column. (*Alexandria Gazette*, Sept. 1, 1891, p. 3.)

VERDICT - Commonwealth vs. Turner Gaines, indicted for maliciously shooting his wife with intent to kill; prisoner pleaded guilty and was sentenced to one year's imprisonment in jail and to pay a fine of $250. (*Alexandria Gazette*, October 16, 1891, p. 3.; *Alexandria Corporation Court Minute Book*, Vol. 9, October 16, 1891, p. 223)

^^*^*^*^*^*^*^*^*^*^*^*^*

MYSTERIOUS DEATH - Yesterday Captain Webster, of the police force, notified Dr. Purvis, the Coroner, that a colored boy about four years old had died in a house on Franklin Street, between Washington and Columbus Streets, that no application for a burial permit had been made, and the circumstances were of such a nature that an investigation should be made, this having been the third child which had died in the same house recently. The Coroner notified Constable Supple, who had the remains removed to Mr. Demaine's undertaking establishment, and this morning summoned a jury. It seems that the colored child had been adopted by Henry Allen and Eliza Smith, colored, who lived at the house where the body was found, and they were accordingly arrested. At the inquest several witnesses who live in the neighborhood testified that they had heard Eliza Smith beating the child, and saying she would kill it before it should be taken from her. One witness averred that on one occasion the prisoner had knocked the child down because it would not place its tongue on a hot stove plate. Two or three neighbors swore that the child was healthy and one said that the prisoner on the occasion of the death of another child in her charge, had said Allen killed it, but she was afraid to tell any one lest he would beat her. Allen and the woman in their statement said the boy which died yesterday had always been delicate and subject to spasms. On Sunday evening, they allege, while in a spasm he fell on the stove and hurt his head and was burned somewhat; that he afterwards died. Dr. T.S. Gibson, stated that he found a wound on the head made by a blunt instrument or a fall. The skull, he said, was fractured, and there was a depression of the brain. The jury returned a verdict that the child's death was caused by a blow upon the top of the head received in a way not known to the jury. The man and woman were committed until this evening, when they were taken before Mayor Strauss, who sent them on to the grand jury. (*Alexandria Gazette*, December 15, 1891, p.3.)

VERDICT - ... The prisoners were led to the bar and pleaded not guilty. After a trial the jury returned to the court and proceeded to give the following verdict: "We the jury find the prisoners not guilty. Therefore it is considered by the court that the prisoners be discharged." ...(*Alexandria Corporation Court Minute Book*, Vol. 9, July 11, 1892, p. 400.)

^^*^*^*^*^*^*^*^*^*^*^*^*^*^*

THE MURDER OF CAPT. REVELLE - An inquest was held at Riverside, Charles County, Maryland, yesterday over the remains of Capt. Benj. F. Revelle, who was murdered by a negro hand on his schooner, the *John A. H. Dixon*, in the Potomac on Monday. Two colored boys who were found on the boat with the body of Capt. Revelle testified that the crime was committed by a colored man named Benjamin Johnson, the mate. Johnson is probably now in Baltimore somewhere, as he left Pope's creek on the train Monday afternoon. The boys testified that the captain and Johnson had been quarreling upon several occasions since leaving Norfolk, and when off Cedar Point Johnson refused to obey the captain's order to lower one of the sails. The captain swore at him and the negro swore back, and when the captain went towards Johnson in a belligerent manner, the latter picked up a hand spike and struck the captain a violent blow and knocked him down. The assailant then remarked: "Damn him, I will finish him," and then struck him two more blows. When the captain was dead the murderer ransacked the cabin, and after telling the boys to remain on board, he left in the small boat for the Maryland shore. The murderer was seen Monday morning making his way to Pope's creek to take the train. He arrived there after the morning train had left, and did not leave the vicinity until the afternoon, when he boarded the train for Baltimore. He shipped his satchel by express to Annie Wilson, Baltimore, to be called for. The murderer is described as a thick, short man, about five feet six inches tall, weighing about 160 pounds, and about twenty-three years of age. John Brown, a colored man, twenty-eight years of age, was arrested at the Seventh Street wharf in Washington last night on suspicion of being the man who murdered Capt. Revelle. Brown declares that he had just arrived in that city from Portsmouth, and had never done any work on the schooner of which Revelle was captain, nor had he ever seen it. He looks like a countryman, and has none of the appearances of a man who would commit such a deed. (*Alexandria Gazette*, September 25, 1895, p. 3)

∧∧*∧*∧*∧*∧*∧*∧*∧*∧*∧*

ATTEMPTED MURDER – Officers Bettis and Beach learned a day or two ago that a colored man named Jerry Dorsey had been seriously assaulted on Christmas Day in the extreme southern portion of the city, and that the injuries he received may result fatally. It seems that the difficulty began in a saloon in that neighborhood, and that Dorsey, who was drunk used some insulting language toward three negroes names. Harry Gambrick, William Saunders and John Howard, Dorsey, it seems. threw one of the men out of the saloon. Later the four left the place and when Dorsey reached his home the trouble was renewed, during which Gambrick and Saunders used a razor and stones. Dorsey defended himself as best he could, and in the midst of the affray Howard appeared, with a gun and discharged it at Dorsey, the load of shot which was in it taking effect in his breast and neck. The assailants then left their victim. The latter crawled into his house and made no complaint to the authorities of the assault, nor did he seek medicial attention. This morning it was necessary to bring him to the Police Court room in a carriage. He was evidently in a critical condition. His legs were cut in several places and his clothing almost converted into ribbons by slashes from the razors; his head was also cut and his breast and neck terribly lacerated by the contents from the gun. After he had given his testimony he was put in a carriage and sent home with instructions to send for a physician at once. His assailants were held to await the results of his injuries. (*Alexandria Gazette*, December 30, 1895, p. 3.)

∧∧*∧*∧*∧*∧*∧*∧*∧*∧*∧*

POLICE COURT – The following cases were disposed of by Mayor Thompson this morning: Harry Gambrick and William Saunders, both colored, charged with assaulting and beating Jerry Dorsey, colored, were fined $10 each, or given 60 days on the chain gang. – John Howard, colored, charged with shooting Jerry Dorsey, was also fined $10, it being claimed the shooting was accidental. He was sent to the chain gang for sixty days in default of the payment of the fine. (*Alexandria Gazette*, January 11, 1896, p.3.)

∧∧*∧*∧*∧*∧*∧*∧*∧*∧*∧*

A MURDEROUS HUSBAND – The tranquility of south Lee street was disturbed this morning by a brutal attempt at wife-murder which occurred in a small brick house on the east side of that thoroughfare, between Gibbon and Franklin Streets. It was about ten o'clock when the murder was attempted, and from that time until now the neighborhood has been in a state of excitement. The would be murderer is Michael Thomas and the victim Mary, his wife. For several years the domestic relations of the couple have not been a sea of happiness, the wife having long ago found marriage, so far as her part in the contract was

110

concerned, a failure, and on more than one occasion has had to invoke the arm of the law for protection. It was one of these cases where the wife seemingly was disposed to do all the work and the husband was perfectly willing she should. The monotonous plod of such a life naturally told on the frame of the weaker vessel until existence was unendurable. They had parted and come together off and on for several years and the domestic broils which followed culminated in the bloody scene of today. It seems that Thomas had of late had the house to himself, the wife having left him, and yesterday he sent word for her to come to the house and get her belongings. It was while this part was being enacted that the murderous act took place. The husband and wife were in an upper room at the time, when a neighbor who was down stairs heard a scuffle and every indication of an angry scene in the room above. Supposing it to be a mere quarrel she called to the couple to cease wrangling, when she was horrified to hear three pistol shots in rapid succession, and before she could gather her senses Mrs. Thomas rolled down the stairs, the blood streaming from her head, face and side. Two bullet holes were in her face from which her life's blood was cascading, another on the left side near the region of the heart and two triangular wounds on the back of the head which had been inflicted with the blunt end of an axe. The axe is said to have been used on her first and the pistol was brought into requisition for the purpose of giving her a coup de grace. The corner of the axe had struck in each wound on the head and the skull was fractured in both places. The lady who was with her at the time gave the alarm and in a few minutes' time the neighborhood was aroused. Mrs. Thomas lay in a pool of blood, apparently dying, and one by one her relatives and friends as they entered wrung their hands in anguish at the spectacle presented. Drs. Jones and O'Brien were summoned and upon their arrival did all that medical science could suggest for the relief of the unfortunate woman, but it was generally conceded that her wounds were fatal. Her son, her only child, soon reached his home, and the anguish he manifested was a scene long to be remembered by all who were present. Leaving the dying woman, we will follow the murderer. After committing the horrid deed he skulked to Franklin street and took a southwesterly course over fields toward Hunting Creek bridge which he crossed, and upon arriving at the forks of the road on the opposite side he managed to summon nerve enough to cut his throat, severing the windpipe. He also cut both wrists. Policemen were immediately dispatched in the direction the murderer took and Mr. F. L. Entwisle loaned his wagon for the purpose of accelerating the pursuit. After some little search Mr. Sidney Pullman discovered Thomas lying in a ditch with his clothing saturated with blood. Later Officer Sherwood and Mr. Walter Cline came to the spot and the officer took the murderer in charge and brought him in Mr. Harry Catt's buggy to the station house in this city. Dr. Purvis, who attended him, found his injuries to be most serious, there being every likelihood of him dying from hemorrhage. In answer to questions Thomas admitted shooting his wife, but laid the responsibility of the affair on his mother-in-law, saying he should have shot her first. He thought he was dying, and said if he recovered he knew he would be hanged. He requested a friend whom he sent for to see that he was buried properly should his death ensue. Thomas came here from New Jersey several years ago. Mrs. Thomas was a Miss Cook, of this city.

During the afternoon it was found necessary to remove Thomas to the Infirmary in order that he could receive proper attention...

The condition of Mrs. Thomas has remained unchanged all the afternoon. Her life is at its lowest ebb and her death is momentarily looked for. (*Alexandria Gazette*, February 27, 1896, p.3.)

HOPE OF RECOVERY - Late yesterday afternoon Mrs. Mary Thomas, who was murderously assaulted by her husband, rallied somewhat and made a statement of the affair to Drs. Jones and O'Brien. She stated that her husband met her upstairs and there shot her three times. She started for the stairway and fell forward. When she fell upon the floor down stairs her husband followed and, seizing the axe, cut her in the head twice. ...The physician found Mrs. Thomas resting comparatively easy this morning. Her pulse was 85, and while her recovery is possible the chances are very slim. Her husband was attended by Drs. Purvis, Snowden and Smith and while there are chances of his recovery from the wound in his throat other complications may follow and prove fatal. He claims that the cause of the trouble was unfaithfulness on the part of his wife. (*Alexandria Gazette*, February 28, 1896, p.3.)

Mrs. Thomas is now thought to be steadily recovering from the injuries inflicted by her husband ten days ago. This morning she was able to sit up in her bed for a short while. (*Alexandria Gazette*, March 7, 1896, p.3.)

Mrs. Thomas's Condition - The condition of Mrs. Mary Thomas, who was murderously assaulted by her husband three weeks ago today, is said to be precarious, and it is feared the purpose of her husband may yet be accomplished. The two wounds made on her head with the axe are still in a bad condition. Last night Mrs. Thomas was semi-delirious and restless, and powerful sedatives had to be frequently used to render her tranquil. ... The self-inflicted wounds of her husband are slowly healing and the physician who is attending him thinks he will be in a condition to be taken from the Infirmary to jail by next week. (*Alexandria Gazette*, March 12, 1896, p.3.)

VERDICT - Commonwealth vs. Michael Thomas ...the prisoner was led to the bar and pleaded not guilty. Thereupon came a jury to wit: ...After a time they returned and presented the verdict: "We the jury find the prisoner guilty as indicted and fix the punishment at five years and six months in the penitentiary." ... (*Alexandria Corporation Court Court Minute Book*, June 22, 1896, Vol. 11, p. 464, 465.)

∧∧*∧*∧*∧*∧*∧*∧*∧*∧*∧*∧*∧*

STILL A MYSTERY - The finding of a body of Richard H. Bayliss in one of the docks of this city yesterday morning is still causing much speculation, and the belief is becoming stronger that the deceased met with foul play. The fact that his teeth had been knocked out and that there was a bruise over one of the eyes gives weight to the theory....

Messrs. Bert Tatsapaugh and George Cogan went in Zimmerman's place to get a lunch and saw Bayliss there in company with Clift and the stranger. They observed that the men were drunk and advised Bayliss to go home. After 12 o'clock they saw Bayliss and his companion whom they afterward learned was named Brown, pass the market building. Brown seemed to be in an angry mood and his mouth was bleeding. Witnesses heard him invite Mr. Bayliss to go on board his boat and spend the night with him, and the two started toward the wharf. This was the last they saw of them. (*Alexandria Gazette*, June 30, 1896, p.3.)

CORONER'S VERDICT – Coroner Purvis yesterday evening concluded his investigation into the circumstances attending the drowning of Richard H. Bayliss, whose body was found floating in one of the docks...

Dr. Arthur Snowden who assisted the coroner at the post mortem, testified that there was a contusion of the left eye of the deceased which had apparently been caused by a blow, and that the lower teeth had been knocked out. ...The jury rendered the following verdict: "That he came to his death by drowning at the hands of party or parties unknown to jury, but from the evidence suspicion points to one Brown, who was last seen with the deceased and who, it is said, lives near Occoquan." (*Alexandria Gazette*, July 1, 1896, p.3.)

INVESTIGATING THE SUPPOSED MURDER – The Police Court room was densely packed last night to witness the examination of George Brown, James Clift and James Reed, who had been arrested on suspicion of murdering Richard H. Bayliss on the night of the 27th ultimo. ...

The first witness was James Richards, who was evasive in his replies when questioned by Mayor Thompson and Commonwealth's Attorney Marbury. He stated that on the night of June 27, when the murder is supposed to have been committed, he went home at 10 o'clock until the following morning, when he was called for by James Clift, who wanted him (Richards) to purchase whisky for him. He pretended he did not know where he bought the liquor. He went with Clift to the Pioneer Mills wharf. He first stated that Clift gave him the money, but later that the whisky money was supplied by another of the party ... Beads of sweat chased each other down his face during the ordeal of his examination. Richards also contradicted himself by stating that he was at the fire which occurred that night about one o'clock. ...

Messrs. George Sutton and William Hayden testified that on the Wednesday following the crime Clift had been accused in their presence of knowing something about the murder, and had said, "Yes, I did it. I took $4.50 from the old man's pockets, hit him in the head with a stone, and threw him overboard." ...

Brown said he had been in company with Mr. Bayliss until after 12 o'clock at night; that he had met Clift during the evening, but he could not tell when he parted company or at what time or place. He left Mr.

113

Bayliss on King street, near Union, and went aboard his vessel a little after 12 o'clock.

James Clift testified that he met Mr. Bayliss and George Brown, both of whom had been drinking, at the corner of King and Union Streets. They wanted to know if he was looking for a fight, when he informed them he was looking for whisky. Then they joined him and all three came up-town and procured whisky at Zimmerman's saloon. This was a little before 12 o'clock. After going out they separated, he walking to the Pioneer Mills wharf, where he was joined by Remus Beach and Carrie Davis who assisted him in consuming the liquor. Between 1 and 2 o'clock Sunday morning he started for the bakery on north Lee street to get buns, when he met Brown and Bayliss near the corner of Cameron and Lee Streets. They wanted whiskey, and he told them he would conduct them to the Pioneer Mills wharf, where they could secure it. The two men accompanied Clift to that place and got the whisky, and, as Clift claims, left after drinking and paying for it....

It is the opinion of some that Mr. Bayliss was dead when seen on the wharf by the last witness. Beach had been summoned to appear last night as a witness, but he could not be found when the case was called. He will be arrested. (*Alexandria Gazette*, July 8, 1896, p. 3.)

...The examination of the witnesses consumed over an hour's time. It resulted in the release of James Reed on his own recognizance, but Brown and Clift were committed for a further hearing, which will take place on the 17th.

RELEASED - George Brown, James Clift and Oremus Beach, suspected of complicity in the murder of R. H. Bayliss, were dismissed in the Police Court last night with the understanding that should any additional evidence be procured they would be arrested. ...Since the arrest of these men there have been no new developments and the defense is prepared to prove that the man asleep on the Pioneer Mills wharf on the night of the alleged murder was Carey Davis. (*Alexandria Gazette*, July 14, 1896, p.3.)

THE KILLING OF JAMES CLIFT - The killing of James Clift by a freight train on the Southern Railway in the Wilkes street tunnel yesterday afternoon was mentioned in the *Gazette* at the time. Clift was very drunk when he entered the tunnel, and it is supposed by some that he fell on the track and went to sleep. Others think that, being a sufferer from heart disease, he may have been stricken with apoplexy.

John Coleman, the engineer of the train, says that at the time of the accident he was running at the rate of 10 or 12 miles an hour; that he saw an object on the tract ahead of his train but could not stop until after he had struck it. Clift was not lying across the rails, but in the middle of the track. The engine passed over him without doing him any injury, but the brake beam of a fruit car caught his clothing and dragged him about two squares. When the train reached the switch in the middle of the square between Royal and Pitt streets the foot of the unfortunate man caught in a frog which threw his leg across the rails, and when the cars were finally stopped what had a few seconds before been a living human being was a mass of quivering flesh. The leg which had been cut off was wedged into the frog so tightly that it required the strength of three men to pull it out. The body laid upon the track for about an hour, during which time a large crowd of people gathered. It was finally removed to the undertaking establishment of Mr. B. Wheatley, where an inquest was held...last night. "We the jury find that the said James Clift came to his death by the unlawful trespassing upon the property of the Southern Railway Company, it being proven that he was intoxicated at the time, and having been warned not to go into the tunnel, and furthermore that the railway company, by not having a flagman out, as they are required to do by ordinance, also running at a greater rate of speed through the city than the city ordinance allows, are co-responsible for the death of said James Clift." ... Clift's body is still at the undertaker's, but will be buried tomorrow from his home on Wilkes street. (416 Wilkes Street) (*Alexandria Gazette*, July 16, 1896, p. 3.)

＊∧＊∧＊∧＊∧＊∧＊∧＊∧＊∧＊∧＊∧＊∧＊

MURDER IN THE COUNTY - Rose Lowe, colored, with her head nearly severed from her body, was found Saturday night lying bathed in blood on the road leading from the Chain Bridge to the little settlement in Alexandria county known as Walker Chapel. Near the body of the woman Jesse Jackson was found with a ghastly wound in his throat, his head and his face beaten almost to a pulp, making a pitiful endeavor to gain his feet. His efforts were spasmodic, however, as he was clearly unconscious and he soon expired. The dead woman had left her husband and with her three children lived with Jackson. She frequently quarreled with her lover, especially when they had been drinking, and both are reported by the neighbors to have been drunken and shiftless persons. About a year ago Arthur Diggs, sometimes called Arthur Parker, a brother of Rose Lowe, took up his residence with her and Jackson. Diggs is now in jail in this city charged with being a murderer. Saturday afternoon Jackson and the woman left their cabin and went to Washington, ostensibly on a shopping tour. Both drank a good deal of liquor and quarreled. The man returned home about 2 o'clock in an intoxicated condition and frightened the children by taking a razor from a bureau drawer and brandishing it about recklessly. Suddenly he ran from the house in the direction of Washington taking with him a heavy cane with an iron pipe ferrule. He only went a short distance, however, as he was seen during the gloom of the evening leaning against the railing of a small bridge less than a mile from his home, but out of sight of any house he waited until nearly 9 o'clock, or until the Lowe woman came along, riding on a wagon in which were Frank and Edward Carter, two boys who drive an ash wagon and who live near the former home of the dead man and woman. Jackson ordered the woman to get out, which she did. The two at once commenced to quarrel and the Carter boys, becoming frightened, urged their jaded horses to a quicker pace up the hill. When they neared the top they heard the woman scream, and, looking back, saw her in the embrace of her lover. It was the embrace of death. Jackson took his razor and cut her throat from ear to ear. The blood gushing from the

115

awful wound soaked the ground about where the body fell. The Carters ran down to the Cabin and called Diggs, the brother, telling him that Jackson was beating Rose, and it is supposed he repaired to the scene. They then proceeded a quarter of a mile father to the home of the grandparents of the woman and roused them out of bed. The party (among whom was Diggs) proceeded down the road to where the body of the woman lay, and where Jackson's life was coming to a speedy close. It was discovered that his head had been beaten and his skull fractured in several places which, even without the gash in his throat, would have been sufficient to have caused his death. Returning to the blood soaked spot where the tragedy occurred, the party found the razor. The heavy cane with the iron pipe ferrule was found in the house where it is believed Diggs returned it after he had assaulted Jackson. This latter bore all the evidences of having been the weapon with which Jackson was beaten. Yesterday Justice Birch held an inquisitorial court, at which the above facts were elicited. The justice ordered Diggs' arrest pending further investiagtion, and he was brought to this city and incarcerated. Diggs stoutly denies the crime. During yesterday the bodies were viewed by neighbors for miles around. Unwatched they lay through the night on rudely constructed biers, the woman's remains in a shanty and those of the man in a blacksmith shop. (*Alexandria Gazette*, March 22, 1897, p.3.)

^^*^*^*^*^*^*^*^*^*^*

ATTEMPTED MURDER - Suicide of the Would-be Wife Slayer by Cutting His Throat with a Razor - 309 Gibbon Street.

The southeastern section of the city was thrown into a great excitement at an early hours this morning by the discovery of a colored man named Clem Dorsey in the alley bounded by Fairfax, Lee, Wilkes and Gibbon streets, with his windpipe severed and a bloody razor at his side. It was soon learned that the suicide had first attempted to kill his wife with an axe, and that she was lying home with a fractured skull and a horrible wound on the left side of the face extending from the forehead to the nose. Shortly after four o'clock this morning one of Dorsey's daughters appeared at the station house and frantically informed those on duty that her father had killed her mother with an axe. Officers started immediately for the scene, but the accused had fled and it was an hour later before his whereabouts were ascertained, when his lifeless body was found where stated above. Dr. Purvis, the Coroner, was notified, and he was soon on the scene, and Dr. Bechtel was called to render assistance to the injured woman. In the meantime the entire southern section of the city had been aroused, and Dorsey's house and the alley in which his body lay were besieged. The trouble which brought about the terrible deed dates back about one year. Dorsey had always been looked upon as an exceptional colored man, in this that he took care of himself, was always at work, was polite and was generally liked by his white acquaintances. He had worked in the press room of the government printing office at one time, had been a waiter at the Tontine, when kept by the Cooney Bros., at the Hygeia Hotel at Old Point, at hotels in Washington and of late had been a waiter at the Exchange and Ballard Hotel in this city. His wife is rather an attractive colored woman, and he has for some time believed her to be remiss in her allegiance to him. Some time ago he opened his mind to Lieutenant Smith, of the police force, and stated to him his suspicions. On that occasion he named Pat L----, a public school teacher, as a co-respondent and said he strongly contemplated killing L----. The lieutenant dissuaded him from any rashness, and told him to wait until he was positive his surmises were correct and then proceed against the parties in a lawful way. He didn't take the lieutenant's advice, however, but borrowed a pistol from Mr. C. W. Bell, telling him he was going into the country and might have use for it, but he intended killing either L---- or another colored man named Thomas G------ who, he alleged, had helped to destroy his domestic peace. On the 10th of last month he wrote a letter to Mr. C. W. Bell requesting him to take charge of his life insurance policy and turn it over to Mr. B. Wheatley in order that he could have a proper burial. The policy called for $50. He protested against being buried in Penny Hill. Dorsey asked Mr. Bell to attend to some other minor matters for him after his decease, and then went into an exhaustive history of his domestic troubles in which he charged his wife with infidelity and with meeting C----- and L----- at the houses of Laura Robinson and Lucy Baltimore. He charged his wife and mother-in-law with being responsible for the crime he was contemplating, and alleged that his wife's mother aided and abetted her daughter in her acts against him. His wife got possession of the pistol and also of another he borrowed for the purpose of killing C---- and L----. Dorsey sent another letter to Mr. Bell on Sunday, in which he confessed to borrowing the pistol for the purpose of killing C----. The remainder of this letter was a recapitulation of his previous charges against his wife, mother-in-law and the two men. He gave minute accounts of surprising his wife and her male friends under questionable circumstances. His letter throughout gave every evidence that he was contemplating a horrid crime. Dorsey also wrote letters to Mr. B. Wheatley and his own daughter Laura. The one to the former chiefly concerned the disposition of his body, and that to his daughter was a recommendation that she apply for assistance in procuring employment to Mrs. Darnell in Washington after his decease....

A coroner's jury met at Mr. Demaine's undertaking establishment, where the body had been taken.... The jury...brought in a verdict to the effect that Dorsey came to his death by his own hand. From the evidence in the case it seems that the deceased approached his wife this morning while she was lying in bed and dealth what he supposed was a fatal blow with an axe. His daughter who was sleeping alongside of her mother awoke and screamed and the would-be murderer fled. As stated above, the daugher proceeded to the station house and reported the matter. Dorsey in the meantime had repaired to the alley where he cut his throat. (*Alexandria Gazette*, April 7, 1897, p.2.)

KILLED HIS SON - A fatal shooting affray occurred at Mero post office, about five miles below this city, in Fairfax county, about 3 o'clock yesterday afternoon, in which Lovelace Brown, colored, killed his oldest son, Ulysses Grant Brown. The trouble occurred over some misunderstanding regarding the taxes on a piece of land about a mile below Mero. It seems that Lovelace Brown and his son were at the former's house, discussing the situation, when the son, on learning that his father had disposed of a portion of the property, grew angry and told him that he could sell the whole piece, and that he would raise no part of the taxes. Some words followed, and the men came to blows. The old man came out second best, and later left the scene and went to his home, which is but a short distance away. After Ulysses had finished his work he started for his home. At Mr. George Bartle's blacksmith shop he encountered his father, who had a revolver, and the trouble was resumed. It ended by the son being shot just over the heart. Mr. Bartle was the first man to reach the prostrate man. He carried him into the shop, where he died without regaining consciousness. The father left the body of his son lying in the blacksmith shop and walked leisurely to his home. The father claims that his son made a further attack on him and that he produced the pistol to frighten him, when it was discharged accidentally. Another account, however, is to the effect that the elder Brown approached bisson and said: "I am going to kill you." The son begged him not to shoot him. Then the old man emptied his gun into him. The reputation of Lovelace Brown throughout Mount Vernon district is said to be bad. A message was sent to the police headquarters in this city from Mount Vernon, asking that an officer be sent to make the arrest, as the inhabitants of that locality were afraid to interfere with Brown. Sergt. Smith and Policeman Knight left immediately, and were met at Mero post office by Justice Kirby, who issued the proper warrant. The officers proceeded to Brown's home, and found him in bed. Lovelace was brought to the station-house in the city where he was kept until this morning, when he was taken back to Fairfax jail to await the action of the grand jury. Brown was represented by Mr. J.M. Johnson of this city. ...The murdered man's wife is a domestic in the residence of Miss Mary Shinn on Pitt street. (*Alexandria Gazette*, January 20, 1898, p.3.)

POLICE COURT - Lovelace Brown, colored, arrested by Sergeant Smith and Officer Knight charged with killing his son, Ulysses Brown, colored in Fairfax County, was turned over to the Fairfax authorities. (*Alexandria Gazette*, January 20, 1898, p. 3.)

^^*^*^*^*^*^*^*^*^*^*^*

COLORED MAN KILLED - William Pinkney, colored, a well-known colored man, a cripple was shot and almost instantly killed about ten o'clock last night at the intersection of Duke and Peyton streets, by John Thomas Elzey, also colored. The motive for the shooting is not manifest, as no one near the scene at the time seems to know of any previous trouble between the two men. Some of the witnesses say Pinkney and Elzey were together at the head of Duke street about ten

118

o'clock last night; that Elzey drew a pistol and taking deliberate aim fired at Pinkney, sending a ball entirely through his heart; that after being shot Pinkney ran to the northwest corner of Duke and Peyton streets, where he fell, dying about five minutes later; that after the shooting Elzey ran north on Peyton street and escaped before the arrival of the police.

The news of the tragedy spread rapidly, and caused considerable excitement in the western portion of the city, and the affair having been reported to police headquarters Officers Knight and Ferguson went to the scene, and ordered Pinkney's body removed to Mr. Demaine's undertaking establishment, where a post mortem examination was held this morning. Later Lieutenant Smith and Officers Bettis, Beach and Knight, who were searching for the man, discovered him at his home on north Pitt street, near the Portner Brewery. He had barricaded the door but made no effort to repulse the officers, who placed him under arrest and carried him to the station house. Walter Elzey, a brother of the prisoner, had previously been arrested by mistake, but he was soon liberated. The murderer, who alleged that the shooting was accidental, told the officers that the pistol could be found near Beach's pond, in the "Petersburg" neighborhood, as after the shooting he had gone to that locality and secreted the weapon under a piece of tin. Search was made, but the pistol was not found. After telling other stories concerning its whereabouts he said he had buried the weapon near the pond, and that a piece of tin was over the spot. The officers made a subsequent search, found a sheet of tin where indicated and saw the earth had been dug up at that spot. Upon removing the earth a few inches the pistol, from which one cartridge had been discharged, was found....

Several colored people were nearby at the time the shot was fired, but the bulk of them pretended they knew nothing about the tragedy nor the cause of it.

Elzey is well known in this city, he having for some time been in the service of the Watkins Brothers, meat dealers, in the market. He was a soldier during the war with Spain and is about 20 years old. Pinkney was well known, especially around the railroad depots. His living has been gained as a blootblack most of the time. His home was on Park row, near the Fayette street depot. He was married and had one child. He was 27 years old....

The autopsy took place at Mr. Demaine's establishment about noon today. It was conducted by Dr. Jones and it was discovered that the ball entered between the fourth and fifth ribs, passing entirely through the heart and lodged in the muscles of the back. The ball was from a 32-calibre pistol.

No witnesses knew of any previous trouble existing between Elzey and Pinkney. Some of the witnesses averred that the prisoner and dead man were laughing together previous to the shooting. A young colored man, who was in a wagon with two others at the scene of the shooting seemed loth to answer questions and when asked if he saw Elzey shoot Pinkney he refused for a while to reply.

After several minutes had elapsed, the Coroner in the mean time having threatened to send him to jail, he answered that he did see the prisoner commit the deed. He was questioned so closely and became so excited that his stomach grew weak and it was soon cleared of its contents in the presence of Coroner, jury and spectators.

The jury subsequently brought in the following verdict:

"We, the jury, find William Pinkney came to his death from a gun shot wound in the heart, inflicted by Thomas Elzey."

The prisoner was later returned to jail. Pinkney's funeral will take place at 3 o'clock tomorrow afternoon. (*Alexandria Gazette*, September 16, 1899, p. 3.)

SENT ON – The case of John Thomas Elzey, colored, charged with the murder of William Pinkney, also colored, on Friday night last, was brought up again in the Mayor's court this morning. The only witness examined was Dr. T. M. Jones, who conducted the autopsy on Pinkney's body. He testified that death was caused by the bullet which penetrated the heart of the deceased, and also that the vest of the dead man had been burned by the powder, showing the close range of the shot. The Mayor sent Elsey on to the grand jury. (*Alexandria Gazette*, September 18, 1899, p. 3.)

VERDICT – Commonwealth vs. John Thomas Elzey..."We the jury find the prisoner guilty of involuntary manslaughter and fix the penalty at a fine of $5.00." (*Alexandria Corporation Court Minute Book*, April 30, 1900, Vol. 13, p.351.)

^^*^*^*^*^*^*^*^*^*^*^*^*

ANOTHER TRAGEDY – A shooting affray occurred in this city about seven o'clock last night, during which Thomas Bryant was shot and killed by Frank Payne, better known as "Nooks." Payne and Bryant it seems had been engaged in a game of cards in Wade's saloon, corner of Columbus and Wolfe streets, previously, when Payne happened to make a misdeal. Bryant attempted to reach for the money at stake, 6 cents, but Payne anticipated the move, and secured the pennies. Bryant demanded the money, but Payne refused to give it up, and later left the place. About 7 o'clock Bryant met Payne at the corner of Prince and Alfred streets and again demanded the money but Payne still refused when the shooting followed. The first statement concerning the tragedy was made by Payne and two other negroes named Lewis Carrington and Dennis Carter, and was to the effect that Bryant had used threatening language toward Payne and had produced a pistol and fired at him, the ball, it being alleged, striking Payne on the right side of the stomach. The three stated that Bryant on firing the shot started to run up Prince street, but had not gone many paces before Payne drew his pistol and fired two shots at Bryant. The latter staggered and turned southward into an alley leading through to Duke street. The shots had attracted considerable attention and persons who made an investigation found Bryant lying beside a fence in the alley, too weak to speak. Drs. Delaney, Purvis and Howard were soon on the spot, but by the time the physician arrived the man was dead. One of the balls had entered the back just below the left shoulder blade, passing through the region of the heart. Bryant's body was removed to the undertaking establishment of William Demaine by order of Coroner Purvis. Payne, who was soon arrested, together with Carrington and Carter, showed the officers a bullet which he alleged had been fired at him by Bryant and a hole the band of his trousers which he said it had cut in the course and some slight abrasions of the skin....

Dr. M. D. Delaney, who conducted the autopsy, was then called. He said that the ball had entered the left side just below the eleventh rib, passed backward and downward, and shattered the left kidney, cutting its artery. The ball was found lying free in the abdominal cavity. He had seen the abrasions on Payne which the latter claimed were made by a shot fired by Bryant, but witness did not think his story probable. The scratches looked like those made by a small knife, and he did not think a bullet could have inflicted them.

Mr. W. A. Brawner testified that the pistol which Bryant had yesterday evening was unloaded and out of order. He did not think it could have been fired. The improbability of finding the bullet which had been fired at close range in the lining of Payne's trousers was brought to the attention of the jury by Commonwealth's Attorney Marbury....

"We, the jury, find from the evidence that Thomas Bryant came to his death by a bullet wound in his body made by a bullet fired from a pistol while in the hands of Frank Payne with malicious and murderous intent. We recommend that the said Payne be held for the grand jury." ...

This is the second tragedy which has occurred in this city during the past few months. ... (*Alexandria Gazette*, March 28, 1900, p. 3.)

PAYNE CONVICTED - ...The jury did not reach an agreement until about eleven o'clock, five, it is reported, at first being for hanging and seven in favor of sending the prisoner to the penitentiary. An agreement was finally effected and the following verdict was brought in: "We, the jury, find the prisoner, Frank Payne, guilty of murder in the second degree and fix his punishment at imprisonement in the penitentiary for eighteen years." Judge Norton pronounced sentence on the prisoner and he was removed to the jail.

Dennis Carter and Lewis Carrington, both colored, who were held as accomplices of Payne, were sent back to jail and will be tried later on. (*Alexandria Gazette*, May 18, 1900, p. 3.)

CHAPTER SEVEN

Prostitution

A DISTURBANCE occurred at a house of ill fame, on North Pitt Street, near King, yesterday afternoon, about 6 o'clock. The front door was broken open and considerable excitement occasioned in the neighborhood, which was quelled by the appearance of the Provost guard. (*Alexandria Gazette*, December 16, 1862, p. 2.)

^^*^*^*^*^*^*^*^*^*^*^*^*

There are in the city of Washington, in ten precincts, one hundred and five houses of ill fame. (*Alexandria Gazette*, January 12, 1863, p. 4.)

^^*^*^*^*^*^*^*^*^*^*^*^*

Four women were arrested and carried before the Mayor this morning, charged with keeping a disorderly house at No. 48 North Henry street. They were fined six dollars each, and ordered to leave the city in twenty-four hours. (*Alexandria Gazette*, May 21, 1863, p. 2.)

^^*^*^*^*^*^*^*^*^*^*^*^*

PROSTITUTION IN CIVIL WAR, ALEXANDRIA, VIRGINIA - Camp of 26th Regiment Michigan Vols., Suffolk, Virginia - June 2nd, 1863 - ...We did Patriot duty in the city of Alexandria until April 20 (1863). Oh, if we didn't have gay times. There were about seventy-five houses of ill fame in that illustrous city and of course duty compelled us (officers) to visit them to see that everything was quiet, etc. The girls would do anything for us in order to keep on the right side of us for if we chose we could clean them out without ceremony - Suffice I never had so much fun in my life.... Lt. Charles E. Grisson.

^^*^*^*^*^*^*^*^*^*^*^*^*

GADSBY'S TAVERN: HOUSE OF PROSTITUTION - The scene of many fancy balls, parties, and receptions for George Washington, Gadsby's Tavern also functioned as a house of ill-repute during the Civil War. Robert McClure, who had been appointed Col. of the Union Cavalry by Governor Pierpoint of the Restored Government of Virginia, was proprietor of the establishment when he was charged with conducting a bawdy house.

123

A grand jury was empaneled as follows: Geo. C. Hewes, W. R. Howard, E. S. Boynton, P. G. Henderson, C. R. Grimes, R. Hodgkins, Samuel Baker, J. H. Baggett, Thomas Dwyer, E. Francis, D. R. Wilson, W. C. Richards, J. H. Robinson, Jas. Rudd, B. Wheatley and A. Moran who presented the following indictments: Against –

Robert McClure for keeping a house of ill fame, a true bill (*Alexandria Gazette*, October 4, 1864, p. 1)

Commonwealth vs. R. McClure, proprietor of the City Hotel – on an indictment for keeping a house of ill fame – witnesses examined and case argued and given to the jury, who not having agreed at the hour when the court adjourned were ordered to seal their verdict, and render it at the meeting of the court in the morning. (*Alexandria Gazette*, October 13, 1864, p.2.)

Wednesday – Commonwealth vs. McClure – on an indictment – verdict of the jury "guilty" and the fine fixed at $25 – motion by defendant to set aside verdict. (*Alexandria Gazette*, October 13, 1864, p. 2.)

Commonwealth vs. McClure – on an indictment – motion to set aside verdict overruled and judgment given for the fine ($25) with an order that the defendant be imprisoned until the fine is paid. R. M. McClure and Samuel Heflebower were recognized in the sum of $2,000 for the appearance of McClure at the next term of the Circuit Court, to await the action of said Court, on the exceptions to the ruling of this Court, and the judgment is stayed. (*Alexandria Gazette*, October 15, 1864, p. 1; Nov. 18, 1863, p.2.)

⋏⋏*⋏*⋏*⋏*⋏*⋏*⋏*⋏*⋏*⋏*

GARROTED – A soldier, from Fort Washington, made his appearance at the watch house last night, and reported that he had just been garroted by a soldier from Battery Rodgers and a man dressed in citizen's clothes, in the southwestern quarter of the city, and robbed of his overcoat, a watch belonging to the orderly sergeant of his company, and his pocketbook, which, luckily, contained but a small sum of money. All the parties had been at a house of bad repute, on West Street, and after leaving there, and when they had reached a point on the street not much frequented, the attack was made upon him. (*Alexandria Gazette*, December 30, 1868, p. 3.)

THE LATE GARROTING CASE – In Wednesday's *Gazette* appeared a notice of a garroting case that had occured here the preceding night. The following is a statement of the affair as narrated by the sufferer Samuel Edwin McClellan, a soldier from Fort Washington. He and George McDonald and two other soldiers from Battery Rodgers, and a man dressed in citizens clothes, had been at a house of bad repute on West street, kept by a woman named Frances Miller. While there he had eaten a cake which he supposed was drugged. At the invitation of one of the party he had started with them to some other house, but had not proceeded far, when having reached a sort of common, one of them said "this is the place", then he was suddenly seized by the throat from behind, bent backwards over a knee, and robbed of everything on his person, including his watch that belonged to sergeant Williams of Company M. 4th U.S. Artillery, stationed at Fort Washington. His assailants then started to walk away, leaving him lying on the ground, but as he attempted to rise, one of them said "the coat the s---of a b---h has on is worth ten dollars; let's have that too;" and fearing that they would murder him if he resisted, he allowed them to take his valuable overcoat. - Having got all he had, the highwaymen ran off rapidly, in one direction, while he, as speedily as he could, made his way to the station house. (*Alexandria Gazette*, January 1, 1869, p. 3.)

DISORDERLY - The police, last night, entered the house of ill fame on the corner of King and West Streets, kept by Frances Schmidt, and arrested George Schmidt, the husband of the proprietess, on a charge of disorderly conduct, a great noise being made in the house. This morning Schmidt preferred a charge of disorderly conduct and selling liquor without a license against his wife and the other inmates of the house. Accordingly Mrs. Schmidt, her two daughters and five other inmates, together with two male visitors were arrested and locked up in the station house, where they will be tried tonight. Their shouts, songs and disorderly conduct kept the neighborhood of the station house in a lively condition this evening. (*Alexandria Gazette*, December 20, 1876, p.3.)

ARRESTED - Mrs. Frances Schmidt was arrested today, at the upper end of King street, by City Sergeant Lucas on a capias issued by the Corporation Court. She was found guilty at the last term of the court of keeping a house of ill fame at the corner of King and West streets, and was sentenced to pay a fine of $200 and be imprisoned for fifteen days. On the rendering of the verdict and before process could be issued, she fled the city, and only returned this morning to see to the sale of her household effects, when the officer captured her as stated. (*Alexandria Gazette*, July 20, 1877, p.3.)

POLICE ITEMS - The women arrested two weeks ago, on complaint of a citizen, charged with keeping a disreputable house on Pitt street, between King and Prince, and released on their own recognizance for further examination before the Mayor to day, put in their appearance at police headquarters promptly at nine o'clock this morning, where the trial of the case took place. After hearing the evidence the Mayor informed the proprietress of the establishment that the law provided that the "general reputation of the house might be proved," and as six witnesses had testified that the house bore the general reputation of being one of ill fame, he would fine her, the proprietress, $100 and sentence her to ninety days in jail. The two girls, inmates of the house, were dismissed. An appeal was taken from the decision of the Mayor to the Corporation Court and bond fixed in the sum of $400, which was given without any trouble, and the parties left together with the large crowd of curious spectators, who had assembled to hear some "rich testimony," in which they were disappointed. (*Alexandria Gazette*, July 29, 1880, p.3.)

^^*^*^*^*^*^*^*^*^*^*^*

A DESOLATE CORNER – That there are many interesting relics of revolutionary days in Alexandria is a well known fact, and there are many places here, too, which ever recall to find scenes enacted in our midst during the four years' civil strife. One spot in particular has often thrown the mind of the writer in a long reverie when his duties or inclination called him to that locality. The place alluded to is the vacant lot at the southeast corner of King and Henry streets. Up to within a few years ago a large but rickety building stood upon that corner, and during the war, when any place where a terrapin could live was converted into a human abode, this edifce was turned into a cheap concert hall for the purpose of catering to the sensual soldiery and others who swarmed here. This corner then teemed with busy life, and the gay danseuse in her tarltan attire performed terpsichorean feats, while coarse paeins resounded through its halls, and the spangled waiter girls glided gleefully along amid the clatter of glasses and the crude jests of the inmates. But what a metamorphosis has taken place since them! The votary at this shrine of Astarte, after steeping his brain in forgetfulness of the serious nature of his soldierly life or the dangers of the battlefield, is sent to the front and dies amid the clash of war; the actors stray off to other parts many of whom die neglected; the first leasee meets his death in a street fight in Memphis; some of the fair actresses embark for a southern city in company with numerous others of like caste; the ships sinks and sea weeds become their winding sheets; the former pretty waiter girls, now grown older, despoiled of flesh enamel, spangles and pink and blue illusion, have long since been compelled to give way to another generation, and eke out miserable existences in divers ways and last of all, the building itself, as it were. unable any longer to stand desolate, with ichabod inscribed on every part, falls of its own volition; the debris is cleared away, a fence erected around the spot, and nothing left to tell the passer-by of its career but the stair-case imprints of the walls of an adjoining house. Truly, "The world passeth away and the lust thereof." (*Alexandria Gazette*, March 29, 1881, p. 3.)

^^*^*^*^*^*^*^*^*^*^*^*

ARREST OF COLORED FEMALE STREET WALKERS – Three colored female street walkers were arrested last night by officer Lawler, and arraigned before acting Mayor Douglass this morning on the charge of disorderly conduct. Two of them, Martha Brown and Sarah Terrell, in default of the payment of the fines assessed against them, were sent to the work house for thirty days. The other, being the party assaulted, was made a witness against her former companions, thus escaping a work house sentence, which she richly deserved. There are numbers of other colored girls whose unseemly conduct on the streets at night justly entitle them to a berth in the work house, or some other place, where respectable people would not be compelled to hear their obscene language and witness their vulgar behaviour. Fannie Boston, another colored street walker, was arrested this afternoon and locked up for trial tomorrow morning. (*Alexandria Gazette*, October 21, 1881, p. 3.)

^^*^*^*^*^*^*^*^*^*^*^*^*

POLICE NOTES – Acting Mayor James S. Douglass had before him this morning a colored girl named Fannie Boston for disorderly conduct on the streets at night...The Boston girl, in default of the payment of a fine assessed against her, was sent to the work house for thirty days.... (*Alexandria Gazette*, October 22, 1881, p.3.)

^^*^*^*^*^*^*^*^*^*^*^*^*

RAID ON A HOUSE IN BUZZARD'S ROOST – Late Saturday night Jackson Beach, white, swore out a warrant against Virginia Nelson, colored, charging her with keeping a house of ill fame. The warrant being given to officers McCann, Bettis and Davis to execute, they went to the house and arrested the proprietress, Virginia Nelson, a colored woman, and two white women, named respectively King and Summers. A number of men who were in the house at the time the officers made their appearance escaped through back doors and windows.

This morning the Mayor, on the evidence of Jackson Beach, and Ella Summers, Alcinda Boswell and King, the three women arrested in the house raided Saturday night fined the Nelson woman $50 and sentenced her to six months in jail. Mr. Edmund Burke, counsel for the accused, appealed from the decision of the Mayor to the Corporation Court. Virginia Nelson then gave bond in the sum of $100, with Lulu Nelson as security, for her appearance before the grand jury. (*Alexandria Gazette*, May 8, 1882, p. 3.)

^^*^*^*^*^*^*^*^*^*^*^*^*

A DISORDERLY HOUSE COMPLAINED OF – Complaint being lodged at police headquarters of the disorderly proceedings of a house on South Columbus St., Police Officer John Nightingill, who was sent to the place this morning, arrested Fanny Helm, colored, the proprietress, and another colored woman, an inmate. Both the women were locked up in the station house, but were soon released for their appearance for trial at 3 o'clock this afternoon, when the Mayor dismissed the warrant against them, and assessed the costs of the case against the complainant, Horace Johnson. (*Alexandria Gazette*, November 8, 1882, p. 3.)

FRIGHTFUL DEPRAVITY - The *Baltimore American* says: Sergeant Jones returned to Baltimore yesterday from Alexandria, with a girl named Mary Augustine, whom he had taken from a house of ill-repute. The arrest of this child discloses a shocking story. Some time ago Mrs. Laura Russell, who is well known among the demi-monde of Baltimore, took Kate Augustine and her sister Mary and her own daughter, a child of only twelve years of age, to a house in Alexandria. The woman took the girl Mary Augustine, but would not even consider harboring the child, saying she was entirely too young. Mary lived in the place some time, and took part in the life there with her sister. The parents of the child thought she was out at service somewhere; but when time passed and nothing was heard from her, they became uneasy, and told the police that their daughter was missing, and Sergeant Jones was sent to Alexandria, and found Mary. The girl is rather good-looking. Her eyes are large brown ones, and her face is quite pretty. She has dark hair, a well developed figure for a child of her age, and a pretty foot and ankle. (*Alexandria Gazette*, May 18, 1889, p. 3.)

^^*^*^*^*^*^*^*^*^*^*^*^*

AFTER AN ERRING HUSBAND - It has often been remarked that ardent swains often when courting can't be kept away from their imamoratas, but when they get married it is difficult to keep them in the house after dark. A young married woman in the southern section of the city who in her reveries recently has pondered this problem, and having her suspicions that certain other daughters of Eve were proving more congenial company to her husband than herself, became desperate it is said, a night or two ago, and wended her way to a house in which she had every reason to believe her "hubby" was ensconced. She entered an alley in the rear of the suspected house where, to her mortification, she beheld through the window the object of her search in an exceedingly happy frame of mind talking volubly with equally loquacious female companions. The neglected wife, after satisfying herself of the truth of the reports and inuendoes which had come to her ears proceeded to the front door of this retreat and knocked loudly. A female tripped to the front door and asked her business. The indignant wife demanded her husband, but the woman who had answered the knock positively denied that he was in the house. The wife was equally positive he was, and a scene was precipitated between the two women which drew a large bunch of people to the pavement. "Hubby" in the meantime escaped by the back way, and later the irate wife left vowing vengeance on the disturbers of her domestic relations. Since the occurrence of the above described scene several other young benedicts of the neighborhood who are charged with similar dereliction by visiting the same house have been staying home at night and probably will until the sensation shall have had its nine days' run, and their wives, who have been victims of neglect, are loud in their praises of the plucky woman who has thrown the bomb in the camp. (*Alexandria Gazette*, June 12, 1894, p. 3.)

DISORDERLY HOUSE RAIDED - A house kept by Gertie Cole, colored, in the alley bounded by Prince, Duke, Alfred and Patrick Streets, was raided last night by Officers Hall and Sherwood and the proprietress, a woman named Nannie Vines and a colored man named Edward Coyle arrested. This morning they were fined $5 each, or given thirty days in the work house. The neighbors have complained to the police often of the orgies carried on in this house, the Cole woman being charged with cursing and disturbing the slumbers of people living in the locality. Such conduct is said to be often kept up all night. (*Alexandria Gazette*, November 30, 1895, p. 3.)

^^*^*^*^*^*^*^*^*^*^*^*

DISORDERLY HOUSE RAIDED - For some time complaint has been made to the authorities of a disorderly house kept by a colored woman named Annie Hughes, near the Midland depot. Whites and blacks frequent the place, and property owners in the neighborhood claim that their property is being deteriorated in value by the existence of this house. The railroad officials also complain of the place, some of the colored firemen of the road being patrons of the house. Officers Bettis and Beach last night raided the place and captured two young colored women, the proprietress and two colored men. The white men escaped. This morning the proprietress was made to give security for her appearance before the Corporation Court for keeping a house of ill-fame and the two young women were sent to the work house under the vagrant act. The men were dismissed with a reprimand. (*Alexandria Gazette*, December 30, 1895, p.3.)

^^*^*^*^*^*^*^*^*^*^*^*

THE MYSTERIOUS CUTTING - It is now said that the man who was so seriously cut one night last week and whose wounds were dressed by Dr. O'Brien is a native of this city, and that he received his injuries in a house of ill-repute here. It will be remembered that the doctor was awakened after midnight and called upon to render assistance to a man who had been cut in several places on his body, and that the injured man and his friends refused to tell the doctor the circumstances of the case. The police are investigating the matter. (*Alexandria Gazette*, February 20, 1896, p.3.)

^^*^*^*^*^*^*^*^*^*^*^*

DISORDERLY HOUSES RAIDED - Officers Proctor, Young and Sherwood last night made a descent upon certain disorderly houses kept by negro women in the northwestern portion of the city near the Fayette street depot, and captured over a dozen of the inmates, about half of whom were women. These houses have long borne the reputation of being disorderly. They are the retreats of dissolute characters of both sexes, and their orgies have often been complained of. In one house nine babies were found nestled together in a bunch like a litter of pigs. The mothers had come here recently from Fairfax county, and from all that could be learned never were married. After this gang had been

129

taken to the station house the officers found John Bright, white, and Georgie Holmes, colored, living together as man and wife, and Georgianna Lucas, white, and Chas. Haskins, colored, and Malzina Swallow, white, and Philip Ford, colored, engaged in the same conduct. They were also put under arrest. This morning they were fined $5 each. Bright and his dusky company paid, but the others, having no money, were sent to the work house and chain gang. (*Alexandria Gazette*, August 19, 1896 p. 3.)

^^*^*^*^*^*^*^*^*^*^*^*

DISORDERLY HOUSES RAIDED - Sergeant Smith, with Officers Young, Beach, Arrington, Deane, Ticer and Sherwood, raided several disorderly houses in the northwestern part of the city last night, and eight of the inmates were arrested and locked up. Four of the prisoners were men and the other four women. People living in the neighborhood of Payne street, between Queen and Princess streets, have several times complained of the orgies in houses of this sort which at present are maintained by negroes who are working on the Washington extension of the Mount Vernon Railroad. The accused were fined $5 each this morning. Only one paid, a man named Gordon. The other three men were sent to the chain gang and the women to the work house. (*Alexandria Gazette*, May 7, 1896, p.3.)

^^*^*^*^*^*^*^*^*^*^*^*

FINED FIFTY DOLLARS - Matilda Poindexter, colored, was brought into the Police Court last night charged with keeping a disorderly house in a respectable neighborhood in the southeastern part of the city. The evidence was to the effect that the house was a nuisance to the locality, that disorderly scenes were often enacted therein, that white women from north Lee street frequented the place, while it was also a rendezvous for dissolute colored women. It was also shown that certain people who did not want to be seen in questionable localities patronized this bagnio. The Poindexter woman had been warned several times by the police, but she persisted in her course, until her neighbors appealed for redress. She was fined $50, and if she fails to pay that sum she will be sent to jail for sixty days. (*Alexandria Gazette*, July 7, 1896, p.3.)

^^*^*^*^*^*^*^*^*^*^*^*

RAID ON A DISORDERLY HOUSE - Lieutenant Smith with Officers Davis, Wilkinson, Lyles, and Bettis raided a disorderly house conducted by negroes on the east side of Alfred street between Prince and Duke about 1 o'clock this morning. The place is run by the Solomon family, and has often been complained of as a nuisance, it being the resort of men and women. Six men and three women were arrested. This morning they were fined $5 each. This house was raided one Sunday last summer, and when the officers entered they found the inmates undressed. (*Alexandria Gazette*, January 1, 1897, p.3.)

ANOTHER DEN RAIDED – On Saturday night about 12 o'clock, Policemen Bettis and Knight raided a house on Peyton street, occupied by colored women. As the officers entered a negro named John Bryant jumped through a second-story window, carrying the lower sash with him, and landed on a pile of bricks below. Before the officers could reach him he made his escape. The remainder of the crowd were brought to the station house, where they gave their names as Wm. Alsop, George Gordon, Edward Carter, Mary Rich, and Mary Pierson. Their cases were disposed of in the Police Court this morning, each being fined $5 or given terms in the work house or on the chain gang. This house has often been complained of. It is of a class which have become numerous in Alexandria in late years, where negroes of both sexes congregate and indulge in all sorts of unseemly conduct. (*Alexandria Gazette*, January 4, 1897, p. 3.)

^^*^*^*^*^*^*^*^*^*^*^*^*

AFTER THE IMMORAL – The calls for city aid still come in to the authorities. Many of the solicitations are from colored women who are "grass widows," whose husbands have left them with helpless children to shift for themselves, and they are, of course, worthy objects for help. This condition of things has often been brought to the attention of the authorities, and efforts have from time to time been made to bring the delinquents to justice. ... The police have been instructed to ferret out all characters who are guilty of this species of misdemeanor not only among colored people but of the white element also (as the authorities have their eyes on several of the Anglo-Saxon race) and bring them to justice. The fine under the State law is from $50 to $500. This afternoon the police were engaged in raiding the houses of women, white and colored, who are known to be leading immoral lives, and a large number were arrested. (*Alexandria Gazette*, February 12, 1897, p. 3.)

RAID ON THE IMMORAL (Continued)... As was stated yesterday, the police have been ordered to ferret out all cases in this city where immorality is carried on, especially those where men and women not married are living together, and to-day a number among the colored element have saved themselves trouble by getting married. Raids were made on many such parties yesterday afternoon and the number brought before the Mayor this morning reached fifty-one. Forty-eight were disposed of and the remainder with additional parties who are to be arrested during the day will be tried tonight. Probably the largest crowd ever attracted to the station house was on hand last night in expectation of witnessing the trials, which, it was expected, would come off, but they were necessarily postponed until this morning. Long before eight o'clock Market alley was crowded with an eager throng, and when the door was opened in five minutes' time every available inch of space in the court room was occupied. There were fifty-one cases on the docket, and an all-day's sitting of the court seemed probable, but after forty-eight cases had been disposed of court adjourned until 7 o'clock to-night. The first case called was that of a young colored man charged with leading a mulatto girl astray. The case was clearly proven and the Mayor told the accused he could marry the girl or go to the grand jury. The prosecutrix was willing, but Barkis was not, and the accused was sent on to court. Then followed the cases which had attracted the crowd. The proprietresses of several well-known dives were brought into the dock. This class had the fines reduced to $12 and ten days in jail. They mostly urged that if released they would shake the dust of the city from their feet immediately. Judgment in these cases and in those of the inmates who had been fined for immoral conduct was suspended for ten days, at the end of which time they were told to appear and answer judgment. A host of negroes of both sexes who were charged with lewdness were fined $6 each. In all the cases the Mayor admonished the accused that if they continued in the commission of this species of misdemeanor he would have them arrested and impose the full penalty of the law upon them, which is from $50 to $500. Last night the station house was crowded to its fullest capacity, and every effort was made to render the female prisoners comfortable. The upper rooms were occupied by the white women and they smoked cigarettes and acted as jovially as though in their own houses. There was considerable sympathy expressed for them on account of their sex, but every one realized that the offense for which they had been apprehended was one which it is necessary to occasionally check. Some in the group have long since become back numbers, age, wrinkles and gray hairs showing that they have seen their day and are destined to die in poverty and neglect. Others, in he midsummer of lives of dissipation, who thoughtlessly imagine they will always attract, made themselves as conspicuous as possible. In a few years they, too, will be compelled to stand aside for another generation, when the gilded halls of vice will be no longer their homes and they will find themselves repudiated and neglected by the very people who are now rushing them through the butterfly existence of a short summer. People naturally feel sorry for the female sex when they get entangled in the law; but in our commiseration the facts should not be ignored that a very large percentage of the ills to which flesh is heir come from the deliberate violations of the law of God and man, and the sins of past ages are often visited upon succeeding generations. While our sympathy is excited the fact remains that to tolerate lasciviousness is a danger more to be dreaded than gambling or any other species of misdemeanor, for those who make it a business steel their consciences to the results, and notwithstanding their mode of life brings people to untimely deaths by the curse of an outraged heaven and is a fruitful cause of murder and attempts to murder, they persist in defying God and man. All will remember the attempted murder and suicide at the corner of Lee and Duke Streets about a year ago, to say nothing of previous tragedies in our streets or attempts on human life in which lewd women figured. (*Alexandria Gazette*, February, 13, 1897, p. 3)

∧∧*∧*∧*∧*∧*∧*∧*∧*∧*∧*∧*∧*

ASSAULT ON A WOMAN - There was a row on north Lee Street last night about 10 o'clock in the house kept by Rosa Moore. Cries of "murder" were heard issuing from the place, and it appeared that Sam

132

Simmons had assaulted Bertie Gibbons, choked her and threw a lamp at her. The lamp had exploded and set fire to the room. The fire was extinguished by some men, and Officers Hall and Goods, who were attracted by the cries, followed the proprietress and the man accused of the assault for about two blocks away from the house and then placed them under arrest. Simmons was fined $5 by the Mayor this morning. (*Alexandria Gazette*, July 30, 1897, p. 3.)

^^*^*^*^*^*^*^*^*^*^*

The Mayor this morning in the trial of cases of disorderly conduct on King Street Saturday night alluded to the difficulty of establishing the disorderly character of houses where disturbances were started and he said that while the police made arrests of disturbers of the peace, the houses could not be punished unless citizens assisted. (*Alexandria Gazette*, November 26, 1900, p. 3.)

^^*^*^*^*^*^*^*^*^*^*

WOMEN FOLDING TENTS - Inmates of North Lee Street Resorts Shaking City's Dust From Their Feet. - Tomorrow night at midnight will witness the final evacuation of the "red-light" district of Alexandria, which for more than fifty years has existed on Lee Street in the northeastern portion of the city. Chief of Police Goods today notified all of the women living in the district that the houses must be closed tomorrow night in accordance with the order which was given by Mayor Thomas A. Fisher, more than a month ago.

The action was taken by Mayor Fisher at the suggestion of Judge Louis C. Barley of the Corporation Court who came to a conclusion that the houses must be closed following the passage of the Kenyon bill in Washington. Conditions had become so bad in Alexandria, due to the influx of male visitors from Washington to Alexandria's district, as to cause serious inconvenience to the passengers on the electric cars between the two cities.

Chief Goods stated today that he did not think that there would be any trouble in closing the houses. A number of the women have already left the city and others were busy packing their belongings today. Police will be stationed in the district tomorrow night to see that the orders are carried out.

Mrs. E. F. Robertson, secretary of the National Florence Crittenton Mission, who made a census of the inhabitants of the district at the request of Judge Barley, has offered to provide homes for any of the women who wish to accept her offer, but it is said that there will be very few who will do so.

Some houses in the segregated district in which nocturnal revels have, been carried on almost as far back as the recollection of the oldest inhabitants have become as Tara's Hall and others will within a few hours be tenantless.

During the past half a century such resorts have been segregated the northeastern section of the city being Alexandria's White Chapel. Almost as soon as any questionable house was established elsewhere the authorities have pounced upon proprietress and inmates and they were kept moving until eventually they have taken up their abode in the tolerated district.

Long before the Civil War this same neighborhood bore the stigma of the scarlet woman, and many of her votaries infested what was known as "Clay Hill" the extreme northeastern section of the city, and "Blackdog Alley," in the square bounded by Lee, Union, Duke and Prince Streets.

The latter was cleansed many years ago, but when the civil war began an army of lewd men and women followed the soldiers to this city. They roosted in every section, some of which now form the residential neighborhoods, where the most disgraceful orgies were conducted. There were five brothels on Prince street, between Royal and Fairfax, and equally as many more on Prince street, between Lee and Union and on Wolfe street, between Fairfax and Royal.

At that time more such resorts were in the western section than in any other portion of the city, especially on West street. Numbers were on King street also, while concert halls, free and easies, and similar places were situated in different places.

At the close of the war the work of eviction began, and in a few years the undesirables gradually took up their abode in the most un-desirable quarter of the city, where they have remained until their nests have been disturbed by the orders of the court. (*Alexandria Gazette*, June 12, 1914, p. 2.)

CHAPTER EIGHT

Rapes

RAPE CASE – We learn that, some two months since, a negro man (slave) committed a diabolical outrage on the person of a little white girl, not more than eleven or twelve years old, in Alexandria county, Virginia, near the west or south end of the Georgetown aqueduct; and further, that Justice Drummond, of that county, promptly issued a warrant for the arrest of the miscreant, who, owing to the subsequent interference of some parties, has not yet been taken into custody. – *Washington Star*. (*Alexandria Gazette*, August 24, 1857, p.3.)

^^*^*^*^*^*^*^*^*^*^*^*^*

BROKE JAIL – The colored man named Wesley Morgan, committed to jail on the 21st ult., for a rape committed the night previous upon Adalina Banks, a colored girl under twelve years age, on the Gas House lot, effected his escape about dark last night, and is still at large. The prisoners were in the jail yard making the usual preparations for the night when the cook, having been called out of the kitchen temporarily, Morgan came to the window of that apartment, on the North side of the jail – a quarter forbidden to the criminals – mounted it, climbed to the window above, from which he jumped to the outside wall, and in an instant, was over it and free. (*Alexandria Gazette*, September 7, 1867, p. 3.)

^^*^*^*^*^*^*^*^*^*^*^*^*

ATTEMPTED OUTRAGE – An attempt was made yesterday by a colored boy between sixteen and eighteen years old to outrage the daughter of Mr. Emanuel Webb, a little girl about twelve years old. Mr. Webb resides near Colross, in the extreme northwestern section of the city, and his daughter was returning from the house of Mr. Philip Rotchford, who lives at "Mush Pot," about a quarter of a mile further out, where she was in the habit of going for milk, when she was met near the bridge in the bottom by her assailant, who threw her down, and would have accomplished his purpose had he not been alarmed by her screams and by the noise made by some one approaching through the adjoining corn field. The villain is known, and efforts are being made to effect his arrest. (*Alexandria Gazette*, September 4, 1869, p.3.)

OUTRAGE - Yesterday morning, about ten o'clock, a man named Henry Church met a little girl, between eleven and twelve years of age, the daughter of Mr. William Brown, who lives on Columbus, between Franklin and Jefferson streets, in the gully running down to Hunting Creek, near the brick-yard of Tucker & Lucas, with a basket full of chips, which she had collected on the creek shore, upon her arm, and brutally outraged her. Some of the police were informed of the circumstances of the case soon after its occurrence, but the affair was kept very quiet until nightfall, when a general attempt was made to capture the villain, and though he successfully eluded the officers, he was caught on Nailor's Hill, between seven and eight o'clock, by George Webster and Thomas Javins, two young men living in that neighborhood, and carried to his victim by whom he was at once recognized and identified. He was then taken by his captors to the jail, on the way to which they were met by constable Burnett, to whom the prisoner was turned over, and Justice Beach, who lives near the jail, being sent for, at once committed him for further examination. The unfortunate little girl, though conscious, is severely injured, is unable to move without the severest pain, and cannot possibly appear against her ravisher for several days. It is needless to say that the greatest excitement was occasioned in the vicinity of the occurence, and when the arrest was made threats of lynching were frequently heard among the crowd which had been attracted by the cries of the prisoner, who had been knocked down by one of his captors for attempting to break away from him, after he had refused the offer of a bribe of twenty dollars to let him go, but he was hustled away so quickly to prison that no time was allowed for these threats to be put into execution. (*Alexandria Gazette*, October 21, 1869, p.3.)

THE LATE OUTRAGE - The rumor current on the streets this morning that an attempt had been made last night to take Henry Church, the man charged with committing the outrage upon Mr. Brown's little daughter on Wednesday morning last, out of jail and lynch him, was without any foundation in fact. - Between nine and ten o'clock last night three unknown men did knock at the jail door, but Mr. Hudgins, the turnkey, would not open it, and when they asked to see Church, the Sheriff, who happened to be there at the time, went out through the door of his private residence and informed them that they could not see the prisoner at that hour. They then left immediately.

The condition of the poor little girl is represented as terrible indeed, and her father says that he believes a knife was used by the perpetrator of the outrage.

As the crime was committed outside of the corporation lines, and within the limits of Fairfax county, Deputy Sheriff Kirby, of that county, says he will start with Church for Fairfax C. H. on Wednesday morning next. (*Alexandria Gazette*, October 23, 1869, p.3.)

TRIAL OF HENRY CHURCH - As no grand jury for the County Court will meet until January, and as the prisoner will then have the privilege of electing to be tried by the Circuit Court, Henry Church, who committed the late outrage in this city, will not be tried before February next. (*Alexandria Gazette*, November 1, 1869, p.3.)

AN UGLY CASE – Last night, between 8 and 9 o'clock, cries of murder were heard proceeding from a house on Pitt street, between Princess and Oronoco streets, located in a place known as Piper's Cove, and the denizens of the neighborhood running in, found a man struggling with an old woman, about sixty years of age, named Fanny Free, alias McCann. This morning the woman McCann came to the station house and swore out a warrant against Frank Lovejoy, a justice of the peace of the city, charging him with having committed an outrageous assault upon her. Before the warrant was issued, Acting Mayor J. T. Beckham and Justice Wm. H. May had a number of witnesses summoned, and heard their testimony in regard to the matter, which was to the effect that Lovejoy went to the house where the old woman lives and entered it through a window. Finding the old woman in bed he got in too, when the old woman pushed him out, and a scuffle ensued, in which the old woman was bruised about the head. He finally succeeded in overpowering her, when she cried for help and when the witnesses entered the house they found the old woman on the floor, in a position that indicated that a brutal assault had been made upon her, Lovejoy still holding her by the throat. The old woman's first statement corroborated this evidence but after she left the station house, and had an interview with Lovejoy, her story was somewhat modified. The witnesses, five or six in number, however, who saw a part of the transaction, adhered to their version of the affiar. After the examination of the witnesses a warrant was issued for Lovejoy's arrest, but up to three o'clock this evening the accused could not be found. The city was alive with the story this morning, and there seemed to be very little sympathy with Lovejoy, but his friends state that he was drunk and had no intention of committing the crime with which he stands charged. The woman upon whom the attempt was made is a little ugly woman, not less than sixty years of age, and Lovejoy is comparatively a young man, with a family. He has been Justice of the peace for some years, elected from the Third ward, and heretofore, no one would have thought of charging him with such a foul crime. (*Alexandria Gazette*, February 24, 1880, p.3.)

LOVEJOY CASE – The case of Justice Frank Lovejoy, charged with having committed an assault upon the old woman Ann McCann, is still the subject of much talk. He is still at large, and is supposed to have left the city. The old woman, who applied for the warrant now says the story is not correct; that Lovejoy came to her house and entered it through the window, but that he did not assault her. The witnesses, however, still maintain the correctness of their story, as related yesterday. The old woman was called upon today, and she stated that she was about sixty-five years of age; that she had been married three times and was the mother of children; that Lovejoy had been in the habit of coming to her house, but when he came Monday night he was very drunk, and she attempted to put him out. This, she says, was the cause of the scuffle in which she received a black eye; that Lovejoy did not attempt to choke her, and that the colored people who testified yesterday were prejudiced against him. The character of the old woman, upon whom the alleged attempt was made, is not above reproach, and it is supposed by the friends of Lovejoy that he had been in the habit of going to her house, but being drunk on Monday night his visit was not acceptable, and hence the charge. It is said by some that Lovejoy was in the city last night and that he intended to give himself up, but being informed by some one, by mistake, that a number of colored men were approaching his house, he left in a hurry. Information received here this evening says that Lovejoy was arrested at Herndon this morning by some wood sawyers, but they having no warrant for his arrest, turned him loose, and the last seen of him he was going toward Centreville. Of course, many of the stories told are exaggerated, and after all the old woman's second story may be the correct one, for it is hard to believe that Lovejoy or any one else, knowing the penalty, would commit such a crime. (*Alexandria Gazette*, February 25, 1880, p.3.)

THE LOVEJOY CASE – The case of Justice Frank Lovejoy, charged with attempting an assault on the old woman McCann, is still the subject of much talk. The statement made in the Gazette yesterday that he had been arrested at Herndon by some colored wood sawyers was correct. When arrested, Lovejoy told them that they would have to pay his fare to Alexandria if they held him. This statement was sufficient, and they let him go immediately. The friends of Lovejoy say that on the morning after the assault he had no knowledge of being at the house, and the old woman stated this morning that it was his custom, when he came to her house, to enter through the window. Policemen Walker and Arnold went on the W. & O. Railroad this morning in search of him. Officer Walker returned this afternoon without him and Officer Arnold went on to Round Hill. It was reported on the streets this morning that he would return this evening and give himself up, but up to four o'clock he had not made his appearace. There is a great deal of sympathy expressed for his family. Lovejoy is said to be a good machinist and is capable of making a living anywhere. Up to the time of his appointment as a magistrate he was an industrious man. (*Alexandria Gazette*, February 26, 1880, p.3.)

^^*^*^*^*^*^*^*^*^*^*^*^*

A DESTESTABLE CRIME – About two or three months ago a Frenchman, calling himself Pietro Leone, came to this city from Norfolk, and renting two rooms in a building on north Royal street, near the Market House, stocked it with tropical fruits, nuts, etc. and soon secured a fair share of public patronage. Though mild and courteous to his customers, there was something in the man's countenance and actions which seemed to indicate that his civility was more assumed than real. Of late he has had in his partial employ a small girl between eleven and twelve years of age, named Melvina Robey, whose parents reside in this city and at whose house he took his meals. This child was occasionally employed by Leone to wait upon the shop, but recent occurrences have caused some to think that the man's real purpose in having her in the shop was for reasons far more base. Adjoining and over the fruit shop is the printing office of Mr. J. M. Hill, the rooms of which are separated only by a wooden partition. For several days past persons at work there and in the room above have grown suspicious of Leone, and openly hinted that the relations between him and his little female clerk were anything but proper. Subsequent events serving to strengthen this conjecture, holes were bored through the floor in order that, if their surmises proved correct, they could have the man arrested. It was not long before they had an opportunity of strengthening their suspicions in the culpability of Leone, as between five and six o'clock yesterday evening, hearing the latter and his victim in the room back of the shop, they peered through the orifices in the floor and soon witnessed enough to satisfy them of the bestial and depraved nature of the girl's employer. The persons in the printing office called to Leone to release the child, which he refused to do, and threatened to kill them should they interfere. John Mills, one of the young men who had witnessed the transaction, hastened around to the Mayor's office, procured a warrant and in a short time the Frenchman was in the hands of policemen. The crowd on Royal street when the officers arrived at Leone's shop was dense, as by that time the nature of the latter's offense had been passed from mouth to mouth, and threats of lynching were more than once heard. The girl had gone to her home, and Leone was as speedily as possible secured in a cell in the station house. The accused is a low-set man, a specimen of the genus homo in whom a phrenologist would immediately determine the sensual exceeds the intellectual nature. He landed here, as above stated, from Norfolk, out of which city, it is said by some he was run for offences similar to that for which he has been arrested here.

The trial was set for twelve o'clock today before the Mayor, and the precincts of the station house were deemed too contracted for the crowd which desired admission; hence it was concluded to try the case in the Corporation Court room. A few minutes after the doors were opened the room was packed to suffocation – so much so that the doors were locked to prevent any others entering – while an equally large concourse was without clamoring for admittance. The young men employed in the printing office, together with others who happened to be there at the time, testified substantially and positively what has been recited above. Dr. T. Marshall Jones, who made the necessary examination of the girl, however, testified that so far as he had been able to discover no traces of assault existed. The girl, too, denied in toto everything that had been urged against Leone, saying the latter was not only innocent of the charge of assault, but of taking any other liberty with her. Upon this testimony the prisoner was released upon the charge of assault, but rearrested on the charge of attempted outrage, and held in the sum of $1,000 for his appearance before the grand jury of the Corporation Court. Leone was defended by Mr. George Mushback.

While being taken down the Court House steps, after the trial, Leone was struck by the brother of another little girl who, it was stated at the trial, the prisoner had been tampering with. He was not hurt, however, and soon after lodged safely in jail. (*Alexandria Gazette*, June 3, 1885, p.3.)

The stock of fruits, etc. belonging to Pietro Leone, who was yesterday sent to jail for assaulting little girls, was sold yesterday evening at his request to pay such debts as he owed in this city. (*Alexandria Gazette*, June 4, 1885, p.3.)

∧∧*∧*∧*∧*∧*∧*∧*∧*∧*∧*∧*∧*

A SERIOUS CHARGE - Ada Jinckins, thirteen years old, went to the station house this morning and made a serious charge against her brother-in-law, Joseph Clark, who, she alleges, attempted to assault her last night. The girl said Clark came to the house where she lived and begged her to come to his residence and minister to her sister (his wife) who, he claimed, had become suddenly ill. Ada at first refused on account of the intense cold to accompany him, but he soon returned and importuned her to go with him, saying his wife's condition had grown much worse. Ada finally assented and followed him down Franklin street. Clarke entered a grove of trees forming what is known as the Mulbery lot, when Ada suggested that he did not live in that neighborhood. Clarke replied that his wife was at his father's house. He then made known his real intention. The screams and resistance of the girl brought about a temporary truce, but she alleges her would-be assailant finally pulled her into a neighboring alley where he renewed his attempt. Her shrieks, however, caused him to desist, and she fled to her home. The complainant reluctantly told her story. A warrant was issued and Clarke was found near a saloon on Gibbon street. He was locked up. It is said that Clark was under the influence of liquor last night. (*Alexandria Gazette*, January 26, 1897, p.3.)

POLICE COURT - Joseph Clarke, charged with criminal assault on Ada Jinckins, was sent on to the grand jury. (*Alexandria Gazette*, January 27, 1897, p.3.)

A special grand jury, with R. P. W. Garnett as foreman, was sworn and returned an indictment against Joseph Clarke for an attempt to commit rape upon Ada Jinckins, a girl of thirteen years. (*Alexandria Gazette*, January 29, 1897, p. 3.)

SHE RECANTS - It having been learned that Ada Jinckins, the complainant in the case of Joseph Clarke, indicted for attempting to commit an assault, had gone before a notary public and made affidavits that the statements she made in the Mayor's Court and before the grand jury recently were not true, and it being believed by the Commonwealth's Attorney that she is being tampered with as a witness, she was today, by order of the Corporation Court, placed in charge of Mrs. John Robey for safekeeping till the case comes up tomorrow. This morning, before the girl was turned over to Mrs. Robey, Commonwealth Attorney Marbury sent Officer Roberts after

140

her. At the station house she acknowledged that she had recanted the charges made at first against Clarke. She said that Clarke went to Mr. Beach's residence, where she was staying, and asked her to go with him to her sister's house; that Clarke was drunk, and on the way he fell and in doing so knocked her down and hurt her. She returned to Mr. Beach's house and told her story, when Mrs. Beach told her to go to the station house and prefer the charge of criminal assault. Mr. Marbury today received an anonymous letter telling him that the girl is being tampered with, and warning him that everything is being done to prevent Clarke from being brought to justice. (*Alexandria Gazette*, February 9, 1897, p.3.)

FOUND GUILTY - Joseph Clarke was today found guilty of attempted criminal assault upon thirteen year old Ada Jinckins, and the jury fixed the term of imprisonment at nine years in the penitentiary. Mr. S. G. Brent appeared for the accused and Mr. Leonard Marbury conducted the prosecution. It was stated yesterday that the complainant had gone before Mr. K. Kemper, a notary public, and made an affidavit to the effect that her evidence before the grand jury was false. This was believed to have been caused by coercion on the part of those interested in the accused, and this morning's developments proved the theory to be correct. When the case was called the little girl was put upon the stand and she reiterated the revolting story she told the officers at the station house, the Mayor and the grand jury, and in childish simplicity recited how the mother of her assailant and "the others," as she termed them, coerced her into going to Mr. W. P. Graves and Mr. Kemper and making different statements. The child is an orphan and before going upon the stand said she had promised her dead mother to always speak the truth and she had made up her mind to do so on this occasion. The child related all the details of Clarke's crime, and she told how he came to Mr. Beach's house twice after her. (This part of her story was fully corroborated by Mr. William Zimmerman and other members of Mr. Beach's family, and the story set afloat yesterday that Mrs. Beach had prompted the child to trump up the charge against Clarke was amply disproven.) The prisoner was asked if he desired to take the stand after the evidence was in, but he declined. When the jury brought in the verdict, before sentence was pronounced, he was asked if he had anything to say, and he answered by saying he was not guilty. Judge Norton then sentenced him to nine year's confinement in the penitentiary. A motion for a new trial was over-ruled, but a stay of judgment for thirty days was allowed in order that counsel could prepare an appeal if such a course is to be adopted. (*Alexandria Gazette*, February 10, 1897, p. 3.)

^^*^*^*^*^*^*^*^*^*^*^*

TAKEN TO FAIRFAX - As was stated in the *Gazette*, James Lewis, the negro who criminally assaulted Mrs. Ida Reidel at her home on Rose Hill farm, in Fairfax county, south of this city, on Tuesday night last, was brought to this city yesterday afternoon by Constable William Webster and Policeman Atkinson. Lewis was arrested by the police in Charlottesville Monday night from the description furnished them by Constable Webster, who was in that city on Friday last in search of the criminal. While on the train Lewis begged the officers not to put him off at Fairfax Courthouse, as he feared he might be subjected to violence. He protested his innocence, and claimed that he had not taken in charge by the authorities at Charlottesville. Lewis, while in his cell at police headquarters, appeared to be in a nervous condition. He at first refused to talk, except to deny any knowledge of the crime. When acquainted with the fact that his wife had made a statement in regard to his visit to his home in this city at a late hour on Tuesday night, and that he had threatened to kill her, Lewis became very much alarmed. He denied everything which had been said by his wife, but acknowledged that he had gone home early in the evening and packed a small bundle of clothing with the intention of going to Charlottesville for employment. The negro failed to explain why he left Alexandria so hurriedly on Tuesday night, and has made conflicting statements in regard to his sudden departure. When arrested in Charlottesville he is said to have asked if he was suspected of the assault on Mrs. Reidel before the crime had been mentioned to him. Sheriff Gordon reached here this morning and took Lewis to Fairfax Courthouse. He was accompanied by Officer Knight.

Over a hundred people were at the depot at Fairfax station when the train having Lewis on board arrived and some of the cried "get a rope," but no trouble ensued. He was put in a vehicle and conveyed to Fairfax three miles distant. Lewis reached Fairfax with his guards without incident and was at once taken to jail. Later Mrs. Reidal went to the prison where Lewis was in a room with about a dozen men and without hesitation identified him as her assailant.

A grand jury was immediately summoned and in a short time they returned an indictment against Lewis charging him with the crime.

In the absence of Judge Chichester, who is still quite sick, Judge Lipscomb, of Prince William, is presiding. A special grand jury has been summoned and the trial of Lewis will commence on Friday. There is no excitement. (*Alexandria Gazett*, April 20, 1897, p. 3.)

THE TRIAL OF LEWIS - The trial of the negro James Lewis, who criminally assaulted Mrs. Ida Reidel, in Fairfax county, a few miles below this city, was called in the Fairfax County Court at 2 o'clock this afternoon. Judge Lipscomb presided. The prisoner was brought from Leesburg without incident. Commonwealth's Attorney J. M. Love opened the case for the prosecution and he was followed by Mr. C. V. Ford for the defense. Both made short addresses. No trouble was experienced in securing a jury, and Mrs. Reidel was the first witness put on the stand. Her evidence was substantially as heretofore published. The complainant being compelled to testify although an interpreter, the process is slow and much time will necessarily be consumed. There is no excitement whatever, nor is any trouble apprehended.

At the conclusion of Mrs. Reidel's testimony and the examination of two or three witnesses for the prosecution the Commonwealth closed its case.

Lewis was then placed on the stand. He denied that he was guilty and gave a rambling account of his movements after the assault. Lewis was still on the stand when this report closed.

The general impression is that the Commonwealth has made out a clear case and that a conviction will follow.

An old colored woman was at the station house yesterday who alleged that Lewis attempted to assault her on the day he attacked Mrs. Reidel. (*Alexandria Gazette*, April 26, 1897, p. 3.)

THE FAIRFAX ASSAULT CASE - When the *Gazette*'s report closed at 4:20 o'clock yesterday evening of the second trial at Fairfax of James Lewis, colored, for an assault on old Mrs. Reidel, nine jurymen had been secured from the Clifton venire. The three others were not secured till 6 o'clock, when the trial was begun with the following jury: A. J. Kidwell, M. M. Payne, F. G. Mayhew, John M. Ford, F. M. Ford, Louis Hunt, Thomas Harrison, Robert N. Ions, A. W. Robinson, Berkley Kidwell, J. F. Johnson and Edward Stalant.

A large crowd was present, many coming from adjoining towns, and the feeling against the prisoner and the action or rather want of action of the former jury was intense.

About 3 o'clock R. E. Thornton, one of the counsel for the defense, received a message from ex-Congressman Meredith, at Manassas, stating that a crowd was coming from Prince William to help hang the negro. Another message was received that a crowd was coming from lower Fairfax. This news seemed to brace up the crowd at the courthouse....

When the jury had been properly sworn, an opening statement was made by the prosecution and defense, and Mrs. Reidel took the stand. Judge Lipscomb announced that he would try the case if it took all night.

The testimony of Mrs. Reidel was without any material change from that given on Monday. She is ill from the intense strain and excitement in attending court. During the night the courthouse was crowded with farmers and farm hands, awaiting patiently the result of the trial. Emanuel Reidel, George Appich, the interpreter, and Sherill Gordon gave their testimony of Monday over again.

Lewis was put upon the stand, and during the cross-examination became impudent. He did not help his case any from his testimony....

At 1:20 o'clock this morning the court finished its charge and the case was given to the jury. After being in their room some time the jury reported that they could not agree as to the punishment. Eleven stood for hanging and one for six years in the penitentiary.

Intense excitement prevailed and at 3 o'clock three pistol shots were fired outside the courthouse. Mr. R. Walton Moore entered the building and announced that he and his friends were not responsible for the disturbance outside, but that the patience of the people of Fairfax was being severely tested. In the meantime a number of men entered the building and took a stand behind the prisoner. The sheriff seeing a rope dangling from under the coat of one of the men took it from him and reported the fact to the court. Judge Lipscomb in a tired way replied, "Oh, throw it away."

The court remained in session till after daybreak and the prisoner and jury were kept in the building as a precautionary measure.

Before leaving the bench at 5 o'clock this morning Judge Lipscomb ordered another jury, the third, and then adjourned court till 10 o'clock this morning.

Much excitement prevailed; indignation was freely expressed and threats of violence were heard.

The jurymen who had voted that the man was guilty and then refused to agree with the others were roundly condemned.

There has been a disposition on the part of the people to give the man a fair and just trial, and this they say he has already had, and it is now time the community should act, in view of the fact that the jury has failed to do so.

RICHMOND, VIRGINIA, April 28 - Governor O'Ferrall this morning ordered the Monticello Guards, of Charlottesville to proceed immediately to Fairfax Courthouse to protect the negro Lewis, who is on trial there for his life for an alleged outrage on Mrs. Reidel. Lynching is feared and the Governor desires to prevent a repetition of the recent mob violence at Alexandria.

FAIRFAX COURTHOUSE, April 28 - 2 p.m. - The courthouse bell is now ringing announcing the opening of court. The late opening was caused by a delay in the arrival of the third venire from the Chantilly and Falls Church neighborhoods. Mr. Geo. Appich, of Alexandria, who had acted as interpretor for Mrs. Reidel, was summoned to appear again today, but did not do so, and Mr. Louis Krafft, of Alexandria, is here to act in that capacity....

4:15 p.m. - The Charlottesville military company reached here at 3 o'clock and were cordially received, though they came, so far as known, without request from the authorities, and when it was known they were coming an effort was made to have them stopped before they reached here. Much indignation is expressed that the Governor should have sent troops here as his action is thought to be unnecessary.

At 3:15 a jury was empaneled and the third trial of Lewis was commenced. Mrs. Reidel is now on the stand.

The military company have quarters at the hotel and are now stationed around the courthouse.

An Alexandria negro who became impudent when he saw that the military had arrived, was warned that if he put on airs he might not be "protected," and he soon quieted down. (*Alexandria Gazette*, April 28, 1897, p. 3.)

LEWIS WILL BE HANGED - At Fairfax Courthouse at 9:30 o'clock last night the jury in the case of James Lewis, the negro who assaulted old Mrs. Reidel on the Rose Hill Farm early on the morning of Wednesday April 14th, rendered a verdict as charged in the indictment, and fixed the penalty at death, after 55 minutes' deliberation. Their return at that moment prevented a lynching. A delay of five minutes more and Lewis would have been strung up inside the courthouse and riddled with bullets. The crowd was on the qui vive and ready to act.

...At 8:25 the jury retired while a crowd waited inside and outside the courthouse.

Fifteen minutes was the general opinion as to the time within which an agreement would be reached. Outside the militia tramped backward, and forward.

Inside the crowd began to get uneasy. Everybody feared the jury was again hung, and it was. Thirty minutes passed and they called for water and by this time the crowd anticipated that they would be unable to agree. Things began to look more serious. During this time the prisoner sat unconcerned between guards and appeared at perfect ease. Sheriff Gordon took his position behind Lewis to prevent a rope from being thrown around his neck. He had good cause for alarm. But a few steps away from the crowd stood a man with a suspicious looking bundle. In it was a rope, knotted and greased, ready for use. Every man in the crowd carried a pistol, and only waited for the signal.

Twenty-three minutes more passed, and the report came that the jury stood eleven for hanging and one for imprisonment.

This was followed by intense excitement. The man with the rope moved toward the prisoner and the crowd followed. In five minutes more Lewis would have been swung from the balcony in the courthouse. Sheriff Gordon was consulting with Lieut. Wingfield and the militia was about to enter the court room. In this five minutes the jury was advised of the situation and promptly reported that they had agreed, after fifty-five minutes deliberation.

When the jury had filed in and taken their seats, Judge Lipscomb requested that the verdict be received in silence. His request, however, was only partially heeded. There was no other demonstration except that the people seemed highly gratified and expressed themselves jubilantly in and outside of the courthouse.

Lewis received the verdict without any apparent emotion or concern and expressed no opinion, except that he was innocent.

The troops were promptly formed in line and the prisoner returned to jail. It is said that one of the jurymen held out awhile for twenty years in the penitentiary, but soon came over with the rest....

The verdict puts an end to the turbulent scenes which had been witnessed ever since the negro was taken there for trial, and last night for the first time this week the village was free from excitement. There is, however, considerable feeling over the fact that Governor O'Ferrall thought it necessary to send troops to maintain order....

At 12 o'clock last night everything was quiet and the militia had been withdrawn. The company returned to Charlottesville this morning....

FAIRFAX COURTHOUSE, April 29 – 12 p.m. – The military company from Charlottesville left here at an early hour this morning for their home. ...Their presence here would not have prevented Lewis from being lynched if the jury had failed to agree, or if they had brought in any other verdict. The plan had been arranged. A rope was to have been thrown over the prisoner and the man jerked through a window, and by the time he touched the ground he would have been shot.

Lewis was brought into court at 10:30 o'clock this morning and was asked the usual question - if there were any reasons why he should not be hanged. He spoke for some minutes and asked for a new trial, and shed some ingenuity in his arguments, most of which, however, were weak. He said if he had been guilty he would not have returned to Alexandria or have gone to Charlottesville, where he is known, nor would he have told his name. He also said Mrs. Reidel could not have recognized his face with the moon shining at his back.

Judge Lipscomb then sentenced Lewis to be hanged between the hours of 5 and 10 o'clock on the morning of Friday, June 4th, and the prisoner was taken back to jail.

Everything is quiet and no trouble is anticipated. The people are still incensed at the action of Gov. O'Ferrall in sending troops here, and he is being roundly censured. (*Alexandria Gazette*, April 29, 1897, p. 2.)

EXECUTION OF LEWIS - The Negro Ravisher Hanged this Morning at 5:03 - His Confession - Mrs. Reidel His Fourth Victim - His Last Night - Scenes and Incidents

The last night of James Lewis, the negro who was hanged at Fairfax Courthouse this morning for a criminal assault upon Mrs. Ida Reidel, was spent about as the others since he had been under sentence of death. He seemed to take his fate philosophically and pretended he had no fear of death, though when hanging, the mode by which he was to make his exit from this world, was mentioned he would assume an air of seriousness. A number of persons from this city, and neighborhood went to Fairfax yesterday and a representative of the *Gazette* spent some time in the jail with the condemned man. He ate a hearty dinner and at supper disposed of a plate of strawberries. Lewis expressed himself as believing he would be forgiven for his crimes and would go to heaven. He made a full confession, and stated that the offense for which he was to hang was the fourth he had committed during the past ten years. The first he asserted was committed in 1887, a seventeen-year-old colored girl named Lucy Meade being his victim. This occurred in Glendower, Albermarle county. A year later he was guilty of a similar offense toward another colored girl, Edmonia Gardner, eighteen years old. This also occured in Albermarle county. His third crime was committed in 1892 at "Red Hill," near Charlottesville. His victim this time was a white lady, twenty-five years of age, whom he met in a secluded place in the night time. Lewis was arrested for his first offense and sent to the Charlottesville jail. He escaped punishment for his second crime, the girl never telling of her experience with him, as he did also the consequences of his crime on the white woman from the fact that she did not know her assailant, though she had passed and repassed him often since. The lady never mentioned the matter to any one, and Lewis took care not to divulge her name in his confession last night. Lewis subsequently went under the name of James Williams. He said he

146

was but fifteen years of age when he was tried for his first offense, and got off with a jail sentence on account of his youth. When he left Alexandria on the night of the 13th of April he had fully determined to commit the act for which he was to hang. He said he denied his guilt at the trial in order to test the abilities of his lawyers and to hear them argue his case. When asked if at any time after his arrest he feared lynching, he replied no; that he never had any apprehension of such a thing. Lewis, however, seemed nervous every time hanging was mentioned, but at other times he appeared to be composed, especially so long as he kept talking. He said he had made his confession for the reason that he had repented of his deeds and had but a short time to live. Later on he volunteered to sign the following:

I am guilty, and know I am paying the penalty for which I deserve and believe I am forgiven. JAMES LEWIS

Lewis had been an incessant cigarette smoker of late. He spoke in the highest terms of his treatment since he had been in jail. He said he was perfectly satisfied with his trial, and that he never expected any other verdict.

The prisoner arose at four o'clock this morning. He drank a cup of coffee and ate two cakes. Later Rev. Brenner, a colored minister, called and was closeted with the doomed man, singing and praying with him until 4:35. Ten minutes later Sheriff Gordon and Mr. Jacobs, his deputy, entered and the death warrant was read to Lewis, after which he was escorted to the scaffold. At 4:55 he ascended the gibbet singing a hymn. He was accompanied by the sheriff, his two deputies and Revs. Mr. Milligan, white, and Brenner, colored. His hands were tied behind him and his feet pinioned. The condemned man walked with a firm step and manifested no sign of weakening. The colored minister read a psalm and offered up a prayer, after which he made a short address. Lewis when asked if he had anything to say before he died, replied in a sort of ceremonious way to the effect that he was sorry for his crime, but he subsequently spoke in a jesting manner of his exploits, saying the pitcher had gone to the well once too often-- referred to his capture and the consequences attending his fourth crime. He closed by warning all present not to presume too much, but to take heed not to be caught.

At 5:03, the trap was sprung and Lewis was launched into eternity. His death was not instanteous, he dying of strangulation. At 5:24 he was pronounced dead by Drs. Quick, Coombs, Russell, Leigh and Moncure, who were in attendance. Six minutes later the body was cut down and placed in a coffin. Later an autopsy was held. The brain weighted 49 ounces, one ounce above normal. The body was not claimed by relatives and was placed in a pauper's grave, after a brief funeral service, conducted by Rev. Brenner, the colored minister. About fifty people were present at the execution.

THE CRIME - The crime for which Lewis was executed is still fresh in the minds of the public. On the night of the 13th of April, Mrs. Ida Reidell, an aged German lady, living alone in a house on Rose Hill farm, in Mt. Vernon district, near this city, was aroused from her slumbers, about midnight, by a knocking on the door of her dwelling. She opened her window and saw a colored man standing below, and understood him to ask for her son. She indicated to him as best she could, that her son lived in the other house, a short distance away. She then lowered the window, but in a short while the knocking was repeated. She again raised her window and told the man that her sons did not live there. A little later she heard the man trying to force an entrance into the house through a window. She supposed it was Lewis's intention to rob the house, and she lowered herself from a window to the ground by a sheet. Lewis witnessed the act and overtook the old woman, after which he accomplished his purpose. Mrs. Reidell knew the negro and fully identified him at the trial. (*Alexandria Gazette*, June 4, 1897, p. 2.)

^^*^*^*^*^*^*^*^*^*^*^*^*

ATTEMPTED ASSAULT – A stranger, giving his name as Benj. Goldsmith, and who says he came from New York, was arrested this evening by Officer Sherwood, charged with an attempted assault on Mrs. Rollins, who is about 48 years old and lives on Queen street, between Fairfax and Lee. The man went to the house for the purpose of selling and enlarging pictures and in a short time took improper liberties with the woman and it is said threw her dress over her head. Mrs. Rollins screamed, when the man fled from the house. He was pursued by the woman and her son, the latter a boy of 12 years who was playing in the street nearby, and at the corner of Fairfax and Queen streets was seized by Mr. Thomas Waddey, who turned him over to Officer Sherwood. Goldsmith was locked up in the station house, but denies all intentions of wrong doing. (*Alexandria Gazette*, May 11, 1900, p.3.)

CASE POSTPONED – The case of Benjamin Goldsmith, charged with an attempted criminal assault on Mrs. Mary Rollins, was called up in the Police Court this morning. The prisoner was represented by Mr. Charles Bendheim. The court room was filled with persons attracted mainly by curiosity, but by order of the Mayor it was cleared of all but witnesses.

Mrs. Rollins's testimony was mainly what was published in the Gazette yesterday; that Goldsmith, who was soliciting orders for pictures and frames, called at her house, entered the parlor and when she returned to the room with some photographs he seized her and attempted the assault. She screamed and he ran from the house and was followed by her and her little boy who was in the street. Mr. Thomas Waddey stopped Goldsmith and with Officer Sherwood conducted him to the station house.

Goldsmith was called on to testify and stated that he had been invited into the house to get an order for enlarging a photograph. He told Mrs. Rollins that she would have to pay 25 cents a week for the picture and she then became excited, calling him a thief and a fraud. He then left the house and on being pursued ran towards the police station.

Mr. Bendheim, as counsel for the defendant, then made an argument, in which he sought to discredit the statements of the woman, but as no testimony of the kind had been brought forward the court could not receive it.

Rev. C. E. Ball, who was present, volunteered a statement as to the immorality, untruthfulness, etc. of the woman, but as his testimony was on hearsay it was not material. He offered, however, to bring witnesses who could testify as to the woman's character.

No effort had been made to furnish testimony to impeach the plaintiff's statement, so Mr. Bendheim asked a postponement of the case. The Mayor consented and the case was continued until five o'clock on Monday afternoon. (*Alexandria Gazette*, May 12, 1900, p.3.)

FINED FIFTY DOLLARS – Yesterday evening the trial of Benjamin Goldsmith, the picture canvasser, charged with an attempted criminal assault on Mrs. Mary Rollins on Friday evening last, was concluded in the police court. ...A large number of witnesses had been summoned to testify against the plaintiff's character, but the court rules out all such evidence, holding that it was a matter of veracity and not of character. A letter from Hon. E. E. Meredith, of Prince William county, stating that the woman had brought a similar but unfounded charge against a man in that county, was also excluded on the same grounds. From the testimony produced it was found that Mrs. Rollins had made the same charge against a colored man when she lived in Gainesville.

Sergeant Parker, of Fort Hunt, testified that he had visited the prisoner on Sunday and told him that he thought Mrs. Rollins would be willing to withdraw the charge for a consideration.

...After hearing all the arguments, the Mayor decided to hold the prisoner guilty of indecent assault and imposed a fine of $50 upon him.

This morning at the request of a number of friends of Goldsmith who had interested themselves in collecting money to pay his fine Mayor Simpson reopened the case and reduced the fine to $37.25, the amount collected. The sum was paid and Goldsmith was released. (*Alexandria Gazette*, May 15, 1900, p.3.)

^^*^*^*^*^*^*^*^*^*^*^*^*^*

CHARGED WITH ASSAULT – Susan Skelton, colored, last night made complaint against "Piggy" Williams, colored, charging him with a criminal assault on her 13-year-old daughter, Daisey McGuire. The woman said the crime had been committed about 4 o'clock yesterday evening, and when Williams had been discovered by two sisters of his victim he escaped. The girl is said to be simple-minded and suffers from epilepsy. Williams has not yet been captured, and the story is discredited by some. (*Alexandria Gazette*, May 15, 1900, p.3.)

Commonwealth vs. John Williams, colored, indicted for rape upon Daisy McGuire, a small colored girl; no. pros. entered. (*Alexandria Gazette*, July 12, 1900, p.3.)

SENT TO THE PENITENTIARY – John, alias "Piggy," Williams, colored, was today found guilty in the Corporation Court of a criminal assault upon a little colored girl named Maud Blackburn, last week, and was sentenced to serve 20 years in the penitentiary. The evidence against him was clear and it took the jury but a short time to reach a verdict. (*Alexandria Gazette*, July 12, 1900, p.3.)

CHAPTER NINE

Riots

A very disgraceful riot and fight took place on Tuesday night last, at the southern end of Washington street. The services at the African Meeting House were broken up, and great noise and confusion prevailed in the neighborhood for a considerable time, disturbing the citizens living there and endangering their property. Parties of whites and colored persons were engaged, pistols were fired, and stones thrown. In the midst of the disturbance the cry of fire was raised, which added to the tumult. Those who participated in this riot, and can be identified, will be duly punished according to law. (*Alexandria Gazette*, December 15, 1853, p. 3.)

^^*^*^*^*^*^*^*^*^*^*^*^*^*

The Washington papers say that during the disturbance raised in Alexandria a few days ago, by a number of soldiers belonging to the Second Fire Zouaves, heretofore referred to the Provost Guard, being attacked, killed one of the rioters, another died of his wounds and another was severely wounded. General Slough complimented the guard for the faithful performance of their duty. (*Alexandria Gazette*, 11/1/1862, p. 4.)

^^*^*^*^*^*^*^*^*^*^*^*^*^*

DISORDER – We regret to state that much disorder prevailed in town yesterday along several of the public streets. Fights, pistol firing, and disturbances generally were frequent. At one time of the day quiet persons were almost afraid to go out of their houses. Several persons were knocked down and injured, and the police threatened with violence if they interfered. A row occurred at Chapel Hall, at the corner of Duke and Washington streets, in which pistols, brickbats, and fists were freely used. A young man had his head severely injured by a stone, another man was shot in the arm, and several others slightly wounded with pistol shots. A man was severely beaten on the street, at the upper end of King street, and a dozen rows took place there, in the course of the day. Up and down, drunken and disorderly persons were moving about. At last the military aid was requested and that being furnished, guards were sent over town, who proceeded to arrest all disorderly characters, white and black, who were found, and this soon restored order and quietness. A number of persons were placed in the guard house, upper end of King street, and will be made to account for their conduct. Altogether, the scenes were most discreditable, and unusual in Alexandria. The civil authority seemed to be, by itself, entirely powerless. We trust not again to have to make such a record about our town, in olden times distinguished for its observance of law and order, and with about the best population of any city in the country. (*Alexandria Gazette*, December 26, 1865, p. 3.)

The Washington *Star* says: "General Augur commanding the Department of Washington, has directed an investigation to be made into the circumstances of the riot in Alexandria on Monday, and will bring all parties responsible for the affair to justice. A number of arrests have already been made. The Washington *Chronicle* says: "General Augur has instructed Lieutenant Colonel Eyre, commanding at Alexandria, not to release any of the persons arrested in connection with the late riot, on the demands of the civil authorities and to report any such demands to department headquarters." (*Alexandria Gazette*, December 28, 1865, p. 3.)

THE "RIOT" AT ALEXANDRIA – Some disorder in the city of Alexandria on Christmas day, and the previous and subsequent days, has given occasion for exciting dispatches to the distant press, in which the serious point was boldly indicated that an organized attempt had been made to revive the broken enginery of rebellion within earshot of the capital. The foundation which appears for this sensation – so opportune during the legislative vacation – is that, of a large number of Christmas roysterers who misbehaved in Alexandria, a due proportion were white men; that a due proportion of these were young; and of these youngsters a due proportion had served in the Confederate army. The distant Northern reader may also need to be told that many of them were dressed in "rebel uniform," i.e. clothes, and bad ones at that, homespun in fabric and gray in color, some in the regulation gray of the Confederate service. But if the "uniform" was the proof, some of the negroes must have afforded a similar presumption, some of them being dressed in like manner.

Distant journals naturally looked to the local publications of the matter; and when they read in a morning paper here an account drawn with startling allegations, it is not surprising that papers like the New York *Tribune* thought it reasonable to treat a drunken outbreak of whites and negroes as a grave complication of national methods of order. (*National Intelligencer*) (*Alexandria Gazette*, December 29, 1865, p. 2.)

THE MILITARY COMMISSION – Trial of the Rioters ... On the cross examination Dogan stated: Was standing on the corner of Pitt and King streets. The two colored men were coming down King street on the south side, towards the wharf. Don't know who knocked off the hat. The man had raised his hat when Lawler hit him with his fist; all took place in about three seconds. Crowd had passed about ten or twelve feet; no one behind but Edds and Lawler. Don't know what was the first difficulty. ...Though the party of young men were in liquor;

were talking very loud and appeared to be pretty happy. Don't remember whether I heard any firing on Sunday night. Heard music in the street on Christmas morning. Met a party of colored young men with musical instruments, almost one hundred of them in number, near the Catholic church. They were pretty gay, but don't know whether they were very drunk. Saw one of them with a gun. Disturbance at Chapel Hall took place at half past eleven o'clock. Chapel Hall is a restaurant; is kept by a colored man, and colored men, as a general thing, go there. It has been used as a dance house for the last three years. Saw Lawler on the northeast corner of Duke and Washington streets, carrying Mitchell away. Noticed that Mitchell was bleeding freely, and was cut in the head. Can't name who threw stones at the house. Simpson ran from the west side of Washington street towards Chapel Hall, and struck the lamppost with a stick about two and a half feet long; ...Saw nothing thrown by a colored man that day. Heard three pistol shots. After Edds threw he called out, "I am shot," and I saw oozing of blood from his arm. About fifty or sixty persons, men and women, white and colored, within one hundred feet of the house; most of them looking on....

Stephen Hamilton (negro) is a United States soldier, was in Alexandria on Christmas day, going to church, when a man jumped on him, and whipped him; struck him back of the neck with a rock; knocked him down and kicked him; started to run, and was tripped and fell and a man caught and held him; ...this took place about the middle of the day; don't know in what part of the city. There were ten or twelve men running after him; one of them swore at him before he was tripped; don't know what part of the city it was, but can show the place; was off duty eight days after he went back to camp from injuries. (*Alexandria Gazette*, January 12, 1866, p. 3.)

...Georgie L. Smith (white) was next called by the prosecution, and testified that she resides on King street, on the corner above West. ...on Christmas day, between 11 and 12 o'clock, heard a negro man using very abusive language to a white man - saw a negro in the street, and heard him say he could whip any "dirty white, rebel, son of a bitch in town" - heard more than one report of a pistol....

Such a scene as was enacted yesterday evening in front of the Military Prison in this city, called the Slave Pen, we trust and sincerely hope, from a decent regard for the instinct of humanity, and out of respect for the authority of law, never to see re-enacted. A rumor that the "Christmas riot" prisoners had been sentenced and were to be sent off had been circulated through the city, and towards the hour for the five o'clock Washington train to start, a large crowd, including many ladies, had collected at the upper end of Duke street, to witness their departure. We will not attempt to express the feelings excited in all the spectators of this sad ending of, at most a Christmas frolic, but the appearance of five residents of this city - born and raised here, and known to all our old citizens, as honest and upright young men, manacled together with iron handcuffs, and carried through the street in charge of a military guard, after the issue of the Peace Proclamation was sufficient cause for anxiety to all. The sobs and cries of some of the ladies were painfully audible, and the feelings of one were so acted upon that she fainted, and fell upon the streets. It is our deliberate impression that the President, when he approved the following findings of the Commission which tried the parties, was not fully informed in regard to the circumstances attending the affair....

WAR DEPARTMENT
ADJUTANT GENERAL'S OFFICE
Washington, April 3, 1866

GEN'L COURT MARTIAL
Orders, No. 95

I. General Court Martial Orders, No. 78, from this Office, dated March 19, 1866, is revoked.

II. Before a Military Commission which convened at Alexandria, Virginia, January 10, 1866, pursuant to Special Orders, No. 3, dated January 4, 1866, and No. 8, dated January 10, 1866, Headquarters Department of Washington, Washington, and of which Major General Francis Fessenden, U.S. Volunteers, is President, were arraigned and tried: John Mankin, John Lawler, John Travis, Joseph Horseman and Gilbert Simpson, citizens:

CHARGE I – "Assault and battery, with intent to kill." SPECIFICATION – "In this: that John Mankin, George Huntington, Oscar Mankin, John L. Heck, Charles Javins, John Heichew, A. D. Warfield, John Lawler, John Travis, John Mitchell, Joseph Horseman, Gilbert Simpson, H. E. Smith, William Wheately, William Edds, Charles Carson, William Allen and divers other persons, whose names are unknown to the United States Government, being unlawfully engaged in the disturbance of the public peace in opposition to and in defiance of the United States Government, did assault, with intent to kill, Stephen Hamilton, Jno. Vaughan, Richard Green and Henry Barrott, all soldiers in the service of the United States, and Robert Saunders, a colored citizen of Alexandria, Virginia, and with kicks, and blows of their fists and with clubs and stones, and with other blunt and deadly weapons, then and there in their hands held, did beat and did inflict on the bodies of the said Stephen Hamilton, John Vaughan, Richard Green and Henry Barrott, soldiers in the service of the United States, and Robert Sanders, a colored resident of Alexandria, Virginia, divers grievous wounds, with intent to kill as aforesaid, to the detriment of the public peace and to the injury of the military service of the United. This on the 25th day of December, 1865, in the city of Alexandria, Virginia."

CHARGE II – "Murder." SPECIFICATION – "In this: that John Mankin, George Huntington, Oscar Mankin, John L. Heck, Charles Javins, John Heichew, A. D. Warfield, John Lawler, John Travis, John Mitchell, Joseph Horseman, Gilbert Simpson, H. E. Smith, William Whately, William Edds, Charles Carson, William Allen and divers other persons, whose names are unknown to the United States Government, being unlawfully engaged in the disturbance of the public peace in opposition to and in defiance of the United States Government, did wilfully and with malice aforethought, assault and shoot at, and shoot with intent to kill and murder, one John Anderson, a colored man, and whilst so engaged in the prosecution of said unlawful disturbance of the public peace, did wilfully, and with malice aforethought, ill and murder the aforesaid John Anderson, being then and there in the peace of the laws of the United States. This on or about the 25th day of December, 1865 in the city of Alexandria, Virginia."

To which charges and specifications the accused, John Mankin, John Lawler, John Travis, Joseph Horseman and Gilbert Simpson, citizens, pleaded each "Not Guilty."...

SENTENCE - And the Commission does therefore sentence them, John Mankin, John Lawler, John Travis, Joseph Horseman and Gilbert Simpson, citizens as follows:

John Mankin - "To be confined at hard labor in such Penitentiary as the proper authorities may direct for the term of fifteen years.

John Lawler - "To be confined at hard labor in such Peniten-tiary...for the term of five years.

John Travis, Joseph Horseman and Gilbert Simpson each - "To be confined at hard labor for the term of six months." ...

III. The proceedings, findings and sentences of the Commission in the foregoing cases of John Mankin, John Lawler, John Travis, Joseph Horseman and Gilbert Simpson, citizens, have been approved by the commander of the Department of Washington and submitted to the President for his orders.

In the case of John Mankin, the sentence is mitigated "To five years' imprisonment."

In the case of John Lawler, the sentence is mitigated "To two years imprisonment.

In other respects the proceedings, findings and sentences of the Commission in the foregoing cases of John Mankin, John Lawler, John Travis, Joseph Horseman and Gilbert Simpson, citizens are approved and the Penitentiary at Albany, New York, designated as the place of confinement, where the prisoners will be sent, in charge of a suitable guard under the orders of the Commanding General, Department of Washington, for the execution of their respective sentences.

By order of the President of the U.S. (*Alexandria Gazette*, April 7, 1866, p.3.) (Other prisoners not sentenced were acquitted of charges filed against them.)

^^*^*^*^*^*^*^*^*^*^*

ROW AT A COLORED DANCE HOUSE - ONE MAN KILLED - On Saturday night last a serious disturbance took place at a negro dance house, near Fort Whipple, about seven miles from this city, near the

Aqueduct. The house is kept by a colored woman named Lizzie Campbell, a notorious character, and formerly residing in Georgetown. It seems that a party of colored men from Georgetown went to this house where a dance was in progress, and some of the men acting rather disorderly from the influence of liquor, attracted to the spot County Officer Vietch, who expostulated with them, and attempted to arrest some of the most disorderly. He was threatened by some of the negroes, and immediately went to the Fort and applied for assistance, when a guard was sent, who were likewise threatened, and the officers fired upon. The command was then given to fire into the house, which was done and a negro named Griffin Burke of Georgetown, instantly killed by a ball.

On the appearance of the military the colored men became defiant, exclaiming "Let us run the white s--s of b--s off." The squad perceiving the threatening attitude of the rioters, and finding persuasion of no avail, were ordered to fire upon them, which they did, killing Burke, and wounding one or two quite severely. The party were then arrested, and will be brought to this place for trial. A coroner's inquest was held upon the body of Burke yesterday by Justice Johnston, acting coroner, and a verdict rendered that the deceased "came to his death from a minnie ball, in a negro riot, fired by some unknown person." (*Alexandria Gazette*, July 1, 1867, p. 3.)

^^*^*^*^*^*^*^*^*^*^*^*^*

RIOTOUS BEHAVIOR - What with "Christmas riots" and "Sunday riots", Alexandria will soon achieve a riotous reputation. It appears that the burial of a colored man, Bachus Keith, formerly a slave of Mr. Bernard Hooe, of this city, who died in Washington last Tuesday morning, but was preserved on ice until yesterday, was made the occasion for a general parade and frolic of the colored people of the District of Columbia. They came here in large numbers - so large that several trips of the ferry boats were necessary for their transportation. Notice of the affair had been given several days before, and as early as one o'clock crowds of the colored people of this city began to assemble at the ferry slip to await the arrival. The deceased was a member of I. F. Wilkerson lodge of Odd Fellows, which lodge together with the Galilean Fishermen, a colored organization of Washington-- and two brass bands acted as an escort. Upon their arrival here they were joined by delegations of R. H. Lancaster, G. W. Parker and Harmony lodges of Odd Fellows of this city, and, accompanied by an immense number of their race, of all ages, sexes and conditions, the procession marched to the burying ground. While at the grave yard the alleged object for which they came here, began to develop itself and an assault was made upon Mr. W. S. Hough, an elderly gentleman, who was remonstrating against their stoning each other. Policeman Jack Nightingill coming to Mr. Hough's assistance, was assaulted and bitten on the hand, but with the assistance of some bystanders, whom he called to his aid, succeeded after much difficulty in making the arrest of the one who struck Mr. Hough. On their way back from the grave yard one of the Washingtonians kicked and badly hurt a son of

Mr. John Devaughn, and Policeman Lyles, in endeavoring to arrest him, was set upon by his friends, but was successful in effecting his arrest. When the procession reached the wharf, the whole space in front of the docks in that vicinity was thronged with people, news of the previous disturbances having spread through the city and caused great excitement among all classes. Here the climax was reached. Not satisfied with their previous difficulties, they seized upon the opportunity afforded them by an attempt to arrest one of those engaged in the former disorderly proceedings, to inaugurate a riot which, had it not been suppressed promptly by the Mayor and the efficient support he received from the members of the police force present, would doubtless have resulted disastrously. Pistols, knives, razors, clubs, stones and all sorts of weapons were freely displayed, inoffensive citizens, the members of the police and the Mayor himself were grossly and personally attacked, and had it not been for the coolness, bravery and discretion of the Mayor, whose conduct upon the occasion cannot be too highly commended, a scene would probably have ensued, in consequence of the bad passions which had been engended by the calls to "rally", "come to the rescue", etc. used by the rioters, which would have rivalled the most famous riots that have occurred in the country during the past few years. About twenty of those engaged in the disturbances were arrested and put in jail and fines to the amount of $115.40 exacted of them this morning. The colored people of this city took no part in the disturbance nor were any of their lodges at the wharf when the assault upon the Mayor was made....

...When the procession had returned to the steamboat wharf, they had become so disorderly that the greatest excitement prevailed in the city, and the members of the 17th Virginia regiment, without any official notification, assembled at the foot of King street, to assist in the preservation of order in the city.
...The disturbance was finally quelled through the exertions of the police, whose movements were directed by Mayor Latham, and the members of the lodges embarked on the boats and returned to Washington. The origin of the disturbance as near as the facts can be reached was caused by the conduct of a crowd of disorderly characters who followed the lodges to Alexandria and became intoxicated, and upon reaching that city began violating the peace by throwing stones, which necessitated the officers in making arrests. (*Alexandria Gazette*, May 6, 1872, p. 3.)

^^*^*^*^*^*^*^*^*^*^*

A NIGHT RIOT IN ALEXANDRIA - Last night about 10 o'clock the people residing on north Fairfax Street were startled by cries of murder, the blowing of whistles and the rushing of police, followed by a large crowd. The cause of the excitement was a regular riot near the Washington and Western railroad depot, between whites and blacks, male and female. The scum of "Buzzard's Roost" and "Petersburg," man and women, had congregated on the corner opposite the depot, while on the other corner was a number of white men. From the crowd of blacks, Robert Beale, a burly negro, sallied forth in quest of the "best white man in the city." He soon picked out Alfonzo Arrington as a man he considered worthy his notice. Arrington, so witnesses say, was not anxious for a fight, and so informed Beale, but Beale insisted, and the melee commenced, which continued until nearly all the men (and women, too) present were involved. Upon some of the young men interfering to stop the fight, the negroes rushed upon them with bricks and compelled them to retreat. The white men rallied, and then commenced a general row, each side fighting for "fair play" for the two men scratching and biting each other on the ground in the middle of the street. The negro women acted as "ammunition monkies" for the men, supplying them with bricks as fast as needed. The riot continued until Mayor Beckham arrived on the ground with a squad of police, when the following were arrested: John Truslow, Charles Leary, Edward Payne and Fannie Grandison. The first two were released for their appearance when wanted, as it was believed they had nothing to do with the row. The battle over, it was found that Arrington, besides being badly scratched and bruised about the face, had had the entire lower portion of his chin bitten off, causing a very ugly wound. Others received wounds in the back and head by flying bricks during the bombardment, which was violent during its continuance. Razors and pistols were displayed by the negroes, but no one was cut or shot. This morning a large crowd assembled at police headquarters expecting a trial of the rioters to take place, but the Mayor committed Payne and the Grandison woman to jail, and continued the examination until Beale and others could be arrested. While the proceedings were in progress at the office Arrington handed to the Mayor a piece of flesh about as large as a silver dollar, covered with short black bristly hair, which he said was the lower portion of his chin, bitten off by Beale. The Mayor ordered Arrington to take the piece of flesh off his desk and cover up the sickening wound on his face, which he did. The piece out of Arrington's chin was picked up early this morning on the ground where the fight took place. Beale, who has not yet been arrested, is reported to have a bad looking face, presenting the appearance of having been caught in a "chewing" machine. (*Alexandria Gazette*, July 12, 1882, p. 3.)

THE NEGRO RIOTERS – Seven of the parties engaged in the row Tuesday night last, near the W. & W. Railroad depot, were before the Mayor this afternoon. The investigation of the affair lasted for nearly three hours, and many witnesses were examined, the evidence showing that the negroes first attacked the whites.

The Mayor fined the persons as follows: Robert Beale $25, Edward Payne, Celia Harris, Milt Welcone, Fannie Grandison, Jeff Poland, all colored, $5 each, and John Truslow, white, $5. All the colored men and women were locked up, and unless they pay the fines assessed against them by 6 o'clock they will go to jail. (*Alexandria Gazette*, July 13, 1882, p. 3.)

ALL HANDS ARRESTED – For the first time in several months a number of the residents of the Whitechapel district were before the Mayor this morning on charges of disorderly conduct. The trouble arose last night by a woman named Ollie Sykes casting slurs at Maud Tippett who was in a partially intoxicated condition. Later in the evening the Sikes woman with a female and several male companions made an attack on the Tippet woman who was being escorted home by two men, and in the melee which resulted, two of the women were knocked down and a general riot seemed imminent. At this point the police appeared and placed the whole party under arrest. The men in the affair were all married. This morning the members of the attacking party were all fined $5 and the others dismissed. (*Alexandria Gazette*, May 19, 1900, p. 3.)

CHAPTER TEN

Sex And Seduction

SEXUAL ABERRATIONS – Officer Keel, while on his beat near the Cotton Factory last night, observed two persons standing on the corner of Oronoko and Washington street whose demeanor and voices satisfied him that, although one wore the costume of a man and the other of a woman, yet neither wore the proper apparel of their sex, in other words they had exchanged clothing with each other. The officer promptly arrested them but upon proceeding to the station house the man accused of being a woman satisfied the officer that the charge was groundless and the couple were dismissed. The voice of the man was so remarkably feminine that all the people who heard him concurred in the officer's suspicion to have them arrested. (*Alexandria Gazette*, April 16, 1872, p. 3.)

^^*^*^*^*^*^*^*^*^*^*^*^*

ARRESTED – A young man, while at work at the ship yard, was arrested yesterday evening and taken before Justice Arnell, where he was confronted by a young lady who lives in the 3d ward who charged him with enticing her from the path of virtue, and thus destroying the good chaaracter which she had enjoyed up to that time. The young man made no attempt to disprove the charge in toto, but disclaimed being the origin of her fall. The mother of the girl offered to compromise the affair upon the payment to her daughter of $50, but the young man, being unable to comply with the agreement, had to answer the charges brought against him and was committed to jail to await the action of the grand jury. This body at its meeting this morning found a true bill against him and he was sent to jail in default of $500 bail for trial. It is thought that bail will be furnished in a day or two. (*Alexandria Gazette*, October 9, 1883, p. 3.)

^^*^*^*^*^*^*^*^*^*^*^*^*

A SENSATION – Considerable sensation was produced at the lower end of King street at any early hour this morning by the cowhiding of a resident of the First ward by an enraged female, who charged the former with conducting himself in an improper manner before the female members of her family. The accused was in a house on the opposite side of the street, when the woman who made the charges sent for him to come over to her house. The man, unconscious as he alleges, of having incurred any guilt, complied with the request, and having entered the house, the door was shut and he found himself a captive. The woman forthwith produced a formidable looking horse-whip and proceeded unmercifully to belabor the man who had excited her ire. The accused finally succeeded in opening the door and reaching the street, but his Nemesis followed him, and inflicted several other blows with the butt end of the weapon. The parties then separated, the man protesting his innocence of the charge and the woman reiterating her allegations. (*Alexandria Gazette*, January 31, 1885, p. 3.)

^^*^*^*^*^*^*^*^*^*^*^*^*

CHARGE OF SEDUCTION – Lieut. Smith today arrested I. S. Lloyd, a dealer in china and earthen ware, whose store is on King street, between Fairfax and Royal, on a charge of seducing Emma Hall, a girl about 22 years of age, last July. She is from Fairfax county and was employed by Mr. Lloyd as a clerk in his store. A warrant was issued for Lloyd at the insistance of the girl's mother and he was taken before the Mayor and Justice May and bailed in the sum of $1,000 for his appearance to morrow. Mr. Lloyd denies the charge emphatically. (*Alexandria Gazette*, December 11, 1889, p. 3.)

THE SEDUCTION CASE – In refutation of the charge against Mr. I. S. Lloyd that he and his wife had ill treated Miss Hall, the following is published:

Alexandria, Virginia, December 13th, 1889 –
    This is to certify that I attended Emma Hall during the past summer from August 17th, 1889, to October 10, 1889, with an attack of typhoid fever of a serious character, and that during her entire illness, Mr. and Mrs. Lloyd gave to the sick woman, not only every attention and care that was proper and necessary, but exerted themselves to have her restored and arranged to pay all medical expenses incurred. In regard to the statement that food tendered by acquaintances had been refused, that was done in accordance with my orders for the benefit of the patient.   Bedford Brown, M.D. (*Alexandria Gazette*, December 13, 1889, p. 3.)

^^*^*^*^*^*^*^*^*^*^*^*^*

INDECENT CONDUCT – The indecent conduct of a stranger on one of the ferry boats yesterday evening caused some excitement among the passengers.   On the arrival of the boat here the man was arrested. (*Alexandria Gazette*, May 23, 1891, p. 3.)

George Carroll, colored, for indecent conduct, was fined $5. (*Alexandria Gazette*, May 25, 1891, p. 3.)

POLICE REPORT – ...The last case was at first supposed to be of a serious nature, but after the evidence had been taken it dwindled down to one of lewdness merely. It seemed that company being at the house of one John Nichols, colored, whose domestic felicity doesn't seem to be of the highest order, it was necessary for three of the family to bunk together – Nichols, his wife and a grown step-daughter. The latter this morning made a serious charge against Nichols, which, however, was not substantiated by the evidence of the girl and her mother and the trio were pronounced guilty of lewdness. They were fined $1.00 each. (*Alexandria Gazette*, September 17, 1892, p. 3.)

^^*^*^*^*^*^*^*^*^*^*^*

CHARGED WITH SEDUCTION – A young woman named Hannah H. Sims appeared at the station house today and swore out a warrant against Eppa H. Padgett, a young man, whom she charged with seducing her under a promise of marriage. The case came before Justice Thompson this evening, and, at the request of the defendant, was continued until next Monday, the accused being released on $500 bail for his appearance. (*Alexandria Gazette*, June 13, 1894, p. 3.)

SEDUCTION CASE – The case of Eppa H. Padgett, charged with seducing Hannah Simms under promise of marriage, came before Justice Thompson in the Police Court this morning. ... The prosecutrix, who is a native of Fairfax county, is comely in appearance. She was positive in the charges she urged against Padgett, and deposed the that previous to the commission of the offense she had been a woman of chastity; that Padgett had promised to marry her and produced letters from him to corroborate her assertion. The letters show that he had called her his prospective wife, and were full of ebullitions of affections for the prosecutrix. She gave a detailed description of the facts charged in the warrant; said the offense was committed on the 5th of last January in an alley in the extreme western part of the city, and, according to her statement, savored more of assault than seduction, and before and after the occurrence said he would marry her. The defense first put Robert Arnold (son of the late policeman Arnold) on the stand in order to prove that the young woman had been guilty of previous indiscretions with the witness. He testified to that effect, but suffered considerably under the cross question fire opened by the Commonwealth's Attorney. He claimed that Miss Simms, Arthur Mankin and himself spent the night on a common near the outlet lock of the old Alexandria canal between seven and eight months ago. Arthur Mankin corroborated Arnold's statement, but said the occurrence was last July, which was three months earlier than the time assigned by Arnold. They both said Miss Simms had accompanied them to Riverside Park that day, and that the two men had spent between nineteen and twenty dollars in whisky and beer which the young woman had helped drink. Upon being recalled, Miss Simms emphatically denied the charges made by the two men, said she never was at Riverside Park in her life, and further that she never drank liquor of any kind. She moreover stated that she never came to this city until October (which was substantiated by her sister, Georgie Simms, who was

163

present); notwithstanding Mankin was positive the lewdness he and Arnold charged her with was committed last July. A man named Willis Petty testified to having seen the young woman with a young man named Siders under questionable circumstances. It was found necessary to postpone the case until next Friday in order to procure additional witnesses, among them the mother of the young lady, by whom the prosecution suppose they can prove that Miss Simms was at her Fairfax home during the time Arnold and Mankin charged her with behaving unseemly. Several witnesses in whose houses Miss Simms had been during her stay in this city testified that the girl had always borne a good character, and one averred that Padgett had told him he intended to marry her. (*Alexandria Gazette*, June 18, 1894, p. 3.)

A NOLLE PROSEQUI ENTERED - The case of Eppa H. Padgett, charged with seducing Hannah Simms under the promise of marriage, which was to have come up in the Police Court this morning, was dismissed at the instance of the mother of the young woman. Mrs. Simms, who lives in Fairfax county, reached here this morning. It was the intention of the prosecution to prove by her that the complainant in the case was at home from the latter part of June, 1893, until the middle of October following, in order that the testimony of the witness Arthur Mankin, who testified she was guilty of impropriety with Robert Arnold in this city in July of that year, might be disproved. Mrs. Simms, while confident her child's statement is correct, revolted at the thought of having her brought into court again, for the reason that should her daughter establish what she believed to be the justness of her cause and the accused be compelled to marry her, she was averse to having a son-in-law incorporated into her family under such circumstances. She, therefore, deemed it best to suffer patiently from the wrong which she is sure had been inflicted upon her fatherless child, than to allow her to pass through the ordeal of another trial and be compelled to listen to statements from witnesses believed by the prosecution to be hostile and irresponsible, and from whose aspersions there could be no redress. Miss Simms is eighteen years old. She was born and reared near Lorton station, on the Washington Southern Railway. Her father is dead, and, like many others, she grew weary of the surroundings of her innocent home and came to this city in order to support herself and see more of the world than it was possible for her to experience in her secluded Fairfax home. She was employed in several houses in this city, and those with whom she lived who appeared as witnesses testified to her correct deportment. She is passably good looking, but is devoid of education, and is of the rural type, bearing evidence of having been inured to honest work. She still emphatically denies the charges the witnesses Arnold, Mankin, Petty and others brought against her. (*Alexandria Gazette*, June 22, 1894, p. 3.)

^^*^*^*^*^*^*^*^*^*^*^*^*

POLICE COURT - A young women, arrested by Officers Beach and Sherwood for indecent conduct, was fined $5, or given 60 days in the work house. (*Alexandria Gazette*, June 12, 1895, p. 3.)

164

A DEN RAIDED – Officer Atkinson this morning raided a house which has recently been occupied by James Clift and some of his companions, male and female. The place is what was known in the olden time as the John Price restaurant, on the west side of Union street, between King and Prince. Clift rented the place upon assuring the owner it was for the purpose of opening an oyster house, but it seems to be used more as a rendezvous for certain improvident people of both sexes, whom it is alleged, hold orgies and endanger other property in the neighborhood, those conducting business nearby being apprehensive lest fire may be started by some accident. Clift and a woman named Maggie O'Brien were arrested by Officer Atkinson, and it was ascertained that the woman's dress had been taken by Clift and sold for whisky. The liquor was captured. The house was found to be in a filthy condition. (*Alexandria Gazette*, January 30, 1896, p. 3.)

^^*^*^*^*^*^*^*^*^*^*^*

CHARGED WITH SEDUCTION – Mrs. Ryan, mother of a young woman named Laura Ryan, appeared at the station house yesterday and swore out a warrant for the arrest of a youth named Samuel Johnson, charging him with leading her daughter astray under promise of marriage. Mrs. Ryan, who was formerly a resident of this city, now lives in Fairfax county with her daughter. Some months ago the latter paid a visit to a family in the First ward, where Johnson resides, and it is alleged that during this visit the offense was committed. The accused is employed on the ferry steamer *Belle Haven* and yesterday afternoon Officer Atkinson boarded the boat for the purpose of arresting him. Johnson saw him coming and hid, and although the officer searched the boat thoroughly his hiding place could not be found. A telephone message was sent to Washington for the officers of that city to be on the lookout for him. (*Alexandria Gazette*, February 11, 1896, p. 3.)

^^*^*^*^*^*^*^*^*^*^*^*

Laura Coleman, a white woman about fifty years of age, was brought before the Mayor last night charged with entertaining minors at her house. The evidence was positive against the woman, among those who testified as to her conduct being a fourteen-year-old boy. She was fined $10. Complaint is often made of the fact that certain women in this city tolerate minors in their houses and all who are convicted will be sentenced and fined. (*Alexandria Gazette*, September 15, 1896.)

^^*^*^*^*^*^*^*^*^*^*^*

ARRESTED IN WASHINGTON – As heretofore stated, a warrant was recently issued in this city for the arrest of Thos. L. Kimball on the charge of seduction under promise of marriage. The charge was preferred by the mother of Miss Temple Jeffries who requested that Kimball be arrested on his return to this city from Washington. Kimball having purposely absented himself from this city, Mrs. Jeffries

165

last night notified the Mayor that he was in Washington and requested that he be arrested. The police authorities of that city were at once notified of the facts in the case and this morning at 6 o'clock the Alexandria police were notified that Kimball had been arrested and was being held in that city awaiting further orders.

This morning Lieutenant Smith went to Washington, took Kimball in charge and later brought him to this city. The case will come up before Mayor Simpson tomorrow. Mr. Kimball denies the charge against him and has employed Mr. J. S. Greene to defend him. (*Alexandria Gazette*, October 21, 1897, p. 3.)

WEDDING AT THE STATION HOUSE - Quite a number of persons assembled in front of the station house last night for the purpose of attending the Police Court, which was to convene at eight o'clock to examine into the charges urged by Miss Temple Jeffries against Thomas M. Kimball. Mayor Simpson, however, had concluded to admit only the witnesses in the case with the court officials and counsel. When the court was convened the young woman stated her grievance in a straightforward manner, although her emotion at times was manifest. She read several letters Kimball had sent her and narrated her relations with the accused, giving the history of her introduction to him, and subsequent events. Kimball, she said, had promised to marry her a number of times, but continued to postpone doing so, until her mother learned of the circumstances. Kimball's demands for money had been responded to when it was within the power of the complainant, as he had always stated that it was necessary to enable him to assist her in the future. Kimball, she said, had returned to the city on Tuesday last and endeavored to get her to withdraw the warrant, but her mother would not permit her to do so. Mrs. Jeffries, the mother, also testified that the accused had promised to marry her daughter a few weeks ago, and that she had received a letter subsequently to this effect. The letter, however, also requested that the necessary funds be furnished to defray expenses. The testimony of Kimball's witnesses was unimportant. He did not deny the allegations. The Mayor in summing up the case stated that the facts in the case were too plain to be ignored. At this juncture Kimball arose and stated that he would marry the girl, but would not support her. Mr. Beach, clerk of the corporation court, was then sent for and furnished the necessary license. Rev. J. T. Williams, of the M. E. Church South, performed the ceremony. Immediately after the marriage Kimball and his wife separated without a word being passed by either and took different streets for their homes. Miss Jeffries is quite a good looking girl, of about nineteen years. Kimball was represented by Mr. John H. Greene.

It is said, however, that shortly after the wedding, Mr. Kimball proceeded to the house where his bride lives and being denied admission by the gentleman of the house, spent most of the night on the sidewalk talking to his bride, who sat at a window. (*Alexandria Gazette*, October 22, 1897, p. 3.)

THE SEDUCTION CASE - The case of R. E. L. Tyler, charged with the seduction of Agnes Robinson, came up before Mayor Simpson at 11 o'clock this morning. ...The police courtroom was crowded during the trial, which lasted over two hours.

The first witness was the plaintiff, Agnes Robinson, who testified that on Tuesday, April 26th, about 8 o'clock p.m., she was lying on a sofa in a room on the first floor of her father's residence when Mr. Tyler entered the room and asked to borrow a hood full of coal, and she told him that the coal was in a shed in the yard and that she did not want to go out there. Mr. Tyler then sat on the sofa by her, and it was then, she claims, that he accomplished her ruin. The witness also testified that this was on the night, and a few hours before, Mr. Tyler's wife died. When asked if any gentlemen visited her, the witness stated that Policemen Wilkinson and Deane, who are old acquaintances, and Mr. Carr, an employee of the Virginia Glass Works, visited her occasionally. The witness also stated that her parents were absent from home on the night in question. Upon being questioned if Policeman Proctor ever visited her she indignantly replied "that she was too much of a lady to have married men paying attention to her."

Mrs. Robinson, mother of the plaintiff testified that on the evening of April 26 last, she left home about 7 o'clock to attend a meeting in the Sunday School room of Christ Church, of which church she was a member, and that on the way she was met by Mr. Tyler, who asked her to lend him some coal and that she told him to go to her house and perhaps her daughter would get it for him. Mrs. Robinson stated that her daughter told her that Mr. Tyler was the cause of her trouble. When asked if Officer Proctor ever visited her house the witness said that officers had visited her home on business connected with the Mayor's office.

Mr. James Deane, sexton of Christ Church, testified that on Tuesday, April 26, there was a meeting of the Bible class of the Brotherhood of St. Andrew in the Sunday Schoolroom of the church for men and that there was no meeting for ladies that night. When asked by the Mayor if on Friday night two weeks ago Policeman Wilkinson had met him in the yard of Christ Church and asked him if he had heard that his son, Policeman Deane, had left town, and that "things would come up in time," Mr. Deane replied that Mr. Wilkinson had said that to him, but that the officer's language was a conundrum to him, as he did not know what Mr. Wilkinson meant.

Mr. Edward Penn testified that he had never seen any questionable conduct on Mr. Tyler's part toward Miss Robinson, and that he had seen Mr. Proctor in Miss Robinson's company frequently on the street.

Mrs. Annie Penn, who is a sister of Mr. Tyler and lives at his house, testified that on the night of April 26, Mr. Tyler left the house about 7 o'clock with the intention of consulting a doctor, as he was suffering with pains in his chest, and returned about 8 o'clock and remained in the house until the next morning.

Wm. Atwell testified that he had seen Miss Robinson talking to Officer Proctor on King Street and in front of her house.

James Mayhew stated that he paid attention to Miss Robinson about a year ago, but that they had quarreled and parted, that he had found the young lady to be of irreproachable character, and that he had seen Officer Deane at the plaintiff's home several times.

Policeman Deane testified that he had known Miss Robinson about one year and a half and that his association with her had been that of a gentleman; that he had frequently met and conversed with her on the street, and had seen officer Wilkinson talking to her, and also officer Proctor while on duty. Mr. Deane said that Officer Proctor had told him that Mrs. Annie Penn had accused him (Deane) of Miss Robinson's trouble; he had seen Policeman Wilkinson in reference to what he had said to his father and Wilkinson said he was only joking.

Officer Wilkinson said that he had known Miss Robinson six years; he denied having engaged in the conversation referred to by Mr. James Deane; that he had seen Officer Proctor at Miss Robinson's home prior to the 26th of April, and had seen them together several times afterward.

Mr. Tyler then took the stand and emphatically denied the charge. He said that on the night of April 26 he went to Dr. O'Brien's office to consult him, as he had been suffering with his chest, and returned to his home a few minutes before 8 o'clock and had laid down on a sofa in the parlor. He was aroused by the entrance of Mr. Edgar Lyles. He stated that he remained in the house at the bedside of his sick wife, who died the next morning a few minutes past 1 o'clock; his first intimation that he was connected with the case was when the girl's mother and brother went to his place of business in Washington and accused him of it.

Mr. Edgar Lyles testified that on the night of April 25, he went to Mr. Tyler's residence about 8 o'clock and remained there until 11:30 o'clock, and on the following night, the 26th, he went there a few minutes past 8 o'clock; on both occasions Mr. Tyler was present. The witness stated that he had known Mr. Tyler for 20 years and had found him a gentleman of unquestionable character.

...George C. Lyles testified that he had repeatedly seen Miss Robinson and Policeman Proctor together at night, and that on one occasion his attention was called to the fact by his mother, who had also noticed their association.

Mrs. Samuel Wade testified that about a year ago Miss Robinson had been employed in her house; that she saw Policeman Proctor talking with the girl and had remonstrated with her for associating with married men.

Mr. Wm. E. Grady said that he had seen Miss Robinson and Policeman Proctor together in front of the young lady's home...

Several other witnesses testified, but their evidence had no special bearing on the case.

After hearing the testimony, Mayor Simpson said: This case is one of ugly environments. A man accused of forsaking the bedside of a dying wife to debauch the child of a neighbor, and, if the evidence could establish this fact, the prisoner should not only have the law's severest penalties inflicted upon him, but in addition thereto, human sympathy should be denied him. The statute governing the crime with which this man is charged does not allow the unsupported evidence of the aggrieved to be accepted as conclusive, but her evidence, with corroborative circumstances, is sufficient. In this case we have neither corroborative circumstances nor undisputed evidence of any kind, for one of the Commonwealth's witnesses stated that a church meeting was attended by her on the night of the offense, and the sexton of the church states that the church was not open the night in question. A Commonwealth witness says no married man visited her and another Commonwealth witness says just as positively that a married man did visit her. Without descanting upon the voluminous evidence that has been adduced I will simply say that the facts elicited in this trial in no wise connect the prisoner with the ruin of the young girl and I can very conscientiously give him an honorable acquittal.

After the trial, Mr. Robinson, the girl's father, attacked Mr. Tyler in front of the station house, but Officer Atkinson arrested Mr. Robinson before the men came to blows. He was reprimanded by the Mayor. (*Alexandria Gazette*, November 1898, p. 3.)

∧∧*∧*∧*∧*∧*∧*∧*∧*∧*∧*∧*∧*

FOUND GUILTY - In the County Court of Fairfax today the jury in the case of Lindsey Jackson, colored, of this city, indicted for an attempted assault on Mrs. James Coxen at Sideburn a few weeks since, rendered a verdict of guilty and fixed his punishment at four years in the penitentiary. A motion to set aside the verdict was made. (*Alexandria Gazette*, October 19, 1900, p. 3.)

VERDICT SET ASIDE - ...The jury returned a verdict of guilty and fixed (Jackson's) punishment at four years in the penitentiary. Upon motion of counsel for the prisoner, the court set aside the verdict and nolle prossed the indictment. Jackson was then carried before Justice Taylor, convicted of indecent exposure and sentenced to serve eight months in jail. (*Alexandria Gazette*, October 20, 1900, p. 3.)

∧∧*∧*∧*∧*∧*∧*∧*∧*∧*∧*∧*∧*

UNSEEMLY CONDUCT IN THE STREET - Justice Beach, who is presiding in the Police Court temporarily, this morning gave instructions to the police to arrest all women making indecent exhibitions of themselves in the northeastern portion of the city. He said complaints had been made of the unseemly conduct of women in that locality who often attract attention by going into the street in a half-clad condition. The complaint is chronic, as the same species of conduct has caused protests to be lodged at police headquarters on other occasions. (*Alexandria Gazette*, July 22, 1902, p. 3.)

CHAPTER ELEVEN

Shootings

Mr. John Peters – Clerk in the Bank of Columbia Shot 2 Miles Outside Alexandria.

Mr. John Peters – a clerk in the Bank of Columbia, is now lying dangerously wounded, in the left side, apparently by a Pistol Ball, at the house of Jonathan Swift Esq., near this town. This gentleman states, that as on his way from George Town, to Alexandria with between 16 & 17,000 dollars in notes of the Bank of Alexandria, for the purpose of exchanging them for cash or Columbia Bank Notes, he was met about 9 o'clock A.M. at a small branch near a hedge of bryers about 2 miles from this town and between the lands of Charles Alexander Sr. and Charles Alexander Jun., by a young man, who approached from one side of the road, and appeared in the act of crossing it. But who getting near the Horse, seized the Bridle and discharged a Pistol at Mr. Peters which occasioned the wound from which he now suffers. This unfortunate young man describes the assassin as of middle height – with a Black Coat and Hat and Nankeen Pataloons, he had shoes on and had a genteel appearance. On falling from his horse Mr. P. supposes he was robbed of his money, as when assistance arrived he had none.

Such were the most correct reports, relative to perhaps the most daring robbery ever perpetrated in America, in circulation yesterday. This morning we have collected a few other facts which we deem it our duty to insert in this day's paper.

As soon as the circumstance was known a general and honorable spirit of indignation was excited – our citizens, military and civil, who could procure horses immediately went in pursuit of the assassin – we are informed about 150 of the inhabitants of Alexandria were engaged in the pursuit – the information obtained from those who returned as follows:

Early yesterday morning two genteel looking men, one exactly answering the description given by Mr. Peters of the assassin crossed at the George Town Ferry and were observed to have pistols, they had with them a black man, apparently a servant – this man might have crossed accidentally – when on the south side of the river they were seen to take the road to the right of the Alexandria road, but were afterwards met in it, but without the negro. Different parties of our citizens met with some waggoners who reported that they had met on

171

the Winchester road, two men answering the above description, riding as fast as their horses could carry them about 3 hours ride ahead of their pursuers.

...It is not improbable but the above were the robbers, that their object now is to gain the back country, and hide themselves in its vastness until the search shall be over...

...We are happy to learn that Mr. Peters (though severely) is not considered dangerously wounded. The ball struck against a rib, and, as it is well known, that a slight resistance will change the direction of a ball, so this gliding under the membranes passed along the side of the bone and lodged itself in the fleshy parts of the back, from which it has been extracted. *The Alexandria Expositor*, July 31, 1805, p. 2.

^^*^*^*^*^*^*^*^*^*^*^*^*^*^*

MAN SHOT – An altercation occurred yesterday morning, in Eldred Restaurant, between James Welch and John Edd, which resulted in the latter's shooting the former in the head, with a pistol. Edd was arrested and examined before Justices English and Summers, and committed to jail. It appeared, on evidence, that Welch was in the Restaurant, and was making a disturbance, when Edd entered and rebuked him. Some words passed between them, and Welch called Edd a liar, which the former told the latter not to repeat. Welch, however, again called Edd a liar, when the latter drew a revolver and shot Welch in the head. Welch fell, exclaiming, "I'm a dead man." Welch was then taken to his home, and Dr. J.C. Broun, called in, who, assisted by Dr. Fairfax, succeeded in extracting a ball from the side of his head, just above the left ear – but it is thought that the pistol was double shotted, and that another shot yet remains, as the eye ball was bursted, which could not have been caused by the shot extracted, which took effect in the forehead, above the left eye. It is probable, that the other shot passed through the ball of his left eye. Welch was still alive at 6 o'clock yesterday evening, though it was considered doubtful whether he could recover. (*Alexandria Gazette*, February 4, 1857, p. 3.)

CONDITION OF JAMES WELCH – At six o'clock, yesterday evening, James Welch, who was shot on Tuesday morning, by John Edd, was much easier, and hopes are entertained of his recovery, though he still lies in a very critical condition. (*Alexandria Gazette*, February 5, 1857, p. 3.)

RE-COMMITTED – John Edd, committed to jail on last Tuesday week, for shooting Jas. Welch, was taken before Justices English, Price, and Summers, yesterday afternoon, and re-committed until Tuesday next, to await the condition of Welch. (*Alexandria Gazette*, February 12, 1857, p.3.)

COMMITTED – John T. Edd, who shot Welch on the morning of the 3d inst., was taken before Justices Price and English yesterday afternoon, for an examination – no new evidence was elicited, and Edd was committed to jail for examination before the next term of the County Court. Messrs. F. L. Smith and David Funsten appeared for the prisoner. C. E. Stuart for the prosecution. (*Alexandria Gazette*, February 26, 1857, p. 3.)

Commonwealth vs. John Edd - indicted for shooting with intent to maim, disfigure & kill - 18 May 1857 - jury could not agree - prisoner dismissed. (*Alexandria County Common Law Court Order Book*, May 19, 1857, Vol. 2, p. 3.)

Commonwealth vs. John Edd - retried - "guilty of unlawful shooting and sentenced to confinement in the county jail." (*Alexandria County Common Law Order Book*, November 10, 1857, Vol. 2, p. 25.)

^^*^*^*^*^*^*^*^*^*^*^*

SAD HOMICIDE IN WASHINGTON - A scene of violence and bloodshed was enacted at about 3 o'clock, yesterday afternoon, at the lager-beer saloon of Joseph Garhard, on Maryland avenue, near its intersection with the canal. Three men from Alexandria, said to be named Rudd, Smith, and Hall, and two from the Navy Yard, called for and obtained drink at Gerhard's, for which they refused to pay. An altercation consequently ensued, in which Mrs. Gerhard participated; and at length blows were passed, the barkeeper, Henry Shulte, assisting his employers. The parties passing out into the avenue, sticks. and stones were freely used, until Gerhard advanced with a pistol, which he is in the habit of keeping in his bar, and fired at the assailants. The shot took effect on one of the Alexandrians, when Gerhard prepared to fire a second time. At this instant the barkeeper turned himself around in front of Gerhard, and so received the shot intended for the other party full in the breast. Poor Shulte fell and almost instantly expired. Gerhard was soon arrested, and the case examined by Justice Donn, who, after hearing twenty-one witnesses, held Gerhard to bail in the sum of $3,000 to appear at the coming term of the Criminal Court. John Robinson, one of the Navy Yard men, was subsequently arrested as a participant in the riot, and held to $300 bail for further examination. The Alexandrians took to flight homewards, but officers have been dispatched to Alexandria to secure their arrest as fugitives from justice. - *Nat. Int.* of yesterday (*Alexandria Gazette*, June 13, 1857, p.3.)

^^*^*^*^*^*^*^*^*^*^*^*

A Federal Soldier who had just landed here this morning and gone to the "Soldier's Rest" at the depot of the Orange and Alexandria Railroad, was shot and instantly killed by the guard, who, it is said, was under the influence of liquor, and who was at once arrested and confined. (*Alexandria Gazette*, February 18, 1929, p. 4. - 65 years ago)

Hayes Tressler, aged 19, was accidentally shot and killed by a boy named Patrick Doran, while they were out gunning near Mr. John Slater's garden, on Wednesday afternoon last. This melancholy affair has caused much distress in the family of the deceased, and in that of the lad who had the misfortune to cause the death. (*Alexandria Gazette*, October 21, 1864, p. 1.)

＊∧＊∧＊∧＊∧＊∧＊∧＊∧＊∧＊∧＊∧＊

SHOOTING – A difficulty occurred today about 11 o'clock, near the corner of Wolfe and Water streets, between a negro man and a soldier belonging to the District volunteers. High words ensued between them, and finally the soldier discharged his musket at the negro, wounding him severely. The matter will be investigated by the military authorities. (*Alexaadria Gazette*, May 23, 1865, p. 3.)

＊∧＊∧＊∧＊∧＊∧＊∧＊∧＊∧＊∧＊∧＊

SHOOTING IN A MAGISTRATE'S OFFICE – In the office of Justice W. L. Penn, in the old market house building, yesterday evening, when the case of Nancy Randal, colored, against Wesley Kinney, colored, for the recovery of $25 was in progress, the defendant, who it appeared in evidence, had at one time been the acknowledged lover of the plaintiff, and had obtained the money which the suit had been brought to recover upon the strength of that relationship, made some remarks which the plaintiff considered as derogatory of her character, and instantly drawing a revolver she leveled it at him, and with her eyes beaming with all the malice of love turned to hate she pulled the trigger. Just as the weapon was discharged, however, her hand was seized by a constable, and the ball, consequently, was diverted from its intended course. The pistol was wrenched from her before she could fire it a second time. The defendant, who had lost the suit, left the office in short order, but after a time returned and had the plaintiff bound over to keep the peace. (*Alex. Gazette*, Aug. 27, 1869, p. 3.)

＊∧＊∧＊∧＊∧＊∧＊∧＊∧＊∧＊∧＊∧＊

SHOOTING WITHIN THE CITY LIMITS – Great complaint is made of the discharge of fire arms within the limits of the corporation and especially of the shooting continually going on in that portion of the city northwest of the Court House. Boys with shot guns are on the commons there daily, banging away at the sparrows and briar birds, to the great danger, however, of the residents of that locality. (*Alexandria Gazette*, September 18, 1869, p.3.)

＊∧＊∧＊∧＊∧＊∧＊∧＊∧＊∧＊∧＊∧＊

ACCIDENTAL SHOOTING – Three gentlemen who came down on the late train, last night, went to Mr. D. C. Thompson's restaurant on St. Asaph street, near King, to get some oysters, and finding it closed, a suggestion was made that a "salute" be fired to wake Mr. Thompson up, which was at once carried out by one of the gentlemen, who fired a shot from his revolver through the lower panel of the door. Unfortunately Mr. Thompson had just reached the inside of the door and was about to open it when the shot came crashing through and struck his right foot near the great toe, and ranging backwards came out near the heel. Dr. Lewis was called in and rendered the necessary surgical assistance. The gentleman who inflicted the injury did all in his power to assist the wounded man. (*Alexandria Gazette*, March 6, 1877, p.3.)

THE THOMPSON CASE – The case of D. C. Thompson vs. G. W. Harrison et al. in which R. J. Daingerfield is sued as an accessory to the shooting of Thompson on the night of the 5th of March, 1877, by George W. Harrison, at the restaurant of Thompson, was concluded in the Circuit Court, before Judge Turner yesterday evening, the jury rendering a verdict in favor of Thompson for $8,000 and the Judge refusing to grant the motion for a new trial. Exceptions were taken to the rulings of the court, and a stay of proceedings was granted for sixty days, in order to give time to apply to the Court of Appeals for a writ of error.... (*Alexandria Gazette*, October 1, 1879, p. 3.)

^^*^*^*^*^*^*^*^*^*^*^*^*

THE SHOOTING YESTERDAY – Mention was made in yesterday's *Gazette* of the shooting of George Edwards by his step father, James Burnett. It appears that Burnett went in company with a grocer to Edwards' house, at the extreme upper end of Prince street, yesterday afternoon, to collect a bill, where they found Edwards in an intoxicated condition, who insisted that before paying the amount claimed by the grocery man, Burnett should leave the premises. Burnett walked off, and Edwards went to the house of a Mrs. Struder, living nearby, for the purpose, he said, of getting the money from his wife. In his absence, Burnett returned and undertook to drive a girl, the daughter of the said Mrs. Struder, out of the yard, applying some harsh epithets to her to which Mrs. Struder took exceptions and called on Burnett for an explanation, when a sort of fight ensued, in which Mrs. Struder and one of her daughters received, in the language of some of the spectactors "a good shaking." During the scuffle, Edwards appeared on the scene with a brick in his hand, and, throwing it at Burnett, struck him on the shoulder. Burnett warned Edwards that if he threw at him again he would kill him, but he (Edwards) did not heed the warning, and, while in the act of throwing another brick, Burnett drew his pistol and fired, the ball striking Edwards in the upper part of the forehead, coursing around the course of the skull and lodging in the top of the head, inflicting a painful, though not serious, wound. Dr. Stabler, who was sent for, extracted the ball, and the wounded man this morning was doing well, although it will be sometime before he will be able to throw another brick. Burnett, as soon as he shot the man, put out towards the grave yards, and, although the police were after him until early this morning, he is still at large. A gentleman from Fairfax this morning reports that Burnett was seen late yesterday evening near Spring field Station, making his way toward Sangster's Cross Roads. (*Alexandria Gazette*, July 21, 1880, p.3.)

175

SHOOTING AFFRAY – Considerable excitement was created last Saturday evening by the shooting of a young man named Jefferson Phillips, of this city, by Frank F. DeLea, of Richmond. The shooting occurred on Union street, between King and Cameron, and in a few minutes crowds had collected in the neighborhood. It appears that the altercation grew out of a game of cards which had been engaged in the day before between Phillips and DeLea, in which the latter had lost between $60 and $70, money it is said, which belonged to Mr. J.H. Chataigne, publisher of the *Alexandria City Directory*. Supposing he had not been dealt fairly with by Phillips, DeLea went to Brodbeck's restaurant, at the foot of King street, shortly after six o'clock and called out Phillips, who was in the house, and the pair proceeded up Union street. Upon reaching Mr. J.H.D. Smoot's lumber yard an altercation took place, DeLea accusing his companion of cheating him out of his money the day before, asserting that the game of cards had not been conducted fairly. Words ensued, during which Phillips called DeLea a ––––– liar. The two men clinched and fought for a few seconds, both falling to the ground. Upon regaining their feet, DeLea drew a pistol and fired at his adversary twice, both shots taking effect, one ball striking him in the right arm and the other taking effect under the left shoulder blade, penetrating the lungs. Upon being shot, Phillips started to run, and rushed into Mr. Smoot's counting room, when DeLea fired the second shot. At this juncture the greatest excitement was produced in that locality, especially in Mr. Smoot's counting room, the occupants of which stampeded in order to avoid injury. After the shooting DeLea walked to King street and out to the wharf, where he was arrested by Officer Nightingill and taken to the station house. A crowd soon gathered around the wounded man who began expectorating blood, and in a short time Dr. Powell, who had been summoned, arrived and rendered all the temporary surgical assistance needed, after which he was removed to his residence, on Royal street. Phillips's injuries, though dangerous are said by Drs. Powell and O'Brien to be not necessarily fatal. He slept comfortably last night but today his symptoms were not so favorable. DeLea was a former student at St. John's Academy, but has recently been living with his father in Richmond. He came to this city on Wednesday last to deliver some directories. He was under the influence of liquor when he shot Phillips and when he became sober seemed much distressed at what he had done.

...Dr. R. C. Powell said he saw Phillips at Mr. Smoot's office; he had been shot twice, once in the right arm and once in the left side below the lower end of the shoulder blade, the ball passing into the lung; the wound in the arm was not serious, but the other was, though not necessarily fatal. He exhibited the ball which he had taken from the arm, and which had been flattened against the bone; had not probed for the other one, as it would be dangerous to do so.

The Mayor, after hearing the evidence, sent the prisoner on to the grand jury, and he was taken to jail.

This evening young DeLea was brought before Judge Stuart on a writ of habeas corpus, sworn out by his counsel, who asked that the prisoner be released on bail.   After hearing the testimony of Dr. Powell, Judge Stuart adjourned the case till Thursday to await the result of Phillips' wounds.

DeLea was then taken back to jail. (*Alexandria Gazette*, July 9, 1888, p.3.)

ADMITTED TO BAIL – The habeas corpus case of Frank DeLea, charged with shooting Jefferson Phillips on Saturday last...but which was continued till today, came up this evening when Drs. Powell and O'Brien stated that the condition of Phillips was favorable and that unless something unforeseen occurred he would recover from his wounds. Judge Stuart thereupon issued an order directing DeLea to be released on bail in the sum of $2,500 for his appearance in court on Tuesday next.

At 5 o'clock this evening DeLea had not furnished bail but he expected to do so later. (*Alexandria Gazette*, July 12, 1888, p. 3.)

The grand jury returned a true bill against Frank DeLea, for feloneously and maliciously shooting Jeff. Phillips with intent to kill and were adjourned until tomorrow.   (*Alexandria Gazette*, July 17, 1888, p.3.)

ACQUITTED – Frank DeLea, who shot Jefferson Phillips on Union street last summer, and whose trial for malicious assault came up in the Corporation Court yesterday, was acquitted, the jury after being out less than half an hour, returning a verdict of not guilty to the indictment.   DeLea, it will be remembered, after losing a sum of money at cards with Phillips, met him, and, after a quarrel on Union street shot him in the side and arm. Phillips, however, soon recovered from his wounds. (*Alexandria Gazette*, October 9, 1888, p.3.)

SHOOTING AFFAIR – Yesterday evening, shortly after 6 o'clock, City Sergeant Smith escorted Frank DeLea (who had just been acquitted in the Corporation Court of maliciously shooting Jeff Phillips) to the depot to take the train for Richmond. On their way to the train they met Mr. B. F. Penn, who accompanied them to the depot.   When the train arrived these gentlemen were standing on Cameron street, a few yards from the depot, talking to Judge James Sangster, of Fairfax, when a burly negro man named Will Smith, who had just gotten off the train, rushed between them, brushing against Judge Sangster and Sergeant Smith with so much force as to almost knock them down. Judge Sangster asked the man if he could not walk along without knocking people down, when Smith turned around and attempted to strike him with a stick, Judge Sangster had a small cane and in defense struck at the negro, shivering the cane.   Smith, who by the way had struck someone else on the platform before he reached Sergeant Smith's party, then attacked Judge Sangster and Sergeant Smith, striking the latter on the cheek with a stick, knocking him down. He then became furious and attacked everyone standing near. A young man in the crowd drew a pistol and snapped it at Smith, but the weapon did not go off, when he handed it to Judge Sangster. By this time Smith had renewed his attack on Sergeant Smith when Judge Sangster shot him, the ball striking him two inches below the ear, penetrating the throat, striking the windpipe and passing to the back of his neck. Much excitement followed and a large crowd of negroes assembled and demanded the arrest of Judge Sangster, but the latter, after warning them to keep off, walked to the station house, where he gave himself up and was released on his own recognizance for his appearance today. Smith was taken to the office of Dr. O'Brien where his wounds were examined and dressed by Drs. O'Brien and Smith. Later he was taken to his home on Wolfe street between Columbus and Alfred, where he now lies in a dangerous condition. He is well known along the wharves and worked for Capt. J. T. Rogers on his pile driving machine.

As before stated, Mayor Downham last night released Judge Sangster for his appearance this morning at 9 o'clock. This was done after hearing the statements of the Judge, Sergeant Smith, Mr. Penn and others. This morning the case was further continued till 1 o'clock. ...The case was continued till Wednesday, the 17th to await the result of Smith's wounds... (*Alexandria Gazette*, October 9, 1888, p.3.)

CASE DISMISSED – The trial of ex-Judge James Sangster, of Fairfax, charged with shooting Wm. Smith, colored, at the local depot in this city on the night of the 8th instant, which had been postponed from time to time, came up before Mayor Downham and Justice May this morning. ...Smith was present, apparently entirely recovered from the wound in his neck. The witnesses examined were Smith, the man who was shot, City Sergeant Smith, B. F. Penn, Isaac Hackley, colored, Fayette Lee, colored, Jos. Purcell, and Judge Sangster. The statements of the colored men were almost identical and were to the effect that Smith in coming off the depot platform, stumbled and almost fell against Judge Sangster when he was assaulted. Smith testified that he had no stick and that he was attacked by several men, all of whom he knocked down. All the other witnesses testified that Smith provoked the row, and assaulted every one in sight, when, after knocking Sergeant Smith down, he was shot by Judge Sangster. The justices without hearing argument of counsel dismissed the case. (*Alexandria Gazette*, October 31, 1888 p. 3.)

^^*^*^*^*^*^*^*^*^*^*^*

A SAD OCCURRENCE – Last night, Wm. Wheatley, son of Mr. Wm. Wheatley, who lives on Columbus street, nearly opposite St. John's Academy, shot Auburn Pridemore Hagan, son of Patrick Hagan, esq. of Scott county, a cadet at that institution, with a self-cocking revolver, Dr. Purvis was called in immediately, but the ball having entered the right eye and penetrated the brain, was necessarily fatal, and the young man, who was a very large and well developed youth in his 18th year, died about two o'clock this morning. Coroner Powell being notified of the occurrence summoned a jury of inquest consisting of

Messrs. G. Ramsay, forman... Wheatley had voluntarily surrendered himself, and young Wheatley himself, rendered the following verdict:

...The jurors sworn to enquire when, where and by what means Auburn P. Hagan came to his death, upon their oaths do say that he came to his death from a gunshot wound inflicted by a pistol in the hands of Wm. S. Wheatley, which pistol was accidentally discharged while being carelessly handled; and we also believe that this occurrence was not due to any want of discipline or care on the part of the superintendent of the academy.

...the Commonwealth's Attorney stated that he did not think a case could be made against him (Wheatley) on the testimony, he was discharged. It is proper to say that young Wheatley is not, and never has been, connected with the Academy. (*Alexandria Gazette*, October 9, 1889, p. 3.)

^^*^*^*^*^*^*^*^*^*^*^*

KILLED BY A POLICEMAN – The depot of the Washington Southern Railway, northeast corner of Cameron and Fayette streets was the scene of a dual tragedy at 7:30 o'clock yesterday evening, Policeman Samuel Ticer shooting two colored men, almost instantly killing one, Fayette Lee, and so seriously wounding the other George Pine, that his death is hourly expected. The neighborhood has for years been rendered disagreeable to quiet people by the assembling there of crowds who sometimes become menacing if not disorderly. Their hilarity generally prevents conversation among other other people, while their buffoonry and skylarking is annoying and disgusting. Last night, during one of these disorderly scenes, officers Ticer and McCuen undertook to disperse the crowd, the two policemen becoming separated in the meantime. Mr. Ticer had occasion to take a colored man named Albert Smith into custody for refusing to obey his order, when Fayette Lee, another negro, interfered. The policeman then undertook to arrest Lee, when the latter struck the former, knocking him down and cutting his nose. Officer McCuen, at this juncture, came to his partner's assistance and struck Lee with his stick. Mr. Ticer immediately regained his feet, shaking off Lee, and defended himself as best he could against the crowd which had gathered thick and menacing. He ordered them to fall back, which order was ignored, and a negro named Geo. Pine, who was in front of the crowd, continued to advance, whereupon the officer drew his pistol and fired two shots. The first bullet struck Pine in the chin, passing up into his head, and the second imbedded itself in Lee's shoulder. The crowd then scattered. The wounded men were taken to a neighboring house, where Doctor O'Brien was summoned, but too late to be of any avail to Lee, who died in ten minutes. Pine was taken to his home where he received medical attention. In the meantime Officer Ticer, who was bruised and bleeding, was taken into a saloon nearby and a large number of negroes gathered in groups outside and listened to speeches of two negro men, who urged them to avenge the death of their fallen comrades using violent language and making dire threats to apply the torch to every house in town and murder the inhabitants saying that

179

this was the time to assert their rights, and that Congress would protect them. The result of the disturbance, however, had a cooling effect upon the bad blood previously exhibited by the negroes, and when re-enforcements arrived the two who were urging the crowd to bloodshed were arrested and taken into custody. Officer Ticer was taken to the station house by Lieut. Smith and an examination of the affair was held by Mayor Downham. ... The evidence adduced was in accordance with the facts given above and that the officer was compelled to act in self-defense. Mr. Ticer was held in the sum of $2,000 for his appearance next Tuesday, Mr. W.P. Woolls becoming his bondsman. This morning the two negroes who had tried to incite a riot (Simon Lee and Webb Roy) were also given a hearing and were fined $5 each for disorderly conduct. ... In the absence of Coroner Purvis, Justice Whittlesey summoned the coroner's jury...Mr. S.G. Brent appeared for Officer Ticer. Lee was about 35 years old and a man of powerful build. Pine's name for some time past has figured in the police report. Officer Ticer, who was a Union soldier during the late war, has been on the police force about eight years, has always proven himself reliable and trustworthy, and during the time he has been employed as a conservator of the peace has more than once been an actor in scenes where both his courage and patience have been strained to their utmost tension, and that, too, with the very element with which he was last night engaged. ... The fact that a tragedy has to be enacted by an officer of the law is, of course, to be deplored by all right-thinking people, but when such officials, in the exercise of their sworn duty, are assaulted and knocked down and their life placed in jeopardy by lawless people – either white or black – there is but one recourse, and that Mr. Ticer availed himself of, as any one else would have done under the circumstances. (*Alexandria Gazette*, July 5, 1890, p. 3.)

VERDICT OF THE CORONER'S JURY – ...About twenty witnesses were examined and the burden of testimony was in accordance with the facts published in the *Gazette*. ... There was an abundance of testimony in reference to the size and temper of the crowd present at the shooting, showing that about 150 negroes were present, most of whom had been indulging in liquor. Constant Ponnett, the leading witness, testified that the officer was kicked several times about the body by Lee. ... The jury returned the following verdict: "We, the jury find that Fayette Lee came to his death by a pistol fired by Police Officer Ticer while in the discharge of his duties." ... The records of the station house show that during the late Mayor Smoot's term of office Lee was arrested by Officer Henry for interfering with an officer while in the discharge of his duty, and that to make the arrest the officer had to call for assistance. Lee was fined for the offense by Mayor Smoot. (*Alexandria Gazette*, July 7, 1890, p.3.)

^^*^*^*^*^*^*^*^*^*^*^*^*

A BOY SHOT – On Saturday morning a group of colored boys were engaged in pitching cents near the intersection of Royal and Pendleton streets when a young colored man, named Arthur Shirley, who was celebrating Christmas by firing ball cartridges from a pistol, appeared on the scene. He discharged the weapon once, but the ball from it did no damage. Another report followed, when the ball struck a colored boy named John Lewis, about 14 years old, in the head. The ball entered at the back of the head, on the left side, fractured the skull and penetrated the brain. The bullet split, one part passing into the head, leaving an ugly wound through which the brain oozed, and the other, after making a scalp wound, passing off. Policemen Lyles and Knight, who had heard of the shooting, soon found Shirley and locked him up, and later Officer Atkinson discovered the pistol where Shirley had hid it. Dr. Purvis was called to render assistance to the boy and he had him removed to the Infirmary, where an examination was made by Drs. Purvis, Snowden and Thomas W. Gibson, and his injuries found to be of a very grave nature. According to the statements of some boys who saw the shooting, it was done deliberately and wantonly, but Shirley claims that after he had fired the first time a boy named Elzey struck his arm and the pistol was accidentally discharged. Shirley has been arrested on previous occasions for misdemeanors, but this is the first time anything serious has been urged against him. He was given a hearing by the Mayor this morning who deemed it best to continue the case. Lewis, it is said, cannot live. (*Alexandria Gazette*, December 27, 1897, p. 3.)

Arthur Shirley, colored, charged with shooting John Lewis, was released on his own recognizance to appear on the 6th day of January, 1898. (*Alexandria Gazette*, December 28, 1897, p. 3.)

CHAPTER TWELVE

Custis And Randolph

GEORGE WASHINGTON PARKE CUSTIS: A YOUTHFUL FELON? – George Washington Parke Custis (April 30, 1781–October 10, 1857) was the grandson of Martha Washington. After the death of his father, John Parke Custis in 1781, young George resided with General and Mrs. Washington at Mt. Vernon until the death of the latter in 1802. As a young man, young "Wash" Custis attended Princeton College in New Jersey and was later commissioned in 1799 a cornet of horse in the U.S. army and became an aide-de-camp to Gen. Charles Pinckney. In 1804, G.W.P. Custis married Mary, the daughter of William Fitzhugh who resided at Ravensworth in Fairfax County and at 607 Oronoco Street in Alexandria. Custis constructed a lovely home for his new bride atop an eminence which he called Mt. Washington. Later the house and plantation became known as Arlington House. In 1831, Mary Randolph, the daughter of G.W.P. Custis, married Robert E. Lee. Renown as a brilliant orator, Mr. Custis was also a playwrite, painter and frequent lecturer in Alexandria. Having grown up at Mt. Vernon, he adored General Washington and cherished the sacred mementos which reminded him of his close association with the first President.

While a very young man, Custis became embroiled in a prank at Gadsby's tavern. Records of the Court of Oyer and Terminer reveal the following:

At an Examining Court appointed & held for the Town of Alexandria 25 June 1798 for the Examination of Geo. W. Custis.

Present – John Dundas, Wm. Harper, Jonah Thompson, Philip Marsteller, and Dennis Ramsay

George W. Custis, who was recognized to appear before the Court this day to answer a suspecion of Felony in entering the house of John Gadsby, an Innkeeper and feloniously Stealing & Carrying away two Silver Spoons of the value of Four Dollars being this day solomnly called & failing to appear it is ordered that his recognizance be prosecuted. John Dundas.

One can just imagine the reaction of General & Mrs. Washington to these charges. No doubt the family must have been highly embarrassed at having their grandson charged with a felony -- namely the theft of silver spoons from Gadsby's Tavern. Of course there are many unanswered questions concerning the case. For instance, why did John Gadsby see fit to bring charges against the grandson of Martha Washington? Who paid G. W. P. Custis' bail? Why did young Custis fail to appear in court? Did General Washington intervene with friends in high places to have young Custis exonerated? Unfortunately, there is no further record of any action taken on the case.

^^*^*^*^*^*^*^*^*^*^*^*

PRESIDENT ANDREW JACKSON ATTACKED WHILE VISITING ALEXANDRIA, VIRGINIA – An incident of a most painful nature occurred on board the steamboat *Sydney*, as she stopped here on her way down, yesterday. An assault was made upon the President of the United States by Mr. Randolph, late of the Navy. At the first blow, we understand, almost a hundred arms fell upon the assailant, and he was with difficulty rescued and carried on shore. We have never known more excitement nor more feeling to be manifested by all our citizens. We are induced to mention this matter, which ought indeed never to be published, only because we know that reports of it will be circulated throughout the country and printed elsewhere. It was an affair of a moment; but it is said, that, from the feeling produced, it is wonderful that the assailant escaped with his life.

So great was the public indignation at this outrage, that we believe almost any measure would have been adopted to express it. The President, was naturally highly excited and exasperated – he departed amidst the cheers and good wishes of the great crowd which had assembled.

In the confusion of the moment, an attempt was made to arrest Mr. Randolph on the instant, but the Court being in session, he was immediately presented to the Grand Jury, and a bench warrant forwith issued for his apprehension. (*Alexandria Gazette*, May 7, 1833, p. 3)

Robert B. Randolph and *Harper's Mag.* – Some person has written a memoir of Gen. Jackson, for *Harper's Magazine*, of January which number Mr. Randolph has been kind enough to place upon our table. In that memoir occurs the following paragraph: "A few months before this occurrence," (the attempt to assassinate Jackson, in 1834) "the President was attacked by a cowardly ruffian, while he was on his way to Fredericksburg, to lay the corner stone of a monument to be erected in honor of the Mother of Washington. While the boat which bore the President, and a large number of distinguished ladies, down the Potomac, was lying at the wharf at Alexandria, the President retired to the cabin and sat behind the table next to the berths, quietly smoking and reading, while many friends were standing round in conversation. A lieutenant recently dismissed from the navy for improper conduct, approached the President as if to give him a friendly salutation, but instantly struck the venerable man in the face. Before he could repeat the blow, he was seized by the captain of the boat, and severely punched in the ribs, by a clerk in one of the Departments. The President was so confined by the table that he could not rise at first, nor use his omnipresent cane; and so anxious were all present to ascertain whether Jackson was injured, that the friends of the ruffian were al-

184

lowed to carry him ashore, and effect his escape. 'Had I been apprised,' said the President, 'that Randolph stood before me, I should have been prepared for him, and I could have defended myself. No villain has ever escaped me before; and he would not but for my confined situation.' A few minutes, afterwards, when a citizen of Alexandria said to the hero, "Sir, if you will pardon me, in case I am tried and convicted, I will kill Randolph for this insult to you, the President immediately replied, "No, sir, I cannot do that. I want no man to stand between me and my assailant, nor none to take revenge on my account. Had I been prepared for this cowardly villain's approach, I assure you all, that he would never had the temerity to undertake such a thing again."

ANOTHER VIEW OF THE JACKSON RANDOLPH AFFAIR – Before this incident at Alexandria, Robert B. Randolph had served for many years in the United States Navy. "When a youth, he entered the service of the United, his midshipman's warrant having been signed by President Madison. In 1812, he was with Decatur when he captured Macedonia, and was distinguished by the cool, courageous manner in which he discharged his duty. ... When Decatur was ordered to the Mediterranean, in 1816, to curb the insolence of the Barbary Powers, Robert B. Randolph again sailed with him – in the same ship – and was again in action, when the Flag ship captured the Algerine Frigate." For seventeen years Randolph served in the U.S. Navy before being dismissed. ... "He had been tried upon a charge of 'improper conduct,' and had been triumphantly acquitted, notwithstanding the whole weight of the government had been thrown against him, and the President himself had manifested the utmost eagerness to have him condemned. It was after this acquittal that he received his dismissal, couched in the most insulting language, and signed by President Jackson himself. He was told that he was dismissed because the President considered him no longer fit to associate with the "sons of chivalry," as he chose to call the officers of the Navy. ... It was this language which excited Mr. Randolph to the pitch, almost, of madness, and which led to the assault upon the President."

"..'He struck the venerable man in the face.' He did no such thing. He merely seized his nose with the hand that was in a sling. He neither struck him, nor attempted to strike him. As to the vaporing here attributed to General Jackson, we do not believe one word of it, though it is but a repetition of what was published at the time. He was too brave a man to play the braggadocio. Besides he knew that it was Lieut. Randolph, for he announced his name and held out his letter to him. He said, 'I do not know you,' and the answer was, 'here is your own letter written to me.' He then told Lieut R. to go away, that he would have nothing to do with him. The latter replied, 'I have something to do with you,' and attempted to seize his nose with the hand which was not injured. Jackson threw his head on one side so as to elude the grasp of that hand, and brought his nose within reach of the other, which was used accordingly. In the melee, the table which was setting out, ready for breakfast was broken down. Randolph was knocked down by the persons about the President, pelted with umbrellas and sticks, and was, with great difficulty, dragged on shore by his friends, having lost his coat, which was torn in the struggle. A gentleman who saw him standing on the wharf in his shirt sleeves, told us that he manifested the most imperturbable calmness, and that the first word he spoke was to order a servant to go on board for his hat, which had fallen off in the scuffle. ..." (*Alexandria Gazette*, December 29, 1854, p. 2.)

TOWN MEETING – At a public meeting of the Citizens of Alexandria, convened at the Market Square on Tuesday, the 7th day of May, 1833, in pursuance of previous notice.

Bernard Hooe, the Mayor, was called to the Chair and Christopher Neale was appointed Secretary. The Mayor having briefly explained the object of the meeting, was succeeded by Thomson F. Mason, who, having made an animated, appropriate and eloquent address, submitted the following resolutions, which were unanimously adopted:

Resolved, That the Citizens of this Town have learned, with mingled sentiments of regret and indignation, that a flagrant violation of the public peace, and of the sanctity of the laws, was, yesterday, committed on board the public Mail Boat, whilst lying at our wharves, by Robert B. Randolph, on the person of the President of the United States.

...Resolved, That, in the outrage which has been committed, the principles of our Free Institutions have been violated; and that, in the manner and circumstances of its perpetration, there is nothing found to extenuate it, or all the feelings of an injured and indignant people.

That, in the history of our country, it is the first time, within the knowledge of this meeting, that an attempt has been made to gratify a personal vengeance, for the results of a high official act – and this blow at the fundamental principles of our institutions has been struck by an arm, to which had once been confided the high trust of upholding the flag, and defending the character and honor of his country.

Resolved, That this outrage on the dignity of the People, in the person of their Chief Magistrate, calls for a general expression of public indignation.

Resolved. That the Chairman be requested to enclose a copy of the proceedings of this meeting to the President of the United States, and also cause them to be published in the public newspapers. B. HOOE, Chairman. (*Alexandria Gazette*, May 9, 1833, p. 3.)

Lieutenant Randolph was never successfully prosecuted for attacking the President because he escaped to Fairfax County, Virginia. During this altercation, Alexandria lay within the legal confines of the District of Columbia (1801-1847). Thus, the arrest warrant could not be served on him. President Jackson chose not to pursue the issue and the case was dropped several years later. At a later date, however, Randolph returned to Alexandria:

THE LATE ROBT. B. RANDOLPH – Some days since we announced the death, in Washington, of Robt. B. Randolph, formerly a lieutenant in the U.S. Navy. He was for many years a citizen of this place, and

186

married here.   ...After assaulting President Jackson he lived in obscurity and poverty - but as has been said - maintained his dignity and integrity to the last. Once afterwards a petty office was given him to assist him to support his family - but he was soon found out, and hunted from his position. The writer of this, in former days, knew him intimately, and can bear testimony to the many estimable traits of character he possessed. (*Alexandria Gazette*, April 27, 1869, p. 3)

APPENDIX

Constables Operating In Fairfax County, Virginia
1749-1800

Fielding Turner, Benjamin Mason, Garrard Trammell, Henry Bogges, George Duren, Benjamin Mason, Samuel Taylor, Wm. Stark, Wm. Ashford, John Simpson, Michael Alton, Samuel Canterbury, Peter Turley, John Higgerson, William Gladdin, Robert Mills, Thomas Bosman, Benjamin Ramey, David Richardson, Richard Shore, Silvester Gardner, Samuel Taylor, James Fletcher, Thomas Bosman, Philip Noland, James Paul, George Simpson, Joseph Gardner, Stephen Lee, Vincent Lewis, Thomas Davis, John Doones, Moses Simpson, John Ratcliff, Thomas Owsley, James Rozier, John Rain, Philip Grimes, Thomas Sorrell, James Whaley, George Haden, James Fletcher, James Saunders, Samuel Compton, John Stephen, Edward Dulin, James Paul, George Ashford, Marcillus Littlejohn, David Davis, John Gibson, John Berkley, Francis Eaton, Wm. Simms, Bennett Hill, John Askins, John Askey, William Johnson, John Rhodes, Wm. Sparks, Wm. James, Richard Hunt, Thomas Tuttle, Wm. Johnston, Samuel Xielder, Thomas Bayliss, Joseph Bennett, William James, Benjamin Grayson, John Ellzey, Henry Brewer, John Fielder, Francis Summers, Samuel Johnson, Jr., Samuel Fielder, Elijah Williams, Robert Jones, William Smith, Gilbert Simpson, Jacob Hubbard, John Frizell, Jonathan Denty, Nehemiah Davis, Jacob Hubbard, John Lomax, Robert Douglass, James Waugh, John Tillett, Elijah Williams, Daniel Summers, George Thrift, Elijah Wood, John Skinner, Daniel Summers, George Thrift, Elijah Wood, James Conner, Daniel Jenkins, Lawrence McKinnis, Grafton Kirk, John Mills, Chandler Spinks, Henry Reardon, Zachariah Scott, James Tayler, Wm. Crump, Wm. P. Bayliss, John Pearson, John Stone, Bazel Ball, John Green, Simon Thomas, James Campbell, James Taylor, Benjamin Starr, Lewis Talbot, Lanty Crowe, John Skinner, Wm. P. Bailiss, James Harris, Andrew Munroe, Simpson Martin, Grigsby Grady, John Goodin, Beale Fowler, David Thomas, John Langley, Daniel Bradley, John H. Manley. Source: *Abstracts of Fairfax County Court Order Books, 1749-1800*, editor, Edith M. Sprouse.

Constables & Night Watchmen For The Town Of Alexandria, Virginia
1780-1904

1780-1787 - Isaac Goetling, Ralph Longdon, John Gretter, William Ward, John Winterbury, John Williams, Charles Bryan, Jacob Moore,

John Ehrmin, William Anderson, Jacob Storm, Henry Lowe, deputy Town Sergeant, Robert Kirk, Michael Delaroche.

1788-1795 - John Winterbury, William Young, Jacob Moore, William Farrell, James McHenry, John Gretter, Alexander McConnel, Morris Warrel. Source: *Town of Alexandria Husting Court Minute Book.*

1801-1803 - James Campbell, James Harris, Robert Abercrombie, James McClish, Peter Veitch, Joseph Bowling, Ralph Longdon.

1804-1810 - John Mandeville, Supervisor of Police, John Nalls, Wm. Dulany, Elijah Chenauts, Robert Abercrombie, John Woodrow, John Longdon - Superintendent of Police, 1809.

1811-1820 - John Mandell, Elijah Chenault, John Neill, Archibald Taylor, John Neale, George Reardon, Thomas Murray, J. Green, Alexander Williams, James Aubrey, Gerrard Arnold, John Wigs, Bryan Johnston, Joseph Nevitt, Levin Walker, Lewis Sherwood, George Coryell - Superintendent of Police - 1817; James McQuire; James Carson - Superintendent of Police - 1820; William Davis, James Aubrey, Benjamin Jefferson, John Clarke, John Chauncey.

1821-1861 - William Veitch, Superintendent of Police - 1832; John B. Hancock, James Birch Watchmen; John Johnston, Richard Rudd, John DeVaughn, George Johnston, Joel Sparks, Henry Mansfield, Henry Tatspaugh - 1832.

1838 - Wm. Mills - Superintendent of Police; Theodore Meade - Superintendant of the Watch; Watchmen: John Kisendaffer, Wm. Hutchins, Thomas Burrage, James Dudley, Edward Clarkson, James Griffin, Philip B. Vernon.

1841 - Wm. N. Mills - Superintendent of Police; Henry Mansfield, Sup. of the Watch; Watchmen: George Johnson, James Dudley, Edward Clarkson, Thomas Burrage, Wm. Trammell, Wm. Hudgins, Theodore Meade, Henry Tatspaugh.

1864-1866 - Joseph Padgett, John R. Gray, S.F. Caton, T.H. Stillwell, Wm. M. Johnson.

1870 - New Police Department - Jos. Horseman, J. C. Nightingill, Henry Crump, John Drowns, James Smith, Abert Fair, Isaac Kell, J. T. Walker, Gilbert Simpson, C. Watkins, W. Johnson, Emmanuel Webb, Basil Warring, W. Mullen.

1877-1878 - James F. Webster, Captain; John L. Smith, Lieutenant; Privates: Peyton C. Bartlett, James Smith, Christopher Lyles, James T. Walker, Thomas Hayes, Rolla Henry, Henry A. Crump, Benjamin F. Bettis, Julian Arnold, Joseph W. Horseman, Edwin Goodrich, Jeremiah Franks, Arthur Simpson, Matthew Lattin, Robert Tomlin, Bernard McCann, Benjamin F. Bettice.

1884 - Jas. F. Webster, Captain; James Smith, Lieutenant; Privates: John Lawler, John C. Nightingill, Rollo Henry, Jeremiah Franks, Julian Arnold, Bernard McCann, Gilbert Simpson, James T. Walker, Benjamin F. Bettice, Edward Goodrich, Thomas Hayes, Matthew Lattin, Patrick Hayes, William E. Grady.

1890 - James F. Webster, Captain; James Smith, Lieut.; Privates: Geo. W. Jones, James L. Housen, Rolla Henry, Gayton Arrington, Wm. H. Price, Keith Davis, Samuel Ticer, Gilbert Simpson, Benjamin F. Bettis, Joshua Sherwood, James McCuen, Stephen Taylor, Patrick Iyes, William E. Grady.

1895 - James F. Webster, Captain; James Smith, Lieutenant; Privates: George W. Jones, James L. Howson, James T. Smith, Gayton Arrington, Keith Davis, Samuel Ticer, James B. Dean, W. A. Ferguson, Benjamin F. Bettis, Joshua Sherwood, Banner T. Young, J. D. Beach, Wm. H. Wilkinson, Wilton Atkinson, James Hall.

1904 - James F. Webster, Chief; James Smith, Lieutenant; Privates: Wm. E. Allen, Gayton Arrington, Jefferson D. Beach, B. Frank Bettis, Wm. A. Ferguson, J. Chris Gill, James L. Howson, Banner T. Young, John F. Henderson, Herbert C. Knight, Wm. E. Lyles, Wm. H. Mayhugh, A. J. Nicholson, John T. Roberts, Joshua Sherwood, James T. Smith, Samuel Ticer.   Source: Alexandria Circuit Court Order Books; The *Alexandria Gazette*; Annual Reports for the City of Alexandria; *Alexandria City Council Minute Book*.

The Alexandria Prison

To the Citizens of Alexandria - Influenced by motives of humanity, I last week visited the jail of this county; and if the philanthropic feelings of a man could ever be touched, it is, when he sees his fellow creatures, immersed in a miserable dungeon, where the breezes of the heavens are not permitted to enter; and the atmosphere they inhale, has the most fetid and offensive smell.

This jail was formerly the back part of a warehouse, and was converted into this receptacle for persons sentenced either for their misfortunes or their crimes. The entrance is on the south side; the prison being debarred from receiving air, on account of the jailor's house being situated directly in front; thus totally excluding both light and air. It is by a narrow passage through the jailor's house, nearly blocked up with barrels of fish, (thus adding to the fetidness of the place and obstructing the passage) that you enter a very small room in the prison of about ten feet by twelve; in which there are three doors, one on the left opening into the apartment of the whites; one on the right to the blacks, and the third, directly opposite the entrance door leads up stairs. In the chamber of the whites there is but one window, which is on the west, and they have not only entirely prevented them from looking out of it, but excluded all air from entering by having erected a very high fence directly against it which extends nearly to the top of the prison. - Thus is this chamber entirely void of air, which is indispensably necessary to prisoners. It is impossible for them even to look into the small yard in the rear of the prison, for there it is entirely blocked up; and the attempt to see from the place where they have made a window is as useless, they only see the high fence directly against them, and they have the melancholy reflection in this miserable dungeon of being not only deprived (as is always the case in prison) of the little enjoyments that life afford, but are even denied that clemency, which in other prisons is extended to the vilest criminal. To add to the horrible situation at this room the prisoners informed me that it was so extremely warm that it would be impossible for them to support existence through the summer; and indeed having merely put my head for a moment through the door into the room the heat which assailed me added to the unhealthy vapour which appeared to be there, quickly compelled me to withdraw; not without a sigh of commisseration, for the poor prisoners confined, and a reflection on the cruel parsimony of our government, in not feeling more for our situation and furnishing us with a better jail, for this would actual be a disgrace among the most barbarous nations of Africa or Asia. The room of the blacks is situated in the same manner, except that their compassion towards the inmates of that chamber, has exceeded that which is extended to the whites, as they have air from one window on the north, which looks into the yard. The heat is here too, very excessive, and the window against the yard admits the most nauseous smell. The two rooms up stairs are situated in the same manner, in one of which the debtors are confined. We may now look at its situation, and show how little comfort can be expected from its external appearance; it being part of a warehouse, the front is occupied as a store, which is on the east, and thus both light and air are prevented from entering the prison. On the west is the high fence as before stated, thus preventing the same from entering on that side of the house. On the south is the jailor's house, which also keeps off both wind and light; and the only side on which the slightest portion of wind can enter, is on the north, which is the back-yard of the prison, from whence there issues a smell, which while it is obnoxious to a man of delicacy, cannot but injure the health of those confined, for the yard extends back about fifteen feet, and is the deposit of every ruffian that may please to contaminate the air, as foul and putrid as it is, and the fence is about the height of 15 feet. — There being but four rooms, while there are debtors, it will be necessary to confine whites and blacks together, as it frequently happens that there are confined males and females of both colors. The above account of the prison of this county is correctly stated, and those of our community who are at a loss to conceive that such can be the enormity of the case are requested to call and examine for themselves; though the writer would go more into a detail of facts relating thereto did not a correct sense of delicacy prevent him from laying such nauseous facts before the public.

Is it in such a place as this, that the unfortunate debtor should be confined? It it in such a place that are to be immersed the wretched sons and daughters of humanity? a jail not fit for the reception of murderers. Yes, it is in a free country where a jail exists that would disgrace the most uncivilized nation in the world and one, which would never be suffered to exist for an hour among them. Can our fellow citizens, even passing that way, avoid exclaiming against the cruel parsimony of government? It is impossible that they can! The external appearance of the prison is sufficient to convince them of the miserable situation of its unfortunate inmates. – Let us then make use of all the means within our power to abate this public nuisance; let us present our grievances to a wise and enlightened congress, particularly pointing out how unfit this prison is, even for the reception of criminals, and I feel confident, that they commisserate with the unfortunate and would pity and relieve their distresses, they will grant a new prison. HOWARD (*Alexandria Gazette*, June 14, 1823, p. 2.)

History Of The City Jail
(N.E. Corner of Princess & St. Asaph Street)

The city jail, which is also used by the county, while in more than one sense a forbidding institution, plays so inconsiderable part in town life. It is, as it were, the outer fortress for the defence of the community against the constantly recounted forces which depravity and ignorance gather to make war upon the peace, life and property of society. The community remains in the language of the old law "in the peace of God and the Commonwealth," against which, what modern society calls "the dangerous classes," wage a constant war. In this view the jail sits like the citadel of the Greek cities to protect the town. It is by not means formidable in appearance, yet it serves its purpose very well. It was built by the United States in 1826-7, and is now quite an old building. The cutting of its iron window bars has been so often effected that there is scarcely an old grating that does not show signs of having been mended, but last year new iron gratings were placed outside of the old gratings so that inmates of the jail who desire to break out have, like gymnasts and lawyers, a double set of bars to practice at. The jail was at first located at the market square, and was then removed to the river side at the foot of Wolfe street where the old wall still remains. In 1816, when the town after the war began an era of improvement, which led to the building of the market, the town clerk, etc, a proposition was made to build a new jail. Congress very generously authorized the town to tax itself and build one, but that did not suit the city court, and no jail was built. But ten years later the old jail became too insecure for protection, and Congress had to build the jail. In May, 1826, the following act passed:

"And the said commissioners shall also select a site in the county of Alexandria for a county jail, on which it shall be the duty of the Commissioner of Public Buildings to cause a county jail for the city and county of Alexandria to be erected on a plan to be approved by the President of the United States. And there is hereby appropriated for the building of said jail the sum of $10,000 to be paid out of any money in the treasury not otherwise appropriated."

Under this act the jail was built.
The jail is in charge of City Sargeant Lucas, with Bernard Cline as

jailor, and Theodore Reed as assistant. There are now confined in jail eleven persons, three white and eight colored. Of the latter five are women. There are also two babies in jail, but the sins of the parents do not seem as yet to be visited on their children, for they appear to flourish, and they suck like steam pumps. The interior jail is as clean as water and as white as lime can make it. Even the floors are whitewashed. Two physicians visit it every morning and see to the health of the inmates. (*Alexandria Gazette*, August 13, 1879.)

Reminiscence Of The Old Jail

About the time Gen. LaFayette made his last visit to this place, October 1824, one of the then old inhabitants, William Harper, whose descendants to the fourth or fifth generation are still here, said, "When I came here from Pennsylvania, in the year 1784, there were two black men's heads stuck on pikes projecting above the western chimney of the jail, (now the station House) and the staples by which the pike staves were fastened are still there." On searching for the staples they were not found, as the jail a few years before had been turned into a Fish Market House. Arches were cut in the walls and afterwards filled up, as may still be seen, the brick work pointed up and the walls painted red but not pencilled. Some few bricks are now loosened, perhaps by removing the staples just about where the pike staves would have come, and there seems to be one of the staples stuck in as a wedge to keep a brick in place. More may be found, as the old jail is soon to be demolished. The town was started in the year 1749, and the old jail is, no doubt one of the oldest buildings here. Would it not be well to have it photographed as well as some other ancient buildings, to be mentioned in another communication? There are several old buildings here, the history and pictures of which should, and no doubt, would possess much interest to the present and next generation. The memory of them should not be lost. ALEXANDRIAN (*Alexandria Gazette*. February 13, 1872, p. 2.)

Other Resources To Ferret Out Criminal Conduct Cases In Alexandria, Virginia

1. Record of trials and examination of criminals, Court of Oyer and Terminer, Corporation of Alexandria. April 1794 - November 1800. 1 vol. Husting Court Records of Alexandria.

2. Trial Dockets. 1802, 1810, 1810-11, 1811, 1813, 1816, 1818, 1820, 1822. 9 vols. Each volume usually contains for each action the name of plaintiff, attorney, and defendant; date when action was presented; date of marshal's return; the plea and nature of offense; and names of witnesses. Separate indexes in each volume to names of parties. Records of the Circuit Court, Alexandria County, D.C.

3. Judgments of the Criminal Court. 1839-42. This court was established by an act of Congress of July 7, 1838, to assure jurisdiction over criminal cases. Its members were the same as those of the Circuit Court.

194

4. List of Prisoners in the Jail. 1802; 1820–33. Gives the name of each prisoner, the nature of the offense, and the date.

5. Warrants and Recognizances. 1794–96. Records of felonies and other violations of law in which the Commonwealth had an interest.

6. List of Judgments for Criminal Court 1839–1842. Source: *Inventory of Records of Alexandria County* by Meredith Colket. Records located at the State Library, Richmond, Virginia.

7. Alexandria County Common Law Circuit Court Order Books 1870 to present. Provides the name of the defendant, nature of the offense, and the specific sentence imposed.

8. Alexandria Corporation Court Order Books. 1870 to present. Includes name of the defendant, date of trial, list of jurors, result of trial and specific sentence imposed.

9. Alexandria Husting Court Order Books, 1780–1801; Alexandria County Court Order Books, 1801–1866. Abstract of court cases including name of defendant, list of jurors, specific fines and sentences imposed, etc.

INDEX

BLACKBURN, Maud 150 Samuel
  85
BLACKWELL, Rev Mr 76 78
BLANDHEIM, Dan 96
BLOUSE, Sefer 97-100
BLOXHAM, Joseph 55 56
BOGGES, Henry 189
BOOTHE, G L 45
BOSMAN, Thomas 189
BOSTON, Fannie 127
BOSWELL, Alcinda 127 James
  85 86
BOWEN, Dr 80
BOWLING, Joseph 190
BOYNTON, E S 124
BRADLEY, Daniel 189
BRADSHAW, P M 51
BRAWNER, W A 121
BRENNER, Rev 147 Rev Mr 147
BRENT, 86 S G 45 141 180
BREWER, Henry 189
BRIGHT, John 130
BRILL, Mr 22
BRODBECK, 176
BRODEN, Mary 11 12
BROUN, J C 56 172
BROWN, Bedford 162 Dr 1 89
  Edward 83 84 George 113 114
  John 109 Justice 54 Lovelace
  118 Martha 126 Ulysses Grant
  118 W N 83 William 136 Wm
  N 84
BRUNER, Mr 37
BRYAN, Captain 41 Charles 189
BRYANT, John 131 Thomas 120
  121
BURCH, James H 61 62
BURKE, Edmund 127 Griffin 156
BURNETT, James 175 Officer 83
BURRAGE, Thomas 190
BUTLER, Al 30 Albert 29
BYRD, Mr 91
CAMPBELL, James 189 190
  Lizzie 156
CANTERBURY, Samuel 189
CARLYLE, Jno vi
CARPENTER, Bab 28 Baptist 29
  30
CARR, J W 6 Mr 167
CARRINGTON, Lewis 120 121
  Officer 25

CARROLL, Ada 8 George 162
  John 102 Ruth 8 Walter 61
CARSON, Charles 154 James 190
CARTER, Dennis 120 121 Edward
  115 116 131 Frank 84 115 116
CARUTHERS, Surgeon 69
CARY, Mary vi
CASH, Joseph vi
CATON, S F 190
CATT, Harry 111
CHAMBERLAIN, 20
CHANCELLOR, C W 55 Coroner
  65 66 Dr 72 90 92
CHAPMAN, Charles 31 Fannie
  94-96
CHASE, T L 106
CHATAIGNE, J H 176
CHAUNCEY, John 190
CHENAULT, Elijah 190
CHENAUTS, Elijah 190
CHESTER, Lieut 82
CHICHESTER, Caroline 68 Judge
  142
CHIPLEY, Officer 55
CHURCH, Henry 136
CLARK, Amy 9 James 61 John 33
  Joseph 140 Lillie 42
CLARKE, James 61 John 190
  Joseph 140 141
CLARKSON, Edward 190
CLIFT, James 113-115 165
CLINE, Bernard 37 193 Keeper 35
  Mr 38 87-89 Walter 111
COGAN, George 113
COLCLOUGH, Robert 47
COLE, Gertie 129 Mr 59
COLEMAN, John 6 114 Laura 165
  Officer 30
COLTON, Justice 84
COLVILLE, John vi 47
COMPTON, Samuel 189
CONNER, James 189
COOK, Miss 112 Mr 12 Mrs 12
  Rev 88
COOMBS, Dr 147
COONEY, 116
CORBETT, Brook 24 25 F E 24
  Mrs 25
CORYELL, James 190
COULTER, Wm 47
COXEN, Mrs James 169

COYLE, Edward 129
CRAVEN, George 107
CROSS, Stephen 102 103
CROSSMAN, Capitola 104 Cappie 104
CROWE, Lanty 189
CRUMP, Bee 55 Emory 55 G W 68 George W 55 56 Henry 190 Henry A 190 Officer 91 Wm 189
CURRAN, Cockey 99 Ed 99 John 97 99-101 Tom 99 William 99 101
CUSTIS, George Washington Parke 183 184 John Parke 183 Mary 183 Mary Randolph 183 Wash 183
DAILY, Walter 28 30
DALTON, John vi
DANIELS, Martha 68
DARNELL, Mrs 117
DAVIS, 3 Carey 114 Carrie 114 David 47 189 Keith 191 Nehemiah 189 Officer 40 75 76 127 130 Rebeckah vi Thomas vi 47 76-78 189 William 50 190
DAY, Ella 5
DEAN, James B 191
DEANE, James 167 168 Officer 130 168 Policeman 167
DELANEY, Dr 120 M D 121
DELAROCHE, Michael 190
DELEA, Frank 105 Frank F 176 177
DEMAINE, Mr 6 9 41 45 103 108 117 119 Undertaker 6 William 9 121
DEMPSEY, James 20
DENTY, Jonathan 189
DEVAUGHN, John 157 190
DEVLIN, Edward 81-83
DICKENSON, James 15 16
DICKINSON, James H 16
DIGGS, Arthur 115 116
DIXON, Arthur J 16 Henry T 71-74 Minnie 16 Turner 61
DOGAN, 152 John 7
DONN, Justice 173
DOONES, John 189
DORAN, Patrick 174
DORSET, Clem 116

DORSEY, Clem 116 117 Jerry 110 Laura 117
DOUGLASS, James S 127 Mayor 126 Robert 189
DOWNEY, 56
DOWNHAM, Mayor 178 180
DRISCOL, Sergeant 82
DROWNS, John 190
DRUMMOND, Justice 135 Noah 57
DUDLEY, James 190 Reuben 31
DUGAN, Anthony 84
DUHANEL, Dr 80
DULANY, Wm 190
DULIN, Edward 189
DUNDAS, John 183
DUREN, George 189
DWYER, Thomas 124
DYSON, J L 71
EATON, Francis 189
ECKLOFF, Lieutenant 80
EDD, John 172 173 John T 172
EDDS, 152 153 William 154
EDELIN, Officer 83
EDGES, Wm vi
EDWARD, Hayden 47
EDWARDS, George 175
EHRLICH, Samuel 22-24
EHRMIN, John 190
EICHBERGH, Mr 22
EICHELBERGER, Samuel 90 91
ELLIOTT, Surgeon 69
ELLSWORTH, Col 70 E E 70 71
ELLZEY, John 189
ELZEY, 181 John Thomas 118-120 Thomas 120 Walter 119
ENGLISH, Justice 53 54 172
ENTWISLE, F L 111
EVANS, Martha vi
EYRE, Lieutenant Colonel 152
FAIR, Abert 190
FAIRFAX, Dr 172
FARRELL, William 190
FEBREY, H W 63 64
FERGURSON, John 90
FERGUSON, Harriet 2 Martha 1 Mrs 3 Officer 119 W A 191 Wm A 191
FESSENDEN, Francis 154
FIELDER, John 189 Samuel 189
FISHER, Julia 15 Thomas A 133
FITZGERALD, John 38

FITZHUGH, Mary 183 Mrs A M
103 William 183
FLETCHER, James 189
FOOT, Daniel vi
FORD, C V 142 F M 143 John M
143 Philip 130
FORTNAY, Jacob 38
FORTNEY, Jacob 38
FOWLER, Beale 189
FRANCIS, E 124
FRANKLIN, Nancy 103
FRANKS, Jeremiah 190 191
FRAZIER, Anthony R 57 Jerry 27
28
FREE, Fanny 137
FRENCH, D M 3 86 Dr 1 81 90
Martha 85
FRIZELL, John 189
FUNSTEN, David 173
G----, Thomas 117
GADSBY, John 183 184
GAFFNEY, Patrick 84
GAFNEY, James 84 Patrick 83 84
GAINES, Lon 107 Lou 108 Turner
107 108
GAMBRICK, Harry 110
GARDNER, Edmonia 146 Joseph
189 Silvester 189
GARHARD, Joseph 173
GARNETT, R P W 140 Samuel 94
GARRETT, Dr 37
GASKINS, Charles 29 Chas 28
Sarah 78
GASSENHEIMER, Sam 100
GERHARD, 173 Mrs 173
GIBBONS, Bertie 133
GIBSON, Dr 81 91 92 John 189 T
S 109 Thomas W 181
GIESSON, George 38
GILL, J Chris 191
GILPIN, George 38
GLADDIN, William 189
GODWIN, Henrietta 11 12
GOETLING, Isaac 189
GOLDSMITH, Benj 148 Benjamin
148 149
GOODIN, John 189
GOODING, Margaret vi
GOODRICH, Edward 30 191 Edwin
190 George 61 George W 69
John 69 Officer 28 30
GOODRICK, Geo 68

GOODS, Chief of Police 133 Of-
ficer 133
GORDON, 130 George 131 Sheriff
142 143 145 147
GRADY, Cud 22 Grigsby 189 Wil-
liam 22 William E 191 Wm E
168
GRAFFORD, Pelitah vi
GRANDISON, Fannie 158
GRAVES, W P 141
GRAY, John R 190 Mr 87
GRAYSON, Benjamin 189
GREEN, 20 J 190 James 21 John
189 Joseph 91 Mr 33 Nelson 91
Nettie 90-92 Richard 154
GREENE, J S 166 John H 166
Nettie 91
GREENWOOD, Ann R 82
GRETTER, John 189 190
GRIFFIN, James 190
GRIMES, C R 124 J W 92 93
James 92 Philip 189
GRISBY, Tazwell 71
GRISSON, Charles E 123
GROVE, Thomas 2
GUY, Mr 15 Mrs 15
HACKLEY, Isaac 178 John 22
HADEN, George 189
HAGAN, Auburn Pridemore 178
179 Patrick 178
HAHN, Frank 89
HALL, 173 Bazil 62 63 Elizabeth
62-64 Emma 162 James 191
Officer 24 133
HAMILTON, Stephen 153 154
HANCOCK, John B 190
HANDBOUGH, Thomas 47
HARLOW, John 105
HARPER, Wells A 20 William
194 Wm 183
HARRIS, 28 Celia 158 Eliz vi
James 189 190
HARRISON, George W 175
Thomas 143
HASKINS, Charles 30 Chas 130
HAYDEN, William 113
HAYES, Officer 103 Pat 28
Patrick 191 Thomas 190 191
HEATON, Solomon G 59
HECK, John L 154
HECKEN, Mr 37
HEFLEBOWER, Samuel 124

PONNETT, Constant 180

POWELL, Coroner 178 Dr 99 176 177 R C 3 5 176

PRICE, B F 23 G E 40 John 165 Justice 55 65 66 172 Wm B 55 Wm H 191

PROCTOR, Officer 129 168 Policeman 167

PULLMAN, Sidney 111

PURCELL, Jos 178

PURVIS, Coroner 113 121 180 Dr 6–9 45 103 108 111 112 116 120 178 181 W R 7

QUICK, Dr 147

RAIN, John 189

RAMEY, Benjamin 189

RAMMELL, I 24 J 22 23

RAMSAY, Dennis 183 G 179

RANDAL, Nancy 174

RANDOLPH, Robert B 184–186

RATCLIFF, John 189

REARDON, George 190 Henry 189

REED, James 113 114 Theodore 194

REIDEL, Emanuel 143 Ida 141–144 146 147 Lewis 39 Mrs 39

REVELLE, Benj F 109

RHODES, John 189

RICH, Mary 131

RICHARDS, 76 James 113 W C 124

RICHARDSON, David 189 Henry 76 77 79

RICKER, Mary 15 16

RIDGEWAY, Maria 14 Susie 13 14

RILEY, Dr 29–31 Jos 68 Joseph 65 66

ROBERTS, Frank 98 100 John T 191 Officer 140

ROBERTSON, Mrs E F 133

ROBEY, Melvina 138 Miss 93 Mrs John 140

ROBINSON, 20 85 A M 16 17 A W 143 Agnes 167 168 Austin 53 J H 124 John 173 Laura 117 Mr 169 Mrs 167 Phoebe 17

ROGERS, J T 178

ROLES, Sarah 1

ROLLINS, Mary 148 149

ROSS, Chas 100

ROTCHFORD, Philip 135

ROXBURY, J 83

ROY, Webb 180

ROZIER, James 189

RUDD, 173 Jas 124 Richard 190

RUSH, John 69

RUSSELL, Carrie 15 Dr 147 Laura 128

RYAN, Laura 165 Mrs 165

RYE, Buck 66 Wm H 66

SANDERS, Robert 154

SANGSTER, James 177 178

SANKSTONE, Isabelle vi

SAUNDERS, James 189 Robert 154 William 110

SCARCE, Frank 103

SCHMIDT, Frances 125 George 125

SCHWAB, F 105

SCOTT, Zachariah 189

SCOTTEN, James 69 James H 69

SERVANT, William 64

SHEEL, Ann vi

SHERMAN, George C 15

SHERWOOD, Joshua 191 Lewis 190 Officer 111 129 130 148 164

SHINN, Mary 118 S 20 Stephen 21

SHIRLEY, Arthur 180 181

SHORE, Richard 189

SHULTE, Henry 173

SIDERS, 164

SIKES, Ollie 159

SIMMONS, Sam 132 133

SIMMS, 30 Georgie 163 Hannah 163 164 Mrs 164 Sarah Jane 28 Susan Jane 29 Wm 189

SIMPSON, 153 Arthur 190 George 189 Gilbert 154 155 189–191 John 189 Mayor 42 44 45 149 166–168 Moses 189

SIMS, Hannah H 163

SIPPLE, Constable 6

SKELTON, Susan 149

SKINNER, John 189

SLATER, John 174

SLAVE, Tony 33 Will 38

SLOUGH, General viii 151

SMITH, 173 Albert 179 B B 51 Dr 6 112 Eliza 108 F L 173 Francis L 61 62 Francis L Jr 86 George S 103–106 Georgie L 153 H E 154 James 42 190 191

204